QUICKSILVER HERITAGE

Frontispiece The Queen Stone, in the horseshoe bend of the
Wye near Symond's Yat. A fine Herefordshire example of
a standing stone with inexplicable clean-cut grooves.
(*Alfred Watkins*)

QUICKSILVER HERITAGE

The Mystic Leys:
Their Legacy of Ancient Wisdom

by
PAUL SCREETON

THORSONS PUBLISHERS LIMITED
Wellingborough, Northamptonshire

First published 1974

© PAUL SCREETON 1974

ISBN 0 7225 0282 6

Typeset by Specialised Offset Services Limited, Liverpool,
printed by Whitstable Litho, Straker Brothers Limited,
Whitstable, Kent, on paper supplied by P.F. Bingham Limited,
Croydon.

Contents

List of Illustrations

Frontispiece The Queen Stone, Herefordshire

The numbers throughout this text refer to
'References and Bibliography', *starting on page 273.*

Acknowledgements

I gratefully acknowledge permission to reproduce the following:

Two photographs taken by the late Alfred Watkins, by permission of his son Allen Watkins and heirs; The formula of Peter Furness on the mathematical probability of leys; The entire text of Tony Wedd's historic work, *Skyways and Landmarks*. I also add my appreciation for the support given by contributors to *The Ley Hunter* magazine, both those credited in these pages, and the many others who have made valuable additions to our understanding of the ancient and modern skills and wisdom.

The Name 'Ley'

'Ley', pronounced 'lay', was not simply chosen by Alfred Watkins for the 'old straight track' because the word appears frequently as a prefix or suffix at ley points, but chiefly for the reason that in Saxon times it meant a cleared glade; not an enclosure or field, as generally used today, or pasture on the sunny side of a hill as in North-East Scotland. Watkins also found evidence to show the 'straight' meaning of the word 'ley'.[59]

There is also the Sanscrit word *lelay* meaning 'to flame', 'to sparkle' or 'to shine', and thought by Mircea Eliade to maybe convey notions of Fire, Light or Spirit, and taken from the root *lila*, meaning cosmic creation, which suggests the esoteric side of leys.[13]

I like the name 'ley' as it does not appear self-explanatory, and when something as complex as the energy alignments concept is found there can be no simple definition.

Preface

'All things begin and end in Albion's Ancient, Druid, Rocky Shore.' — William Blake.

Charismatic Albion, a country with a great heritage, eventful history and inspiring future is awakening from its enchantment, and a growing proportion of the populace is becoming aware of formerly hidden truths which lay spellbound in suspended animation, and which are now pressing their influence upon areas of consciousness which were once a vast wilderness. The barriers of the wasteland continents are falling, and frontiersmen of the awakened state are exploring new lands. There is a time for the times to come together, and just as astronauts of our decadent, materialistic society reach out for the Moon and outer space, a new breed of Britons look to the countryside for a true vision of the past and find themselves also exploring the infinity of the mind's inner space.

The quest outlined in this volume not only comprises a complete reappraisal of prehistory, but leads to a recognition of powers at work in the landscape and man's psyche, and also brings into focus a vision of the future. The reader is introduced to a world in which time and space have only relevance in the great cycles of the cosmic clock; where the outer landscape has four dimensions, those of length, breadth, height and timelessness; where the mind takes on wings and is free to wander the paths of extradimensional experience.

One of the paths to enlightenment has a firm foundation in the physical world. There exists a striking network of lines of subtle force across Britain, and elsewhere on spaceship Earth, understood and marked in prehistoric times by men of wisdom and cosmic consciousness. These lines of inspiration hold one of the keys to universal knowledge and spirituality for mankind today. They provide access to the heart of Albion's enchantment, to revelations that the past comprises ages not so dark and glimmerings of an attainable golden future.

The complex, elusive, quicksilver lines of force, manifested as the Earth cooled, and exerting subtle influences on sensitives through aeons of time, lie as a matrix around which the speculations of this book are woven. For centuries, knowledge of the current flowing over hill and vale lay submerged in the deepest recesses of human consciousness, until the system was revealed in a vision to the late Alfred Watkins.

Fifty years have elapsed since Alfred Watkins gained his insight into our marvellous past, and those who have chosen to study and expand his discoveries have become aware that the lines traced by him are not truly ancient roads, but a geometric network of lines along which energy currents flow. Research has led to students evaluating both the exoteric factuality and also the esoteric significance of the lines.

Alfred Watkins termed the lines 'leys', and he believed them to mark prehistoric pathways, 'the old straight track'. He was aware that his study bordered upon the occult, but chose to concentrate upon creating a solid body of evidence to substantiate a physical reality for his discovery, which would be acceptable to archaeology. Further research has shown that only by delving into occult realms can we hope to comprehend fully the significance of leys and the enormous programme carried out by prehistoric man to live his life in accordance with an invisible force which inspired his every act.

This book attempts to present a balance between an antiquarian's re-evaluation of prehistory, and a spiritual conception of a 'live' power understood by our distant forefathers and which can be tapped today. My thesis is the existence in prehistoric times of an active science of spiritual physics, whereby the functions of mind and body were integrated with currents in the earth and powers from the cosmos.

Newcomers to the subject and seasoned investigators will find in these pages basic information on recognizing ley points and tracing alignments on maps and in the field, a history of ley hunting and allied research, speculations on astrology, astronomy, alchemy, unidentified flying objects, giantlore and dragonlore, conclusions upon the spiritual nature of the quest for leys, and to aid those who wish to read more deeply into the subject I have included a comprehensive bibliography.

I have attempted to present my researches in an objective manner, allowing the reader to decide for himself the validity of the material, and also where authorities hold divergent views give each theory as objectively as possible. Suggestions as to where further investigation seems particularly worthwhile are given, in the hope that the reader will pursue one or more of these avenues of research, and thus add to our knowledge of the subject.

No serious study can be wholly the author's own, and I must pay tribute to several people whose ideas I have found stimulating and whose friendship I value. They are John Michell, Philip Heselton, Jimmy Goddard, Frank Lockwood and Allen Watkins.

PAUL SCREETON

Part 1

THE QUEST

1. Seeking the Truth

'The world with all its resources and permutations, is not large enough or complex to keep the truth out.' – Richard Grossinger.

For the seeker after the truth of leys, those lines of subtle energy pulsing along a dead straight course and knowing no boundaries, and first marked by alignments of Stone Age monuments, his path will be an inspiring one. He will walk through sunlit glades, meditate under gospel oaks, rest his weary feet on special mounds while listening to highflying skylarks, pass by duckponds swarming with tadpoles, point himself towards a distant notch on the skyline, go beyond to a strategically positioned stone circle, marvel at strange faces on small wayside stones.

He will learn to see the landscape as men did several thousand years ago. He will note how long ago features were subtly altered to create an indefinable harmony. At noon he will note formations reflecting the midnight constellations spread across the land. Slowly he will become attuned to the scene; his perception having shifted, there will appear a vibrant countryside humming not only with the buzz of bumblebees, the call of the curlew, or the scamper of rabbits, but throughout it all the energy of nature, and criss-crossing it, always straight, the heartbeat of magic power which keeps it alive.

His studies will be of the ancient sites themselves, legends, myths, old parish churches, flora and fauna, the heavens, astrology, cosmic rays, flying saucers, the occult, vanished civilizations, elementals.

He will become a walking encyclopaedia of the country-side, having made many new entries for himself; see flowers as though through a microscope and stars as though through a telescope; eventually know by intuition, feel, or sight just where the power is flowing and tap it for himself; if he be sensitive, perhaps tune in to past ages, which may reveal themselves through the quartz crystals of a solitary standing stone; receive physical and spiritual sustenance from the invisible power emanating from a heather-clad tumulus; stand by an enigmatic clump of Scots firs and glare with distaste at a horizon steelworks belching out its poison into skies where summer swallows skim.

As he gazes towards Orion's Belt he will become an astronaut of inner space, becoming calm, becoming at one with the cosmos, expanding into a timeless consciousness where the truths of man's unbreakable link with the heavens enfold untold centuries, and he will withdraw facts as intuitions and truth as comprehension. There are no barriers to time, only those we pretend exist, and leys offer us the positive negation of time in that they are, were, and always will be. They are there. They were there a long, long, long time ago.

He who believes in the reality of the ley system is engaged in a quest. His aim is to further his knowledge of a mysterious force and its many manifestations and incredible implications. He will become footsore, his head will burst with ideas, he will be coming to terms with himself and learning about spiritual truths rather than material falsities.

For his pains he will meet a degree of derision. A study which encompasses a belief in a high technology several thousand years ago, astrology, dowsing, flying saucers, and psychic faculties, must sound like a crank's paradise. It is no use asking professional archaeologists to certify the validity of the alignments, which are plainly traceable on any map.

He will be a pioneer in a New Age study which is only fifty years old. There will be ample room for him to make his own significant discoveries and know that others will be only too eager to give them a sympathetic hearing, discuss them, suggest new directions, provide encouragement and give him full credit. The goals are many. Simply adding piece by piece is important, but it is also a fact that no one is yet sure of the cosmic purpose of the ley system; why it was marked so clearly, the exact nature of the power and how it was, and maybe still is, utilized.

Hours of armchair study are far from sufficient. Little has yet been published on the subject, and until the planners have covered every acre of Britain, the evidence will remain, laid across our land, written in the curves of hills, the transformed courses of rivers, the stone circles, the tumuli, the dolmens, punctuated by flash ponds, mark stones and menhirs.

No one need be an expert in any field, no 'A' levels are needed to gain admittance to the growing band of ley hunters, there is no requirement to know that the Iron Age followed the Bronze Age; all that is necessary is a love of the countryside, an ability to observe, a willingness to consider the incredible, a huge reserve of perseverance and tolerance when inspiration seems lacking, and above all determination to find the truth.

No archaeological knowledge is required to find the evidence on a map or in the field. No long-winded phraseology is demanded for setting out discoveries for further study. Results will be immediately forthcoming. Proof will be there before your eyes.

2. A Heretical Study

'There have been many attempts to recover this lost history; but every one of those writers has come against the blank wall of intellectual obstinacy in the form of hostile criticism and the deadly inertia of official education.' – Alan V. Insole.

He who travels the leys will be in good company. Several generations of ley hunters have already trodden the path and made the way a little clearer for those now seeking to reveal its whole identity.

Fifty years ago Alfred Watkins had a vision of the ley system and since then interest has ebbed and flowed. Few of the original ley hunters are still alive, but others who are younger have been attracted to these rich veins of the living Earth in search of a once and future golden age.

Many are the reasons for following leys, and all are enriching. Those who turn from the twentieth-century motorways to the serenity of the timeless leys, all seek a quality of living which is not present in the urban chaos of gasworks, skyscraper flats, petro-chemical complexes, offices, schools, universities and the sprawling neon-lit garden cities. It is true that leys traverse towns, but lust for land has meant a mark stone may have been destroyed to make way for a bingo parlour, or a mound levelled for a slaughterhouse.

Yet in the city tenements and tentacles of suburbia live ley hunters. The lucky ones live in the country. Ley hunters may be on the shop floor or in the directors' boardroom. For those who tramp the leys there will be friends along the way. Hippies and housewives, Anglican vicars and white witches, occultists and geologists, ufologists and ornithologists, Druids and spiritualists, gypsies and ramblers, schoolboys and schoolgirls, the young and old.

All are people with the common denominators of a belief in the uniqueness of leys, a wish to learn more of their mysterious properties and value, a mistrust of current archaeological thinking and a love of the countryside.

Ley hunting is one of the few pursuits where there is no generation gap and no dogma.

Alfred Watkins was the father of ley hunting. He rode and strode the leys of Herefordshire, and since then the subject has passed from being a purely archaeological pursuit along many other lines of research. Archaeology scorned Watkins fifty years ago and still does. We are on our own. We revere Alfred Watkins, but do not worship him; our quest may be likened to that of the Holy Grail, but the Church can hardly help us; we may wish to preach a doctrine of leys, but must take care not to bore or coerce those to whom it is unbelievable and invisible; no God, no priests, just ley hunters, each an individual and equal. If there is a God, He is infinity, and in His cosmogony it would be foolish to worship leys and not motorways; stone circles and not locomotive depots; standing stones and not parking meters; the Moon and not an electric light bulb; clumps of Scots firs and not plastic Christmas trees.

To say that leys do not exist, is to say that motorways do not exist. Both can be found on maps.

To say that ley power does not exist, is to say that electricity does not exist. Both can be felt.

Nevertheless orthodox archaeologists deny the existence of leys. Leys are a heresy. Leys upset preconceived notions about prehistoric culture.

However, mainstream archaeology is undergoing a turbulent revolution — a (r)evolution — as there has been a reluctant acceptance that among other things stone circles were astronomical computers, and new dating methods have laid waste the diffusionist theory. The findings of Prof. Alexander Thom on stone circles are receiving grudging attention from them. Yet Prof. Lyle B. Borst, whose 'deplorable astro-archaeology' so upset Dr Glyn Daniel, has been considered unworthy of serious consideration. The most damning view is that of Prof. Stuart Piggott, who told television viewers in 1971: 'You have to be an archaeologist before you can put forward ideas about archaeology.'

It is sad that archaeologists do not favour others, however

well qualified they may be, to trespass on their patch. They guard zealously the structure of prehistory they have created on ill-founded suppositions, and wilfully refuse to examine any data which might lead to their having to make even the slightest modification to their theories. The foundations of their prehistoric archaeology are hopelessly unsound, and the cracks are ever-widening.

A recent example of how the archaeologists have been proved wrong by scientists from another field, is that a new method of dating has shown that the megalithic culture in Britain is 700 years older than had been assumed, and that consequently the diffusionist theory, with culture spreading from the Mediterranean region, is invalid. Dr Colin Renfrew, writing in *The Listener* of 7 January, 1971, though referring unkindly to Megalithic Man as a barbarian, has some pertinent points to make on the current position of pre-historic archaeology:

> The rejection of the diffusionist model leaves something of a void in European prehistoric studies. In consequence our profession is in a state of flux ... we have to adjust our thinking to the realisation that our barbarian predecessors and ancestors were just as creative as we ourselves.... The next decade's work in prehistory promises to be very exciting.

This followed the disturbing revelations on stone circles by academics such as Professors Thom, Borst, Hawkins and Hoyle, none of whom is an archaeologist. It is, unfortunately, as Ian Rodger wrote: 'People like Borst and Thom are men trained in measurement and the observation of factual data. Unfortunately it seems that most archaeologists are not mathematicians or astronomers and they tend to dismiss the findings of men who are more qualified to appreciate megalithic geometry.'[104]

Leys, of course, are more ethereal than Thom's circles and Borst's cathedrals, and consequently less likely to be considered a reality than stone circles as astronomical instruments or cathedrals as being based on megalithic plans. Imagine what would happen if an eminent academic archaeologist did accept leys as a fact. He would have to admit a previous misconception of the skills and spirituality of prehistoric man; would need to reconsider and entirely rebuild a lifetime's study and work; would put his career and reputation in jeopardy; would invite derision from his colleagues and students.

Academic institutions and educationalists disgracefully neglect the most speculative kinds of intelligence in students, and conformist thinking is rewarded against creative and emotionally involved thinking.

Academics indoctrinate archaeology students with a remarkable fabrication of lies. They are unable to see the wider implications of the researches we amateurs have undertaken. Somehow they cannot, or will not, accept leys. They do not fit into their narrow concept of the past, and so cannot be incorporated. Leys are dismissed, but cannot be argued against. To accept them would require a complete reappraisal of prehistory. There has been a furious debate over the findings of Thom, whose observations make it patently clear that the technological and intellectual level generally accepted for prehistoric man has been placed hopelessly low.

The discoveries made by Thom, and the implications of Borst's work, are far from fully appreciated, as are those of ley hunters, and it is obvious that a stupendous upgrading of prehistoric man's abilities is necessary now, and will need to be continually reassessed as new facts emerge. The relative acceptance that stone circles had a technical use·has been made possible because men of high academic standing have postulated the theories. As for leys, so far there is no one in the scientific hierarchy championing this line of research.

What must be stressed is that the issue over the ley system does not involve a schism in the ranks of archaeologists. Few, if any, of the people studying leys regard themselves as archaeologists. Maybe none of us have any training in the discipline. We would not take kindly to being associated with a study whose foundations are the plunder of tumuli, the amassing and categorization of broken pottery and implements, and the scratching away of soil with incredible patience.

This is dead archaeology.

Ley hunters are interested in a form of living archaeology.

Through the study of the ley system and its mechanics we are dealing with a continuous tradition which endured from Neolithic times through Celtic invasions, Roman occupation, the Dark Ages, the siting of parish churches, the splendour of the Gothic cathedrals, secret societies, to Alfred Watkins, up to present-day New Age groups.

Megalithic Man utilized a force which is present today and available to us. This is the live current which presents a live alternative to the barrow bounty hunting. It is a retracing of long-forgotten sciences whose significance is still somewhat obscure but nevertheless real. I wish to see a revival of those sciences for mankind's benefit.

However much scorn and derision is aimed at live archaeology by the academics, researchers will continue to make progress and eventually we shall overcome and the thesis will become accepted. Meanwhile we shall continue to outrage those who have derided Alfred Watkins, Major F.C. Tyler, Arthur Lawton, Lewis Spence, John Foster Forbes, T.C. Lethbridge, John Michell and Guy Underwood, and all others who have shed light into the dark recesses of prehistory, where orthodoxy dare not venture for fear of finding something beyond its sadly limited comprehension.

For several years ley hunting and ufology were closely allied, but our paths have since strayed. On the face of it the two subjects make strange bedfellows, and ufology has produced some vociferous detractors. Dr John Cleary-Baker has written:

> Will someone please tell me how and why the prehistoric population of Britain, lacking means or incentive to do anything of the sort, laid out a vast and countrywide system of straight trackways? . . . Belief in leys seems to be a matter of faith rather than proof or logic. An elementary knowledge of prehistoric archaeology suffices to disprove the idea. Why clutter up the field of UFO-research with such notions?[73]

Why not?

3. Fifty Years

'I knew nothing on June 30th last of what I now communicate, and had no theories. A visit to Blackwardine led me to note on the map a straight line starting from Croft Ambury, lying on parts of Croft Lane past the Broad, over hill points, through Blackwardine, over Risbury Camp, and through the high ground at Stretton Grandison, where I surmise a Roman station. I followed up the clue of sighting from hill top, unhampered by other theories, found it yielding astounding results in all districts, the straight lines to my amazement passing over and over again through the same class of objects, which I soon found to be (or to have been) practical sighting points.' – Alfred Watkins.[58]

It sounds simple. A man sits down, opens a map, is casually casting his eyes over it and notes that a number of ancient sites happen to be in a straight line. If anyone else on 30 June, 1921 had been looking at a map and noted such an alignment he would have thought no more of it. In fact, others had noted alignments and failed to see the significance. But Alfred Watkins's discovery was in the nature of a vision. The alignment struck a responsive chord, the magnitude of whose significance was inspiration unparalleled before or since in archaeology. The revelation took the form of a rush of images forming a coherent whole. This insight into the truth of what lay directly between Croft Ambury and Stretton Grandison was as breathtaking as any vision any shaman, guru or mystic has experienced.

This illumination was unforeseen; but for a man who knew every nook and cranny of his native countryside, it was, on reflection, probably not so unexpected.

Confirmation of his vision was provided in excess as he marked ancient sites and old parish churches on one-inch Ordnance Survey maps, and linked them into dead straight lines. He wandered the countryside corroborating the evidence on the map with the evidence of his own eyes, and with his camera he recorded the reality of the alignments.

Alfred Watkins wasted no time in plotting where leys exist and what marks them. In addition to the basic prehistoric structures which fit into the pattern, he also included primary peaks, tree clumps of significance or special centuries-old trees, parish churches, wayside crosses and castles.

The ley system seemed to offer new insights into the study of the historical development of paths and roads, and he presented it as such. But there are indications in his *magnum opus, The Old Straight Track*, that he considered there to be occult connotations which he preferred not to enlarge upon.

He was a past president of the Woolhope Naturalists' Club in Hereford, and it was to this society in September of the year of his discovery that he lectured upon the subject. In 1922 this lecture, with illustrations by the author and additional material, was published as *Early British Trackways, Moats, Mounds, Camps, and Sites.*

Watkins had firstly come to the conclusion that his discovery was simply a proof that prehistoric man had taken steps to mark the landscape in such a way as to make travel easy. A man would set off from one place and aim for a notch, cairn or mound on the skyline; where there were no hills he kept straight on and reached ponds, mark stones, moats, mounds and significant tree clumps.

His best-known book is *The Old Straight Track*, which was published in 1925, and which brought him fame and infamy. O.G.S. Crawford, then editor of *Antiquity* magazine, refused a paid advertisement from Watkins for the book (just as the present editor of that magazine, Dr Glyn Daniel, similarly refused a paid advertisement for *The Ley Hunter* magazine, edited by the author of this book).

Academic archaeologists derided Watkins's discovery, but interest was sufficient for Watkins to start the Straight Track Club, at the instigation of Mrs B.M. Carbonnel. A year later – 1927 – saw the publication of *The Ley Hunter's Manual*, a practical handbook required to meet the increasing demand for what the *Birmingham Post* had described as 'a new outdoor hobby'.

I have climbed Castle Mound, in Cambridge, and can well understand its extraordinary attraction for Alfred Watkins when he visited his son, Allen, in the city for a few days. He knew Cambridge as a ley centre, and spent his visit never far from the mound. It inspired him to write his last book, *Archaic Tracks Around Cambridge*, published in 1932.

The subject was undergoing its first flush of popularity, and the hard core of serious ley hunters in the Straight Track Club started a postal folios scheme, whereby members circulated papers on the subject and added their comments to articles written by other members. The folios are now in Hereford City Library.

A later development was a series of Summer Field Meetings between 1933 and 1939, which gave members of the club an opportunity to meet one another, following leys together and examining sites of interest. Meetings were held at Cheltenham, Exeter, Hereford, Salisbury, Harrogate, Fishguard and Anglesey. These lasted for three or four days, and each was led by a member who knew the area being visited. These were interrupted by the 1939-45 War, and in 1948 the decision was taken to wind up the club.

The North-West Pembrokeshire meeting in June 1939 was the club's last, and was led by Mr A.T. Morley Hewitt. They visited stone circles, standing stones, cromlechs, chapels, churchyards, a cathedral and other sites of interest. The itinerary describes delightfully the stopping place for tea on 23 June as, 'Primitive but Tea!!'

Not until July 1971 did ley hunters gather again as a body out-of-doors; on this occasion to celebrate the fiftieth anniversary of Watkins's discovery, in the form of a picnic at Risbury Camp, on Watkins's first ley.

Readers may be interested in a few biographical details of Alfred Watkins, and I regard these as being specially important, for they emphasize two points: that his interests involved more than just leys, and that he was a man of integrity. He was born on 27 January, 1855. The school he attended was so bad that he had to educate himself. His father had several businesses, and after working in the brewery trade as a traveller he studied flour milling, and again became a traveller. In 1886 he married Marion Mendham Cross and fathered two children, Allen, born 1889, and Marion a year later.

In public life he became a county councillor, a magistrate, schools' governor, hotel director, and spoke for the Liberal cause. His photographic inventions were many and he was president of the Royal Photographic Society in 1908, and was made a Fellow of the Society in 1910. He also created a perfect form of brown bread. He kept bees, did conjuring tricks, and was a proficient skater.

Alfred Watkins applied logic to whatever interested him, and his researches into the ley system were carried out accordingly. However, the vision which led him to the alignments was something of an embarrassment, as revelations are not yet regarded as scientific. In fact he was a gifted psychic, but after childhood experiments he repressed it in favour of reason — until he was given no choice on 30 June, 1921.

He died on 7 April, 1935.

Watkins had rediscovered leys, but others before him had come close to deducing the plan, but were not blessed with the revelation which came to him. A number of references can be found in old books which suggest a vestige of mankind's memory of the reality and importance of leys. Watkins recorded that a number of other observers had found confirmatory evidence.[58] Mr G.H. Piper entered in the Wollhope Club Transactions for 1882: 'A line drawn from Skerrid-Fawr [a mountain] northwards to Arthur's Stone would pass over the camp and the southernmost part of the Hatterill Hill, Old Castle, Longtown Castle, and Urishay and Snodhill Castles.' Also in the Wollhope Club Transactions, for 1910, Mr James G. Wood wrote of a line of tumps (mounds) across South Monmouthshire and West Gloucestershire. Long before this John Bunyan, in Pilgrim's Progress, described the way 'as straight as a rule can make it' and 'cast up by

Patriarchs of old'. Michael Drayton, in *Polyolbion*, wrote:

> To guide my course aright.
> What mound or steady mere
> Is offered to my sight?

F.W. Andrew published *Memorials of Old Derbyshire* in 1907, in which he noted that Derbyshire stone circles were geometrically arranged at even distances. A year later, the Revd Hadrian Allcroft's *Earthwork of England* drew attention to the alignment of Maiden Castle, Eggardon and Pilsdon Pen earthworks. Sir Norman Lockyer, in the second edition of *Stonehenge*, noted that Stonehenge, Old Sarum and Grovelly Castle earthwork lay at the angles of an equilateral triangle.

Watkins was pleased to give these researchers credit for their discoveries, and from 1921 until his death, he and his co-researchers continued to build up an impressive case for the alignments. Overwhelming evidence had been collected. Leys were found in every county which they studied. Leys were followed below the ripening buds of spring, under the glare of the summer sun's rays, trodden through fallen autumn leaves, and paced through glistening winter snow.

But there was a niggling doubt. The validity of leys was unquestionable. But were they trackways? Were they traders' routes? Was travel the true key to the enigmatic network?

The greatness of Watkins is not just his vision, but the untiring manner in which he sought to confirm it for everyone. No one could have tried harder or been more painstaking in noting the features and writing about them. His insight and verve were enormous. We owe him a great debt for making his vision so clear, and for not allowing the derision of detractors to create doubts or cause him to lessen the will to make his discovery public.

Nevertheless it cannot be stressed too strongly that the placing of stones, piling up of earth and planting tree clumps in alignments was not to provide a trackway system, even though parts were undoubtedly used as such, but the programme was carried out to mark, and maybe manipulate, the subtle earth current. Watkins himself was mystified when he noted that leys would climb precipices where the easiest route would be elsewhere, would cross rivers where shallower reaches existed upstream or downstream, go through bogs, were duplicated in close proximity, and crossed lakes.

According to his son Allen Watkins, the founder of ley hunting was a man with his feet firmly on the ground, but with something of the psychic in his make-up. Allen Watkins told me that since 1925 he had believed the leys to have a great deal to do with traditional occultism. Alfred Watkins was fond of quoting passages from the Bible dealing with the straight and narrow, so we might suppose that he had more than an inkling of a spiritual attribute to leys.

Increasingly, the subject of ley hunting is attracting people from such interests as occultism, spiritualism and ufology, all with highly speculative ideas of their own. It would, however, be a great shame and unforgivable if Alfred Watkins's pioneer work were to be overshadowed. In ascribing leys primarily to trackways he made a fundamental error, but this in no way makes his vision and judgment of what constitutes a ley any less meaningful. His view of leys is completely in harmony with my own, in that leys have a scientific viability, and have a magic of their very own.

During the 1930s ley hunting continued to attract supporters, and the topographist Donald Maxwell wrote on the subject in a light-hearted way in several of his books. Maxwell, who died in 1937, did much to popularize the subject. Reviewing Maxwell's *A Detective in Sussex*, Vita Sackville-West wrote of ley hunting, somewhat frivolously: 'A new sort of game which one can play oneself. I can imagine no more entertaining way of spending a summer holiday, and I advise you to get the book.'

Leys startled Donald Maxwell, for he had hardly taken them seriously at first, but being an observant man who walked the country byways, he checked for himself and came to the conclusion that Watkins's theory was sound. In the preface to *A Detective in Essex* he made several points which are as valid today as they were in 1933. He wrote:

Mr. Alfred Watkins has been treated by the archaeological world very much as Galileo was treated by the scientific world of his time — the only difference being that the anti-Watkinsian has not dragged the Church into this dispute. No doubt many of Galileo's arguments for a moving world were unsound. No doubt many of his friends gave silly reasons for the hypothesis.

However, the world still moves and leys or 'sighting lines', in spite of the ridicule of 'experts', still exist.

Another of his points was a plea that the evidence of amateurs be compiled, because the Straight Track Club had only partly recorded prehistoric remains.

That there is no such help (as with radiant points of meteors compiled from amateur astronomers' observations) from amateur explorers is largely the fault of archaeologists themselves. It would seem that any fresh evidence — as in the case of that discovered by Mr Alfred Watkins — of methods and matters concerning archaic England is almost invariably treated with scepticism, which is natural to the wise and prudent, or with antagonism — which is just unscientific.

Where one man of vision had led, two other men followed, applying mathematics as they went. In 1939 two extremely important works were published, by Major F.C. Tyler and Arthur Lawton; the former having analysed geometrical arrangements created by· leys, and the latter rediscovering standard distances and more remarkably the existence of ley power and geomantic divination.

While brooding over a map, just as Alfred Watkins had, Arthur Lawton realized the geometrical significance of sites, and subsequently communicated his observations through the Straight Track Club portfolios. This new dimension in ley hunting was also investigated by Major Tyler, who became magnetized by the uncanny incidence of parallel alignments, so close as to be impractical if leys were to be considered simply as trackways. He also considered the theory that from a common centre a series of concentric circles can be drawn, taking up two or more sites. He presumed that these related to a geometric plan of exceptional complexity and mystery, whereby sacred sites were related to geometry. His findings, first communicated in a lecture in 1938, were posthumously published as *The Geometrical Arrangement of Ancient Sites*. It seems that Lawton was the first to suggest that the mathematically precise mesh could be interpreted in a spiritual/occult context, and was furthermore related to a terrestrial power system. His deductions were undeveloped, but he had come closer than anyone since Watkins to the truth of leys.

The grandeur of the system had been given a strict mathematical basis with undercurrents of spirituality. What could have been a point for the subject to take on momentum, was instead the beginning of a period of decline coinciding with the fury unleashed upon Europe by Hitler, his astrologers, the Horsemen of Poseidon and the Ultima Thule Group.

One person who was active during the war years was the formidable speculative archaeologist John Foster Forbes. It could be said that he was obsessed by megaliths. For a period he produced a number of inspirational paintings, not one picture being without his signatory trademark — a standing stone. He struck up a partnership with Iris Campbell, a gifted psychometrist (a psychometrist is able to detect by psychic intuition the knowledge of what happened in the past at a site), and their results over a number of years produced some astonishing data. He was an earnest follower of the seer and mystic, the Revd J. Todd Ferrier, and the work of Forbes and Miss Campbell is very much of a spiritual nature.

After the war a new phase of ley hunting activity sprang up. The Straight Track Club members had become fairly elderly, and under the aegis of the Research Centre Group the initiative had been taken over by The Avalon Society, formed by Egerton Sykes in 1946. When the group began its magazine *Research* in 1948, the vice-chairman of The Avalon Society was Iris Campbell, and two noteworthy members of the council were Lewis Edwards and K.H. Koop. The aims of the society were laid down as:

> To investigate the probability that from the Megalithic Culture had evolved:
>
> (i)   A system of orientation of sacred and secular sites based upon a common astronomical knowledge.
> (ii) A system of measurement for the construction of these sites for their linking together.

(iii)   A system of surveying indicated by alignments, tracks, standing stones and other objects.

(iv)   An interlocking arrangement of the sites based upon triangles, straight lines and circles.

(v)   A system of naming sites which has left its traces in the place-names of today.

(vi)   A calendar system based upon the formulation of the Zodiac and its application to daily use by means of stone circles and other structures.

(vii)   To consider whether the Arthurian Legends, the Welsh Triads, the Nordic Sagas and Eddas, the Celtic legends may not all contain confused recollections of this period.

It seems, however, that consideration may not have been given by The Avalon Society to Lawton's speculations. From the published work of this period, by such people as K.H. Koop, F.R. Watts and M.C. Carr-Gomm, it would appear that research had taken a step backwards, investigators having gone back to the grass roots of ley hunting. Watts, a schoolmaster, was producing fascinating illustrated articles on trackways in the area of Oxfordshire around Charlbury, and several of these appeared in his school's magazine.

Nevertheless, the 1950s was a generally dormant decade, though a number of present-day ley hunters were then working along traditional or speculative lines related to ley research.

What was undoubtedly the subject's turning point, and the occurrence which sparked off a new boost of energy in ley research, was the highly controversial deduction made by Tony Wedd which related leys and flying saucers. This association between leys and UFOs is so crucial as to warrant full explanations in a later section, but it is worth noting at this point that it was in a sixpenny booklet in 1961 that Tony Wedd first promoted a link between prehistoric sites and extraterrestrial visitants.

The result was that a new breed of ley hunters, with a fresh approach, were introduced to prehistoric alignments, and they began tracing leys and seeking correspondences between ley points and UFO sighting locations. The Straight Track Club had been wound up, The Avalon Society had gone its separate way, and so a band of keen ufologists, fascinated by Watkins's discovery, set about forming the Ley Hunters' Club.

It was formed in 1962, following a suggestion by Tony Wedd, then secretary of STAR Fellowship, to Philip Heselton. Philip contacted Egerton Sykes, who gave advice. and' a list of names and addresses of those who had been members of the Straight Track Club. Eleven replies were received.

On 15 July, 1962, a joint field trip with members of the Pendragon Society was undertaken by coach to Avebury. As a result Jimmy Goddard appeared on television, and gave a brief account of the outing.

On 17 November, 1962, the club held a public meeting in Kensington Central Library, London. Allen Watkins, the club's president, talked about his father's discovery, and colour slides of mark points were shown.

In January 1963, a bulletin was issued, edited by the club's chairman, Philip Heselton, in which a scheme to compile a national ley index was proposed. The aim was to plot every acceptable ley in Britain for analysis into possible patterns, and to have orderly, scientific evidence for presentation to professional archaeologists.

In the summer of 1964, Philip visited several of the original members of the Straight Track Club, and in October of that year a second bulletin was issued.

In April 1965, the first issue of *The Ley Hunter* magazine appeared, and subsequently six further issues were published, the last in November 1966. Philip Heselton edited all but the last two, which were edited by Ken Rogers. In fact, an eighth issue was put on stencil, but never reached the duplicator because a decision was taken to disband the club.

I learned of leys from an article by John Michell in 1967, and noting a mention of the Ley Hunters' Club in a book, I contacted Jimmy Goddard, who had acted as secretary to the club. Learning that the club no longer existed, I agreed to Jimmy Goddard's suggestion that I take over the magazine's title and subscriptions list, and publish it myself. *The Ley Hunter* reappeared in November 1969, and I have since published it at monthly intervals.

The present popularity of ley hunting owes a great deal to the writings of John Michell, the first of which was published in 1967. It was inevitable that 1967, with its bells, beads, flowerpower and psychedelia, the year when a generation thought the Age of Aquarius had dawned, would be a springboard for an active period of ley hunting. The underground newspaper *International Times* published an article by John Michell, 'Centres and Lines of the Latent Power in Britain'. Later that year his first book was published. Throughout 1968 he continued to develop his ideas, lecture and publish articles in alternative media publications. In 1969 he published *The View Over Atlantis*; in 1969 *The Ley Hunter* was reborn.

The history of ley hunting has shown a waxing and waning of interest, and at present the study is enjoying its greatest popularity since the 1930s. This work is dedicated to those who helped to shed light upon this subject, and provides information for those who wish to follow in their footsteps.

Visitors to foreign lands require tourist guidebooks. Mechanics who wish to understand the workings of machines require manuals. Those who wish to read further on a subject require a bibliography. Between the covers of this book is a guidebook, which leads the reader from stylish stone circles, to gaunt standing stones, to crumbling tumuli, to towering pines, by way of lines, straight and true. Here too is a manual on the workings of a system of spiritual physics. Here are suggestions for further reading; books to be studied while regaining strength at wayside crosses or on grassy mounds.

This is not a book written to entertain or educate. Those who seek within these pages for great truths will be disappointed; those who wish to be titillated by sensationalism will be displeased; those who think that there may be easy answers to the puzzles of prehistory will be disheartened; but those who wish to learn by their own efforts will find guidance.

If this book should help the student of leys, by making his journey a little easier and clearer, then it will have fulfilled its purpose. It is a practical guide, a manual. It details the points of leys, speculates on the system's creation, its purposes, its uses, its value, its dangers, its qualities, its layout, its future. It is an evaluation of all the hypotheses regarding leys, and how we may come to learn more. It is an advertisement for leys: an invitation to find them.

4. *Mapwork Ley Hunting*

'Both indoor map and outdoor field exploration are necessary.' – Alfred Watkins.[59]

Mapwork ley hunting is essential, but only as a prerequisite for fieldwork, the real work. Its value is only equal to that of a railway timetable to the traveller, which lists where he should go but does not take him there.

Before the stage is reached where a ley hunter need only travel in the countryside and note leys intuitively as he walks, cycles, drives or is driven, the map will provide examples for study. The best maps to use are the Ordnance Survey one inch to one mile. These cover a sufficiently large area and give reasonable detail. Larger scale maps are helpful in providing additional local detail, and are specially useful for tracing an exact route taken by a ley through a build-up district. Smaller scale maps are necessary when tracing primary leys, which cross several counties.

Leys are to be found on any one-inch map, and evidence of the system can be discovered even in the most densely built-up towns and cities. However, it is preferable to begin one's ley hunting in one's native district; not simply because fieldwork is made easier, but local knowledge is invaluable in determining whether certain features are ancient or modern.

Lay the map on a perfectly flat surface, and with ruler in one hand (a three-foot perspex ruler, giving the advantage of length and ability to read what is on both sides of the straight edge, is preferable), and pencil in the other (a pencil with a sharp point and fairly hard lead is essential), you are ready to begin.

Alignments are numerous, so you rapidly find a series of lines emerging on the map. The exercise need not necessarily be to find every single ley on the map, because quantity is not the yardstick by which to gauge successful ley hunting. However, as many leys as possible should be found if the aim is to determine whether any particular pattern of leys will emerge: If a map such as that of the Cleveland district of the North Yorkshire Moors be taken as an example, then if each tumulus were to be ringed and each alignment of four or more acceptable points be joined, not only would the map become one blanket of graphite, but you would find it a wearying task. The point of the exercise is to be selective.

Begin by circling several of the prominent sites. Then lay the ruler against any two. If the total of sites found to align adds up to four or more, then the ley is acceptable, and all points on it may be joined. Another worthwhile method of finding leys is to choose a particular point and turn the rule slowly in a circle, paying attention to note alignments radiating in different directions. When several leys cross at one point you will have discovered a ley centre.

If a ley centre appears on a map and there is no ancient site marked there, this will act as a spur to the ley hunter to visit the location and seek the explanation. Most likely at least a tree clump will be found, differentiated from the surrounding flora either by species of tree or the form of the clump. If not a clump, it may well be that a mark stone will be discovered. By making such a calculation on a map, F.R. Watts went to the exact location, found nothing suggestive of a ley point above ground, but unearthed a mark stone buried in the precise spot in the field.

In a later portion of this section I will deal in detail with all the acceptable ley points, and the many pitfalls which must be avoided.

Nevertheless this is the place for a couple of warnings. Leys are exactly straight. Do not accept any point for an alignment if the ley does not pass directly through it (except in the cases of camps, where leys generally only touch a side or sides).

Also an alignment of three or less points is not a ley. Alfred Watkins and Major Tyler accepted a minimum of four points, though five are accepted as a minimum by many ley hunters. However, and this is where fieldwork can be shown

to be of immeasurable value, it may be that if a four-point
alignment is followed on foot, one or more additional points
may be discovered, thus making it absolutely acceptable as a
ley. Also it may be found from publications of yesteryear,
particularly the records of local archaeological societies, that
details are given of mounds removed by ploughing, or ancient
stones destroyed for handy wall-building material.

If an exact location be given, then these are acceptable. It
is also a fact that the Ordnance Survey has not marked every
single tumulus, and careful fieldwork may bring these to
light, and also mark stones.

The destruction of a sizeable proportion of our prehistoric
heritage is to be deplored, and makes the ley hunter's task
difficult, as the discovery of ley patterns in an area is made
impossible except for practised geomancers. The location of
Budbury stone circle, Bradford-on-Avon, is recorded, but
apparently it is now partially covered by prefabricated
dwellings. Other sites have been even less fortunate. F.R.
Watts has referred to a historian of the last century who
deplored the destruction of crossroads stones to provide
metalling for roads by which they had stood for centuries,
and added that only those forming convenient boundary
marks had been spared.[113]

Wayside crosses were destroyed much earlier too. During
the early 1640s orders were given by the Puritans for their
destruction, owing to the idolatrous worship of the figures
carved on them. The Parliamentary army obeyed orders by
breaking the shafts and destroying the heads.

Hadrian's Wall, 73 miles long, with its typical square
dressed stones, provided much easy material for walls and
farm buildings, and was incorporated into these up to as
recently as the 1939-45 War.

Another shameful practice is the removal of prehistoric
stones for their curiosity value. At the eastern end of
Wallington Hall boating lake, Northumberland, is a 10-foot
monolith, which was originally the larger of two standing
stones called the Poind and his Man. The Poind was
supposedly removed from Shaftoe by Sir William Blackett in
the eighteenth century. The 6-foot high Man still remains *in
situ*.

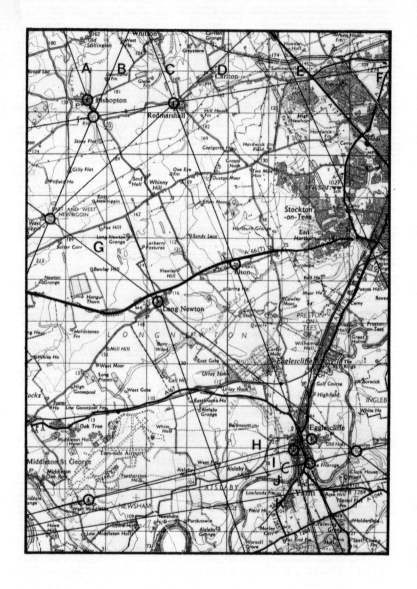

With regard to acceptable ley points, one prominent researcher, John G. Williams of Herefordshire, only accepts a limited number of features on alignments. His Scemb line system accepts:

S standing stones, stone circles
C cairns or tumuli, camps of pre-Roman origin
E earthworks of pre-Roman origin
M moats and mounds of pre-Roman origin
B burial barrows

KEY TO SOUTH DURHAM LEYS
(*See illustration*)

A. Bishop Middleham Church — Bishopton Church — Castle Hill Mound — Long Newton Church — Picton Church.

B. Stillington Church — Castle Hill Mound — Moat — Eryholme Church.

C. Sedgefield Church — Stillington Church — Redmarshall Church — Elton Church — Yarm Friarage — Kirklevington Church.

D. St Hilda's, Hartlepool — Stranton Church — Redmarshall Church — Moat — Scotch Corner Tumulus.

E. Finchale Priory — Sherburn Church — Kelloe Church — Beacon Hill — Grindon Church — Hilton Church.

F. Billingham Church — Norton Church — Redmarshall Church — Castle Hill Mound — Walworth Castle.

G. South Church, Bishop Auckland — Middridge Church — Moat — Long Newton Church — Egglescliffe Tumulus.

H. Egglescliffe Church — West Middleton Church — Low Dinsdale Church — Hurworth Church.

I. Yarm Church — West Middleton Church — Low Dinsdale Church — Croft Church.

J. Egglescliffe Tumulus — Yarm Friarage — Low Dinsdale Manor House — Hurworth Church.

K. High Leven Church — Hurworth Church — Croft Church — Barton Church — Melsonby Church — Ravensworth Castle.

5. Fieldwork Ley Hunting

'Experience and practice brings an insight, which quickly spots a ley. Often one can be first seen on the map, but I more often see it out of doors in "the ley of the land" itself, and this before the mark points are found.' – Alfred Watkins.[60]

Most of the particularly intriguing aspects of leys have not been discovered by poring over maps, though, as with Alfred Watkins's original insight into the system, maps have been responsible for such findings as the 'dragon lines' and other discoveries connected with celestial formations in the land.

It is as Alfred Watkins wrote, fieldwork 'should be the chief objective'.[60]

Anyone with a little skill and a spare hour or two can produce an acceptable ley pattern on a map, but it requires a certain ability to perceive intuitively where extra evidence may be found by fieldwork.

While out in the countryside or town keep half an eye open for the unusual, for clues. An idle glance at a row of trees in the grounds of a modern school in Hartlepool, as I cycled by, called my attention to a large mark stone in alignment with the trees. While taking the corgi dog belonging to my parents-in-law for a walk in Gildersome, in Yorkshire's West Riding, his sniffing at a boulder led me to note what may be one of the most remarkable mark stones yet found.

Allen Watkins, the son of Alfred Watkins, wrote an account of his first ley hunt, and it is a very fine example of what may happen to a ley hunter.[111] It was in 1931, and he was living in Cambridge. His father wrote asking if he would report on one of many leys which all touch the ancient camp around the city's castle mound. Eager to test the validity of the ley, he took the day off, took the train to Royston, and set off on foot for Strethall. As he strode through the beautiful Sky Counties scenery he noted a solitary figure ahead, walking towards him. They exchanged pleasantries about the weather, and Allen Watkins told him he had walked from Royston.

'Ah! Then you must 'a' come by the old Roman road, sir,' said the farm labourer. 'Now when I first came to these parts some of the older folk did used to say as they'd seen another old Roman road. It went straight from Strethall church towards Cambridge.'

This was Alfred Watkins's ley.

Allen Watkins, by simply indicating his route, as anyone would do normally, had received valuable information. He commented in the article: 'He must have read my mind in the way that a native countryman often does.'

Allen Watkins asked the man if he had ever seen the second road.

'No, sir, I never did,' he replied. 'But I'll tell you a funny thing about that old road. You can't see it at all on the ground, but when the corn grows you can see exactly where the old road went by the poorer crop. I've often seen it.'

Not everyone will be treated to such agreeable beginner's luck.

It is as Allen Watkins wrote:

I go out in search of confirmatory evidence, and at the first place I stop, in the middle of a field miles from anywhere, a man marches up and, unasked, gives me exactly the kind of evidence I am looking for — first-hand field observation.

You may call this coincidence. But is it? In the ley hunter's notebook these 'coincidences' begin to accumulate. My father had a score of such experiences. Nothing gives so much confidence as unsolicited evidence from an unexpected quarter. In this instance the casual memories of an elderly man unearthed a valuable clue.

If you have never done any previous fieldwork, choose a particularly well-marked ley from your map and walk along a section of it as closely as possible, taking due regard not to trespass or damage crops. Be alert to notice any indications of a trackway, mark stones, clumps of trees or faint traces of earthworks. You may well eventually develop an intuitive feeling for knowing when you are on a ley. Also, as already mentioned, points where leys cross can produce results.

It is interesting to be in a position where more than two ley points become visible to you on a ley. One summer afternoon, while cycling between Middlesbrough and Carlton-in-Cleveland, I stopped to examine a series of unusual earthworks in a roadside field, not marked on the map. I found that on looking eastwards I had a direct view of Roseberry Topping on the horizon, and between it and the earthworks, a pond and tree clump lay in perfect alignment. By moving several yards either way, I found the alignment to be displaced.

The success of one's ley hunting will be dependent upon one's personality, degree of affinity with the countryside, perception by normal eyesight and 'third eye', knowledge of what to look for and what to discard, and stamina.

When on leys in the countryside, you will become aware of senses outside the range of scientifically accepted ones, where intuition may reign and subtle power may be perceived.

6. Geometrical Patterns

'Establish the triangle and the problem is two thirds solved.' – Plato.

Whatever the properties of leys may be, they have relationships with one another, and these are geometrical. The ley system has been found to include parallel alignments, isosceles and equilateral triangles, regularly recurring angles of intersection and standard distances between points.

As mentioned, two of the factors to cast doubt upon the leys-as-trackways premise were the exceptional number of leys and their close parallelism. These factors were recognized by Alfred Watkins, but he was unable to satisfactorily account for them.

He related that he had discovered six equidistant parallel leys one-sixth of a mile apart.[58] Applying his trackways notion, he surmised that maybe one would take the place of an older one, and so on.

When drawing leys on maps, one should check if parallel leys occur. If several appear, the widths between should be recorded and checked with other examples, to see if these are repeated, either exactly or as multiples.

Leys abound, and parallel leys are not uncommon. As for a geometrical basis to the ley system, this is now accepted by ley hunters, except for the fact that very little has been done to substantiate this beyond doubt.

Leys, in themselves, are perhaps too exciting a visionary's discovery to be associated with the cold, analytical business of geometry. Triangles, being straightforward geometrical figures, are the obvious starting point for those wishing to research this aspect of the mystery. Few have been interested in analysing this, and few examples of geometric relationships have been committed to print. Yet there are three fine lines

of research which have been explored. Enclosing a vast area
of England is a remarkable isosceles triangle, on Salisbury
Plain lies a marvellous system of equilateral triangles and
there is the white horses triangles enigma.

In 1964, Philip Heselton announced the existence of what
has become known as 'the Great Isosceles Triangle of
England'. Its apex is Arbor Low stone circle in Derbyshire,
and its base links St Michael's Church, Othery, Somerset,
near Glastonbury, and West Mersea, in Essex. Arbor Low is a
ley focal, reputedly having between 50 and 150 leys passing
through it. 'Low' is the general name for stone circles in this
area, and 'arbor' has an old meaning of 'the central axis about
which a wheel turns, the central support for a machine'.
Machine it almost certainly is. A machine of prehistoric
spiritual physics. Jimmy Goddard, several years ago, suggested that Arbor Low could be 'the central "support" of the
ley system in Britain'.[19] I believe this to be correct.

From Arbor Low, two primary leys extend 152 miles. The
perpendicular is also a primary ley, it seems, and meets the
base line of the triangle at the Reading ley centre.[85]

Also, Sir Norman Lockyer drew attention to the fact that
Stonehenge, Old Sarum and Grovelly Castle form an equilateral triangle of six-mile sides.[30] As with certain astronomical
observations he made regarding Stonehenge, and a number of
other sites, he failed to see the full scale of the plan and
wider implications.

K.H. Koop found that extensions of two of the sides of
Lockyer's equilateral triangle by 7½ miles each way pass
through other ancient sites – Sidbury, Clearbury Rings,
'Castle Ditches' and Pertwood Down crossroads.[93] Parallel
leys through the north and south vallums of Yarnbury Castle
pass through south to Bulford Church and through Woodhenge. These are crossed at exactly 90 degrees by a line
through the east vallum of Yarnbury from Pottern Church to
Barford St Martin Church. Further extensions of these lines
seem to indicate a hexagon pattern of six such triangles
centring on Grovelly Castle, and a second centring on Old
Sarum.

The most frequent angles of intersection to be discovered

are 23½, 30, 45, 60 and 90 degrees. The tilt of the Earth's axis is 23½ degrees, which suggests that it is more than coincidental that this should be one of the common angles of intersection, as at Kelloe church, County Durham. Also multiples of this figure – 47, 70½ and 94 degrees – often occur.

Also the direction which leys take would seem to be significant in a proportion of cases. Alfred Watkins recorded eight north-south alignments, crossed by six running east-west, with no greater error than two degrees of true north. This was in Cambridgeshire, and one of these leys passes through two places, more than ten miles apart, both called Noon's Folly.[61]

There are examples of standing stones which align north-south, but these need to be checked as to whether they also mark leys. Within a distance of seventeen miles in Gloucestershire, the monoliths of Winstone, Elkstone and Tibblestone align north-south.

One of the most interesting discoveries in connection with leys and sacred sites is that from certain sites, concentric circles can be drawn to reveal the placing of selected sites, as with leys; lying outside mathematical probability. Colonel A.T. Powell in an appendix to Major Tyler's book[54] writes:

A circle can be drawn through any three points not in a straight line. If, however, one can be drawn through four points or two concentric circles through four points (two on each circle) then there must be a definite geometrical relation between the points. This may be chance or design. More than four points falling on one circle or two concentric circles so diminishes the mathematical probability of chance that design alone must be considered. The circular arrangement may have been definitely planned as such or have arisen geometrically out of quite a different idea of the designer. If a 'grid' had been the basic idea it would also give a design of other regular figures. The converse is not necessarily true. Regular figures may be so arranged that no reasonable grid exists.

Stonehenge, with half-a-dozen leys, has twenty-two arcs on which there are as many as seven or eight sites. Churchingford church, with eight leys and eleven arcs, has forty-two sites, of which thirty-eight are now occupied by churches.

Woodburn church, Buckinghamshire, with seven leys and twenty-five arcs, has seventy sites.

Tyler stated that on concentric circles from a given centre, two or more points give confidence that they are beyond the realms of chance.

J. Robin Allen has shown how he tested the theory on Kelsall Iron Age camp in Cheshire. He found four churches on one circle, six on another and seven on a third.[64]

Another point to note is that the radii of all Tyler's examples are multiples of 950.4 feet, a key distance.

No significance attaches to the actual circles themselves; these are not power lines, as are leys.

For those interested in the mathematical relationships between sites, several researchers have done pioneer work on this aspect, and the best-known standard measurement in this study is the megalithic yard.

But the first person to write on prehistoric standard distances was Edward Milles Nelson (1851-1938). He was foremost a microscopist, not, as he put it, interested in 'bugs and slugs', but 'brass and glass'. However, our concern is with his views on the dimensions of stone circles, and his deductions on the unit of length used by their builders. He wrote of visiting Hestinsgarth stone circle, in the Shetland Islands, in 1905, and discovering the measure used by its builders, 12.96 inches.[42] He also claimed to have found the use of the secret number of the 'Sun god', 666. He also wrote of a 'cult of the trigonometrical functions, and of the areas of the right-angled triangles' in England. The 12.96 inch measure was found throughout Britain by Nelson, also the hidden, sacred number 666 of 'The Beast', which is also the number for solar energy, being the total of the numbers in the magic square of the Sun. The number 1296 is also 6^4 — Plato's 'marriage number'.

Sir Norman Lockyer's equilateral triangle (Stonehenge, Old Sarum, Grovelly Castle), referred to previously, has three sides of six miles, making a perimeter of eighteen miles.

The Revd Hadrian Allcroft also attached significance to the length eighteen miles. He pointed out that in Dorset, Maiden Castle, Eggardon and Pilsdon Pen earthworks are in alignment, Eggardon being dead centre, and the total distance being eighteen miles.[1]

F.W. Andrew found divisions of 950.4 feet between cromlechs and their attendant long stones in Devon.[2]

Ludovic MacLennan Mann called this measure of 950.4 feet (which is 1/100 of 18 miles) the 'alpha unit', and attributed it to Palaeolithic origin.

Major F.C. Tyler related 950.4 feet to the length of the base-side of the Great Pyramid (1/480 part of a degree of the equatorial circumference of the Earth). The radii of the concentric circles he drew from various sites were multiples of this unit.[54]

The 'alpha unit' was also related to the old measurement the reed by Arthur Lawton and G.M. Hayton. Lawton also related it to a multiple of the Greek cubit.

Professor Alexander Thom has provided evidence that 2.72 feet, his megalithic yard, was used in the construction of Britain's stone circles. It was naively suggested that Thom's standard measurement would be the average pace of prehistoric man. We cannot, of course, measure prehistoric man's pace, but the standard Roman pace appears to have measured 2.43 feet, according to Professor Richard Atkinson. The significance of this figure is somewhat complex, and John Michell has investigated this thoroughly.[40]

John Michell noted that 2.72 miles is also a standard distance, having the same relationship to our mile as the megalithic yard has to our foot. He named it the geomantic mile. Distances from Glastonbury Tor to certain significant sites are measured in its multiples (St Michael's Tower, Burrow Bridge, 4 geomantic miles; Stoke St Michael, 4; Camelot, 4; Avebury, 15), and elsewhere, including Silbury Hill to Stonehenge, 6. Michell believes it to have been a universal unit, and states that in small units it has been found elsewhere in Europe and South America.[95]

With leys being so thick on the ground it would be surprising if we did indeed find each to be of equal length, equal in richness of type of aligned sites and equal in number of sites. A ley's requirement for validity is the alignment of four or more points. No one has yet produced a stipulation regarding primary leys – those to which we might attach a greater importance. The only examples so far recorded in print with the name 'primary' are the three sides and perpendicular of the Great Isosceles Triangle of England, the respective lengths of these being 125, 152, 152 and 170 miles. Such lengths are not inconsiderable and with the moderate frequency of spacing on leys between sites, should link a great many points or else a fair number of important sites. A couple of churches, a mark stone, a solitary pine and a monolith in a 100-mile alignment would be far from sufficient. An equation based on length, number of sites on alignment, and number of possible sites in districts covered is really necessary, but extremely complex to calculate. Commonsense would, I think, be the simplest answer to the problem.

The extended base line of the Great Isosceles Triangle of England is probably the most famous primary ley, and among the points on it are: Ashbrittle church, Devon – Othery church, Somerset – West Bradley church, Somerset Zodiac – Pylle church, Somerset – Roddenbury Camp – skirts Cley Hill and Cradle Hill, Warminster – Casterley Camp – Everleigh barrows – Inkpen Beacon – through Reading and North London – Stapleford Abbots church, Essex – Margaretting church, Essex – Mersea Island, Essex.

Saints slaying dragons, lords of the manor being summoned to combat with dragons, maidens being devoured by dragons, treasure being guarded by dragons, lone dragons winging through starry skies, dragons on hilltops. Inextricably, the legends connect with the ley system. Dragonlore is far from straightforward and can be best understood through application to the many properties manifested by the leys. However, in such a section as this, dealing primarily with the business of discovering the whereabouts of leys, the associations between places with dragon legends and saints connected with the legend may be usefully stated here.

The first person to discover alignments of dragon legend sites and churches dedicated to 'dragon saints' was John Michell, and he found that many such sites fall on three lines, all of which we may consider as primary leys.

Southern dragon line: St Michael's Mount – Hurlers stone circles – St Michael's church, Brentor – site of serpent killing at Trull, near Taunton – St Michael's, Burrow Bridge – St Michael's, Othery – St Michael's, Glastonbury Tor – Stoke St Michael – entrance to Avebury rings – Ogborne St George – St Michael's, Clifton Hamden – castle mound, Bury St Edmund's, Suffolk.

Western dragon line: Includes dragon legend sites associated with Brinsop, Bromfield, Moston, Unsworth and Longwitton.

Eastern dragon line: Dragon legend sites of St Osyth's, Essex; Slingsby and Sexhow in Yorkshire; Lambton, County Durham; crosses eastern dragon line at Longwitton, and Linton, Roxburghshire.

Useful work can be done in discovering which old parish churches are dedicated to 'dragon saints', and an attempt made to see if alignments occur. St Michael, St George and St Margaret are traditionally dragon slayers, and St Catherine is associated with the aerial phenomenon of the fiery wheel.

Also note barrows with the name Drakelow. This means dragon's barrow, dragons being associated as guardians of the treasure, supposedly within tumuli, but more likely it is a confused memory of ley power.

Within the context of this discussion mention must be made of 'Arthur lines'.

'That he [Arthur] belongs to mythology rather than to history has been made so plainly evident by recent research that the argument for his humanity must at last be regarded as futile.'
– Lewis Spence.[48]

'Arthur . . . was a human being if he was anything.'
– Geoffrey Ashe.[3]

Arthur is the central character in the Matter of Britain, the legendary history of Albion. Of all our native myths, that of Arthur has flourished strongest. Whether he was an historical character is not of prime importance, for symbolically he is very powerful – immortal, haunting, romantic, rich, spell-binding and visionary. He is the once and future king, awaiting reawakening to influence the rising of Albion's majesty.

As for keys, there are 200 prehistoric sites with Arthurian connections. These appear as widely dispersed as Argyllshire and Berkshire, Dumfriesshire and Hertfordshire, Cumberland and Surrey, Westmoreland and Glamorganshire.

These also form alignments, and this fact was discovered independently by John G. Williams and Maurice Clark.

Maps and books can be used to find these Arthurian sites. Examples of Arthur's Seat occur near Moffat, at Edinburgh, in Dumfriesshire and Surrey. Arthur's Stone is found near Swansea, near Coupar Angus, and in south-west Hertford-shire. There is Ben Arthur, Arthur's Pike and Arthur's Round Table.

John G. Williams has suggested that the name Arthur came from Welsh names for the Great Bear constellation, and Brinsley le Poer Trench has applied this vexing question to visitations by extraterrestrials.[53]

However, on a more basic level, further work on plotting these alignments could provide interesting results and estab-lish – if a large number of other sites of interest fall on the lines – whether such alignments are primary leys.

7. Distribution of Leys

'A most surprising fact is the enormous number of leys.' — Alfred Watkins.[58]

Leys lie thick on the landscape, running in many directions, some long, some short, some parallel, some higgledy-piggledy, some forming intricate patterns, but their sheer number is astounding, and remains outside the bounds of statistical probability.

Whether leys are evenly distributed throughout Britain is not easy to determine. A number of factors make an accurate assessment impossible. In an area where the population is densely concentrated there will be more ley hunters investigating the system, and so one would presume that a compilation of each's results would, when collected, reveal every single ley. However, modern development has removed a great many mark points, such as tree clumps and mark stones, and so many leys may be lost — except to psychics — for both mapwork and fieldwork. Also if one were to follow the Scemb line system, created by John G. Williams, County Durham would only produce a handful of mark points, as so far no stone circles or standing stones have been discovered in that county, yet I can vouch for the system being still active between the Tees and Tyne.

As for differences in the geometrical patterns throughout the country, some preliminary work has been done, and in certain parts parallel lines have been discovered but not in others, yet nothing which may be regarded as conclusive has emerged. Much work can be done on this aspect, comparing for instance the flat Sky Counties of East Anglia with rugged Dartmoor, or the similar geological limestone districts of the Mendips or Peak District to seek correspondences and divergences.

Also worth seeking are what, to coin a phrase, may be called ley focals. Arbor Low stone circle has been described by different investigators as having between 50 and 150 leys passing through it; Cley Hill, Warminster, having 13.

The system is, of course, not solely British, yet nowhere else in the world is it studied to any great extent, and I have chosen to concentrate in this work on Albion's leys.

Mathematical Probability and Leys

'Four-point alignments are seldom accidental.'
— Alfred Watkins.[59]

The vexing question of the mathematical probability of leys has been asked and answered several times, but requires explanation here in order that the reader can be assured of the scientific viability of leys.

Alfred Watkins dealt briefly with the accidental coincidence objection by showing that on the Andover map, containing fifty-one churches, eight separate instances occurred where four churches fell on a straight line, and in one case five aligned. He then marked haphazardly fifty-one crosses on a blank sheet of paper of similar size and found only one instance of four points aligning and none of five. In addition, he found the haphazard map had thirty-four cases of three or more aligning, and on the real map thirty-eight cases of three or more aligning. This indicated that three-point alignments are valueless, but that four-point alignments give ample evidence that such is design, not accident.[59]

Two equations to prove the mathematical probability of leys have been formulated, one by Tony Northwood,[100] and the other, reproduced here, by Peter Furness.[84]

Since the early days of research, the ley hunter has never been absolutely sure that leys are not merely due to chance alignment. Some methods have been devised for showing that random points do not line up to the same degree as ley points — but these have always been experimental. Such methods are clumsy and inefficient for the simple reason that reliable results can only be obtained by repeating the experiment a large number of times.

In this article I shall only outline a theoretical solution to the problem — fuller details may be obtained by writing to me.

Consider a one inch Ordnance Survey map of area A square miles, upon which is drawn a thick line representing a ley of length y miles and breadth x miles. If a random point is dropped on the map, the probability that it will fall in the line will be the fraction (f) of the area of the map that the line occupies.

i.e. Probability $= f = xy/A$

Similarly, the probability that m such points fall in the line is f^m

Now; if we scatter n points on the map, the probability that exactly m of these will fall in the line is given by:

$$P(n,m) = f^m(1-f)^{n-m}\binom{n}{m}$$

where $(1-f)^{n-m}$ represents the probability that the remaining $(n-m)$ points do not fall in the line, and $\binom{n}{m}$ is the number of ways of selecting m points out of n.

It can be shown that $\binom{n}{m} = \dfrac{n!}{m!(n-m)!}$ where $n!$ denotes the product of all the numbers from n down to one; i.e. $3! = 3 \times 2 \times 1.$ $= 6$

If the line is first fixed on the map by two of the points (the method used in ley hunting), the probability of getting an exact alignment of m points becomes:

$$P(n, m) = \binom{n-2}{m-2}f^{m-2}(1-f)^{n-m} \quad \text{(Equation 1)}$$

If there is a total of W alignments in the n points (including two-point lines) then the number $N(m)$ of m point lines to be expected by chance is given by:

$$N(m) = W\,P(n, m) \qquad \text{(Equation 2)}$$

It can be shown that: $\quad W = \binom{n}{2} - \sum_{3}^{n} [\binom{m}{2} - 1]\,P(n, m)W$

rearranging: $\quad W = \dfrac{\binom{n}{2}}{1 + \sum_{3}^{n}[\binom{m}{2}-1]\,P(n, m)} \qquad \text{(Equation 3)}$

If we assume that ley points are random, we can find n for a particular map of area A. If the length of the ley is y miles, what can we reasonably take as its width x? The ultimate minimum for this is the breadth of the pencil or ink line representing the ley, but inaccuracies in drawing, in symbolism on the map itself, make it reasonable to take x to be 1/100 of a mile of 17.6 yards.

The following are results of calculations performed using a typical one-inch Ordnance Survey map.

Counting gave the total number of good ley points as 200. The area of land A of the map was 625 sq. mls. I took the length of a typical ley on this map to be 30 mls.

From equations 1 and 3, $W = 16,500$.

From equation 2 $N(3) = 1,570$, i.e. 1,570 3-point leys by pure chance.

similarly $N(4) = 72$, i.e. 72 4-point leys by pure chance.

similarly $N(5) - 2$.

similarly $N(6) = 0.05$.

similarly $N(7) = 0.001$.

These figures indicate that for the particular map used, any ley with less than six points could be expected by chance. The value of $N(7)$ suggests that if leys are chance alignments, one would only find one seven-point ley in a collection of 1,000 different maps!

Thus we can show with certainty that leys of more than a fixed number of points are unlikely to be due to chance.

Geomancy, Dowsing and Geodetic Lines

'The potential value of diviners to archaeology is indisputable.' — Guy Underwood.[55]

Ley power is invisible to all but the most sensitive psychics, yet at times a fair proportion of people can feel it. Those who regard this as superstitious nonsense, beware. Almost invariably geologists and physicists regard water divining as fraudulent, yet dowsers discover water where all other means have failed to locate it. When this ability is related to the location of leys and currents of psychic energy, it is termed geomancy.

In addition to finding water, dowsing has been responsible for making clearer the notion that a great proportion of minor topographical features were engineered by man, and that certain major features have been considerably altered by man, such as hill-top shapes and river courses.

What the dowser can achieve baffles the scientist. The diviner walks with an instrument, usually a hazel twig, and when his subconscious or superconscious perceives water, or any other object of his search, this causes neuro-muscular reflexes to indicate the presence.

Major F.C. Tyler believed dowsers were not only able to locate water, but prehistoric sites. In suggesting this, he added: 'This is a suggestion of my own, and I do not ascribe this idea to others. Anyway, it is a romantic one, even if not based on logical reasoning.'

Arthur Lawton was in complete agreement with Tyler. His researches led him to coin the word 'eustasia', which he related to the 'right-sightedness' of prehistoric sites. In support of his belief in what is now called geomancy, he quoted[27] from *Dawn of a New Age*, by Eleanor C. Merry:

> How much more significance places have than we even imagine today! How little we realize with what care and what vision they were chosen, so that the living earth should pour into the atmosphere what was needed for a particular cult – whether of moisture, or dryness, or heat, or cold, whether of iron or copper or lead or sparkling silica, or the magnet's invisible passion!

Is this an insight or shrewd guess that prehistoric man controlled the weather, controlled the forces of the earth currents, and knew later where to site his mining operations? Lawton also refers to a letter by L. Palen, in June 1939 issue of *The Journal of the British Society of Dowsers*, which gives examples of bad living conditions in houses caused by unhealthy radiations, and their cure after having been found by dowsers. Palen suggested the formation of a government department board which would advise on new housing sites. Lawton believed this was done six thousand years ago. Similar care would be taken over religious sites, where large numbers of people met.

Before describing further examples of geomancy, a brief review of the late Guy Underwood's work in this field should provide ample evidence of the reality and importance of such a practice. In his posthumously published book *The Pattern of the Past* he set out his remarkable conclusions on the existence of what he termed geodetic lines.[55] The reality of these lines is of immense importance in ley study, as they occur at prehistoric sites and give insights into not only the location of sites, but the type of monument chosen for a particular place.

The patterns created by the subtle geodetic lines of force were assigned to particular topographical monuments, and Underwood believed that these enabled persons initiated into that code to find them distinguishable. This theory that lines of force were responsible for the choice of structure and layout is the most interesting point in his book.

What we must, however, be sure to recognize is that geodetic lines and leys must not be confused. Leys are straight; geodetic lines wander in curves, spirals and many other shapes. It may be helpful if we consider the three main forms of geodetic lines as a secondary phenomenon, and leys as a primary phenomenon. Nevertheless, the sites where Underwood mapped the geodetic lines are the same sites which ley hunters link into alignments.

Underwood mentions Alfred Watkins briefly twice, but there is no attempt to relate leys and geodetic lines. It must be presumed that he was unaware of the theories relating leys to power lines akin to his geodetic lines, for if he had known so, it is hard to believe that he would not have investigated leys, to determine the relationship between the currents he had discovered and the ley current.

In the detailed examination of each feature related to the ley system, I will describe Underwood's findings with regard to them. However, so that the reader will be conversant with the three main types of line categorized by Underwood, it will be profitable to give here a synopsis of each. What they all have in common is their being generated within the Earth, wave motion is involved, they have great penetrative power and form a network all over the Earth. Apart from the primary forms of geodetic phenomena, there are many secondary phenomena. The following are the three primary types:

Water line — To a dowser is 'negative', i.e. affects the left side of his body. Ground has been lowered to denote their presence. They are denoted by ditches, lower parts of lynchets, and in the case of multiple water lines by marks on stones. They mark the course of underground streams.

Track line – To a dowser is 'positive', i.e. affects his right side. They have little significance in the layout of sacred sites, though sometimes affect minor details or were specially marked. Animals follow them. Old roads are aligned on them. They are denoted by lanes, tracks, field divisions and solifluction lines.

Aquastat – To a dowser is 'positive'. Ground was raised to denote these. An aquastat had not to be obstructed so that it could not be followed. It was denoted by linear mounds, terraces, upper ridges of lynchets, stone rows and stone circles.

Blind springs are also worthy of mention. They are centres where primary lines converge and emerge. Their significance will be made abundantly clear in later pages. Important ones were denoted by stone circles, barrows, monoliths, dolmens, logan stones, rostra, basin stones, hut circles, pit dwellings, pond barrows, pits and ponds.

Geomancy, however, does not necessarily require the use of a divining instrument. It was the ancient art of divining centres of power and the currents flowing between them. As with water divining, the ability may still be inherent in a large proportion of the population, and many ley students are capable of utilizing it. I can often sense the presence of a ley without the landscape giving any clues as to there being a power alignment, while occasionally I can actually 'feel' the power. For me it is usually only an 'intuition'.

Leys were marked in prehistoric times by those competent in this faculty, and major sites were designated to points where several leys met and there was a strong focus of power. Divination was also responsible for the siting of barrows, stones, wells, beacons and astronomical observatories.

It is difficult to determine when – if ever – geomancy vanished, but sites of ancient sanctity were often chosen for the sites of Christian churches. In A.D. 601, Abbot Mellitus wrote to Pope Gregory concerning the pagan places of worship he had found in Britain. The reply was:

> I have, upon mature deliberation on the affair of the English, determined . . . that the temples of the idols in that nation ought not to be destroyed; but let the idols that are in them be destroyed. . . . For if these temples be well built, it is requisite that they be converted from the worship of devils to the worship of the true God; that the nation, seeing that their temples are not destroyed, may remove error from their hearts, and knowing and adoring the true God may they more faithfully resort to the places to which they have been accustomed.

Whether the Pope assumed that the Britons had temples along Roman lines with great statues, his answer appears to reveal somewhat secular reasoning, and indicates the unlikelihood of his having knowledge of the sacred power inherent at these sites.

King Cnut repeated this injunction, it being obvious that for a long time after the introduction of Christianity, the stone monuments continued to exert an influence on the populace.

Dion Fortune gives a reason for the wisdom of retaining pagan sites for worship:

> Whenever a place has had prayers and concentrated desires directed towards it, it forms an electrical vortex that gathers to itself a force, and it is for a time a coherent body that can be felt and used by man. It is round these bodies of force that shrines, temples, and in later days churches are built; they are the Cups that receive the Cosmic downpouring focused on each particular place.[16]

Many are the legends associated with the siting of churches, abbeys and cathedrals, and it seems that until the Reformation, geomancy was practised and the continuity of placing religious sites on the power lines remained. Was it coincidence that the Benedictines chose to build monasteries at the foot of both the Man of Wilmington hill figure in Sussex and the Cerne Abbas giant in Dorset?

H.J. Massingham, whose vision of the ancient megalithic culture was light years ahead of his fellow archaeologists, sensed something of the geomantic principles when he wrote that prehistoric man had a 'special faculty for selecting a site which both reveals and gathers up the true values of a landscape'.[36]

Dowsing, generally an outdoor pursuit, can also be practised in the home. One night at a friend's home, my wife and I experimented with a sealing wax pendulum. With the map of South Durham in front of her, my wife dangled the pendulum over St Cuthbert's church, Billingham, closed her eyes, and concentrated on finding a ley from it. After a short while she received a clear impression of a streak of white light. I told her to keep her eyes closed and move the pendulum in the direction where she sensed the ley. It was exactly on the alignment to Norton church, Redmarshall church, castle mound at Bishopton and Walworth Castle. When I made a similar attempt from St Hilda's church, Hartlepool, with eyes closed and the map turned so I could not establish the directions, the result was less spectacular. However, I received a distinct impression of the Cleveland Hills, and could indicate the correct direction without opening my eyes.

A special form of divination which has been utilized to probe into prehistory is psychometry, and as data from this practice will be found throughout this book, a few words of explanation are necessary. Psychometry is basically the art of receiving tactile impressions which in a part of the brain are transformed into pictures or visions. The means by which information from a standing stone, for instance, can be gained, is to allow the mind to become blank and receptive. Touching the stone lightly, impressions will form, and eventually definite conclusions will be gained. However, a great deal of subjective, wishful thinking may be involved, though the insights claimed by certain psychometrists recorded in this work are being backed up by further evidence from other sources — albeit currently psychic rather than physical.

Part 2

THE MEGALITHIC CULTURE

8. The Neolithic Period

'Here you may enter upon the very holy of holies of the moorland and shake off the mean thoughts of cities in the visible presence of the Great God Pan.' – Michael Temple (The Gytrash of Goathland).

The Neolithic period can be dated as lying roughly between 3,000 B.C. and 1,800 B.C. Britain was on the fringe of civilization, untouched by the metal users of the Near East. Its people were farmers, to whom was introduced the practice of collective burial in long barrows and new types of stone tombs. Stock-raising and cereal growing, with mutual protection, made them a settled people. Surplus food was traded for tools, equipment and ornaments, made by specialists. Bushes and small trees were felled with polished stone or flint axes and burnt to enrich the soil. Domesticated animals ate new shoots and helped clear woodland. The people never exceeded 20,000 at any one time. They occupied Sussex, Wessex, East Anglia, Lincolnshire, Yorkshire, the South West, the coast of Western Scotland, Orkney, the Moray Firth and Aberdeenshire. The climate was warm and moist, with alder, oak, elm and lime growing. The megalithic (megalith = stone) culture was brought either by prospectors for metals (many tombs in metalliferous districts), by colonists (most in good farming districts) or by purveyors of a new kind of tomb, perhaps missionaries of the Mother Goddess religion.

This is a typically orthodox viewpoint. Needless to say, much of this bears little resemblance to my view, and virtually nothing whatsoever to fact and truth.

Orthodox archaeologists are now realizing that two major suppositions about prehistoric life are false – those regarding stone circles and the dating of sites. Recent advances in dating have shown that many sites are very much older than had been previously supposed. Radiocarbon results have not only placed the European megalithic culture back about 700 years, but swept away the diffusionist basis of prehistory. It has shown how various assumptions in dating have given a patently false conception of the time relationships between the Egyptian and Mesopotamian civilizations, whose calendars afford accurate dating, and the civilizations of Europe. Previously it was thought that a diffusion of ideas from the Near East created the advances in Western Europe. Now we know that the megaliths of Albion and Brittany are a great deal older than the Egyptian pyramids, and that the builders of Stonehenge did not have any help from Mediterranean civilization. This new calibration of radiocarbon dating, though not universally accepted, makes untenable the diffusionist theory. This put the beginning of the megalithic culture before 4,000 B.C., and showed that specifically technological advances, such as metallurgy, were first achieved in Europe.

Diffusionist theories are popular with both orthodox and speculative archaeologists — though not the same examples — and the bolder thinkers enjoy seeking for information on vanished civilizations and researching the possibilities of early voyages of discovery. Lemuria; the Piri Reis Map; Scandinavians discovering North America, proceeding through Central America and on to Easter Island and back; not to mention the dogged determination of those who believe in a former physical existence of Atlantis.

These are no less fanciful than a belief that Western Europe's megalithic culture originated in Twelfth Dynasty Egypt, with Middle Minoan Crete as the distributor. The latter belief was H.J. Massingham's. He wrote:

'In Egypt, agriculture, astronomy and mathematics were essential parts of one whole, and it seems we can only read any meaning into Stanton Drew and Avebury by the aid of Egyptian pictographs.'[35]

Apart from his emphasis on a diffusionist colonization for mining theory, Massingham came nearer than any of his contemporaries to putting the megalithic culture into perspective.

Many are the pitfalls for those who navigate in the wake of Atlantean colonists or disaster survivors and inter-continental

voyagers across the Atlantic or Pacific or from the Mediterranean. This book is specifically about Britain and its leys,
but some attempt must be made to relate the beginnings of
the marking of the system, and application of ley power, to
the influences which brought about a truly remarkable
revolution in thinking and behaviour, and to its timing. We
may safely, I believe, describe the Neolithic period as the
time of the foundation of the marking of the ley system, but
the origin of the first 'ley men' remains uncertain.

Alfred Watkins reserved his right to remain undogmatic
about the age of the marking of leys, and also the time they
fell into decay. However, from the evidence of the monuments upon them, he postulated a Neolithic origin.

Guy Underwood reckoned that the time necessary to mark
the geodetic lines was excessive and required much effort. He
suggested guardedly, and I believe quite wrongly, that mass
hypnotism was utilized. He was mystified as to why such
lines should be marked, and to explain this seemingly obscure
exercise he postulated that it might have been as simple as
keeping folk out of mischief in uneventful times or in winter
periods.

A re-evaluation of the megalithic culture is necessary as
this will provide us with the background to the inspiration
which led to the creation of the working ley system, and its
remains give us some indication of how this was achieved.
The Neolithic period must be reappraised to determine the
true extent of the cultural and technological advances made
by a people who were in no way primitive savages, but
sophisticated philosophers and astronomers living in harmony
with one another, their countryside and the cosmos itself. As
a starting point, before their remains are shown in a new
light, it can be shown that the orthodox archaeologists have
created a ludicrously insupportable view of the Neolithic
period and the megalithic culture which thrived during those
distant times.

The distribution of this culture may firstly be examined.
To relegate the population, which I believe must have
numbered far in excess of 20,000 at any one time, to the
areas neatly apportioned for it by archaeologists is grossly

inadequate. I have discovered sufficient evidence of Neolithic occupation in County Durham to rule out anything but a certainty that large numbers of settlers at that time inhabited this particular area. Yet the remains produced by professionals are dreadfully scanty.

The whole notion of their settling in high areas, because of widespread afforestation, is extremely suspect. Alfred Watkins disbelieved this, but for the reason that dense forests would make his theory of sighting from point to point untenable. Mark stones would be lost in thickets, and flashes of water would be undetected from high points. Solitary tree clumps would be an impossibility. I think we can assume that the Neolithic landscape was little different from our own natural countryside. Since the Neolithic period it may, however, have been left to become more afforested.

There is ample evidence, especially with false hills, tree clumps and mark stones, that the lowlands were inhabited by Neolithic man, and that as such areas became the basic territory of mankind from Roman times onwards, traces of his habitation of such districts has been almost completely eradicated. Nevertheless, I believe he had a greater affinity with the high ground. It was closer to the heavens and afforded greater vistas of the cosmos. From the escarpments he could see the stars spinning in their orbits above at night, and see the lush vegetation and winding streams of the valleys below in the daytime. By day he hunted deer in the valleys and as evening fell he climbed to see the Great Bear move across dark infinity.

Dartmoor was a supposed wasteland, yet contained more villages than any other ground of the same area in Britain. As Massingham said, prehistoric man settled 'at the dictation not of his body but of his mind'. It was important for him to be in the correct place, and if possible nearer the heavens.

He appreciated the landscape and the sky in a way we can now only dimly comprehend. The wonder of the hills, valleys, peaks and the sea; the majesty of the Sun, the Moon and the stars.

He was not on the fringe of civilization, but at its earthly centre, attempting to reach out physically and spiritually for a universal knowledge and belonging with the infinite. His manipulation of ley power was not a conquering of nature, but a partnership as equals. The next stage was space travel, and his space programme was not material but spiritual; not in the nature of exploitation, but exploration. His attempts seemingly lay on two levels, that of inner space whereby he received visionary information on its movements, constitution and astrological significance, and perhaps also on the plane of actual space travel — astrally.

His harmony with nature gave him an understanding of the properties of stone, wood, plants, animals, his fellow men, and above all, a oneness with the universe. What was natural, he accepted and used. He utilized ley power, the most potent expression of the divinity of the infinite, including nature and his environment. Metal, once treated, was repugnant to him. Why otherwise would it be that no metal objects have been found in any long barrows? A metal object placed on a blind spring obliterates for a while all geodetic reactions around it. Leys are the dragon pulse, and dragon spirits in China detest iron. If a piece of iron is thrown into a pond where such a spirit dwells, the dragon will spiral into the sky and rain is caused. Bronze was seemingly less abhorrent to our early ancestors. However, all metals, unlike stone and wood, will not hold ley power, but repel it.

They were farmers, but they were also technicians in a huge programme of marking leys and applying the power to their needs. They collaborated as one, joined in a common purpose and a bond of brotherhood. They were also astronomers, mathematicians and philosophers, bound by a peaceful instinct to create and retain a perfect society.

To a great many people it seems inconceivable that the physical and mental resources of the Neolithic Britons were adequate for them to have achieved such a technologically advanced civilization as this book strives to make clear. A not inconsiderable number of those who accept the fact of the ley-based civilization believe there was an impetus from outside the indigenous population to establish the megalithic culture, and their theories generally favour outer space or fabled Atlantis as the source of inspiration.

Atlantis – a drowned Atlantic Atlantis – is the major contender for being the source of the megalithic knowledge. The reasoning is that when the legendary continent was submerged around 9,500 B.C., survivors arrived in Britain and marked the ley system. Others, particularly those who believe there to be a definite link between leys and the flight paths of UFOs, contend that beneficent extra-terrestrials taught earthmen the megalithic culture, and that this period was the golden age of mythology. Evidence for the megalithic culture to have grown in Britain without outside influences is as difficult to establish as the Atlantean and extra-terrestrial theories. This book is intended to be a practical guide for the reader to do his own research and his own thinking, and he must decide for himself how the megalithic culture came into being. The fact that the culture involved enormous undertakings with regard to leys and allied matters is indisputable. How it came into being is still something of a mystery.

It is also worth considering at what point in history the system and culture became misunderstood and its value degraded. It must be remembered that the megalithic culture we are visualizing was a peaceful one, where each man was in harmony with his fellows. Perhaps the breakdown into warfare was the result of invasions, of greed, of black magic, or drugs, of metal usage or the departure of extra-terrestrial overlords. It would seem that in a short space of time the system fell into general disuse, and the masses began to treat its potency with superstition, the heavenly bodies as gods and goddesses, the strong and the rich as masters, and UFOs as dragons. Legends may give us the answer, or a part at least, as to how a great civilization began its downward path.

Neolithic science dealt with in this book is varied, but underlying it all is the dual requirement of fertility and health. Natural arts come to the fore, and are the domain of agriculture and medicine. Without the farmer or the doctor plants would grow and mankind would continue; but Neolithic man, with farming prominent in his life, sought to manipulate natural processes and conquer the vagaries of climate and disease. This book reveals the ways in which he exploited natural currents for a wide variety of harmonious purposes. The artificial crafts, whereby man intervened to produce artefacts, is the archaeologists' territory — metalworking, pottery, etc. — where man created what nature could not, and this debatable step forward is of far less interest and of little significance. The introduction of metal into prehistoric man's universe was probably the death knell of his quest for spiritual enlightenment.

Mastery of agriculture, husbandry and medicine, and the consequent development of religious thought, was responsible for an integrated moral, philosophical and cosmic awareness. These pursuits were ruled by seasons and were immediate and immutable, whereas the production of artefacts depended in no way upon the cycles of time.

Metal production followed simple laws, but agriculture depended upon the unpredictable complex force, weather. Consequently everything which might lead to a better life, for man's inner contentment in addition to his material comfort, was studied, built into a scientific intellectual system, and expertly applied. Neolithic man's efforts went not into making things, but making himself more perfect. He built his stone circles not simply to make astronomical calculations, either for intellectual or astrological reasons, but created places where ritual was harmonized with mathematical skill and terrestrial power manipulation techniques so as to link himself to the infinity of the cosmos where he played no small part.

Metal-working brought a radical change to society, and the spiritual age ended. Metal's only real interest to us, and its only real value in society, was in the workings of alchemical practice, and here the manipulation of metal was only secondary to the manipulation of consciousness.

9. The Mark Points

*'Since all prehistoric monuments are enclosed by
spirals produced by one or more springs, the
reasonable assumption is that their positions were
determined by these phenomena. The blind spring
designated the spiritual centre of the site.' – Guy.
Underwood.*[55]

Stone Circles

*'Let it suffice to put forward these discoveries or
"coincidences" at Stonehenge, primed with the
thoughts of Hawkins' 2,000 men's seven-year
work. What nature of men were capable of this
task? What forces drove or integrated them?
Finally, and possibly vital to our own survival how
much have we yet to learn?' – Keith Critchlow.*[80]

Sun Honey is perhaps the nastiest prehistoric site in Britain.
It looms forebodingly on an Aberdeenshire hilltop enclosed
by a wall and overgrown with unfriendly vegetation and
shadowed by tall trees. One September afternoon I
approached it. On the wall a hapless crow hopped, one wing
broken. I climbed inside among the nettles, rosebay willow-
herb, deadly nightshade, poisonous ash, sycamores and larch
seemingly blasted by lightning. The ground was turfy and the
impression was that I might suddenly disappear into it.
Midges were everywhere, and crows flew in from all
directions and circled, cawing their annoyance at my intru-
sion. A big hare lolloped ahead of me and disappeared
through a gap in the wall with a backwards glance of disdain.

The atmosphere was distinctly colder within the circle,
with its gaunt, misshapen stones, yet I was sweating. I was
not afraid, but my companions would not venture within.
The last visit of one of them had been made particularly
unpleasant by the sight of rows of dead crows, placed in neat

rows on the huge recumbent stone, and live crows on dead, central trees, now removed. The psychic atmosphere is one of saturated evil; a sinister place of grim stones and a particularly grotesque recumbent stone.

The foul undergrowth runs rampant and bedevils one's footsteps. It protects the stones, which are nevertheless interesting: one has a pronounced V-mark, another purposely indented and a third bearing a face. Here is no mountain ash, no love, no hope or beneficent spiritual feeling. I would not like to revisit it. Standing with its circle of tall firs, it is welcome to remain a black magicians' site.

Nearby Midmar stone circle, by contrast, is cosy. It stands in a neat churchyard and now consists of a recumbent stone flanked by two large stones, and completed by five other upright stones. A partridge was nosing around in the undergrowth by it, and it felt a very peaceful place to me, though my wife was convinced it had once been psychically evil. Such influences having since been nullified. Birds twittered in the trees and the firs leaned with the breeze. The stones suggested the faces of a lion, a baboon and elephants. On the recumbent stone were a variety of symbols, difficult to interpret, but one struck me as a symbol for the etheric — a diamond pattern.

Tomnaverie is another typical Aberdeenshire stone circle, with the same bouncing turf feeling as at Sun Honey, but its atmosphere is not bad. It was a cold morning when I visited it. Midway between two peaks and on level land beside a former quarry, broom grew in profusion around it. Its great granite stones were hardly communicative, but the site made my wife feel very big, and the name means 'hill of the giant's grave'. I had the distinct feeling that the positioning of the stones was meant to reveal a definite spiral.

Melgum stone circles are tiny by comparison, with a wonderful atmosphere, the stones poking up among lush vegetation in a wood. Here my visit was cut short by a pigeon, continually toppling on to its face, which I caught, examined for wounds or a broken wing, and on finding it unharmed physically took it out of the vicinity. It remained tranquil, and when released had recovered much of its balance, and it led me to surmise that the circle had perhaps created a soporific effect. Ley energy has been felt by many to have the same effect as alcohol or other drugs.

It would be as well, before discussing the significance of stone circles, whose attributes must be split into various sections of this book, to give a few generalizations on them. Firstly, the archaeologists have created a division of these into true stone circles and henges. Briefly a henge is a stone or wood circle enclosed in earthen banks with one or more entrances. The wooden ones include the Sanctuary on Overton Hill, near Avebury; Arminghall, near Norwich; and Woodhenge, which has been suggested as being at one time roofed. Class I henges, with one entrance, are known only in Britain. Class II have two or more entrances and include Arbor Low and Penrith. The greatest examples are Avebury and Stonehenge.

Stone circles have no ditches and are usually on rocky ground. Some are in groups as at Stanton Drew, Somerset. A special class are the recumbent circles of Aberdeenshire, Banffshire and Kincardineshire. Here two tall stones flank a space across which lies prostrate another menhir, and the other stones diminish in size from the two tall ones on either side of the recumbent stone.

Before taking my arguments any further, I will dispose of the ludicrously cautious approach of Geoffrey Grigson, who thinks it possible that Stonehenge was a very large roofed round house inside its enclosure; Avebury a pair of such, with a great stockade of stone posts whose infilling has disappeared.[21] The mind boggles.

Standing Stones

> 'Let it be confessed that scientific archaeology has brought us little nearer to understand them.' — Grahame Clark.[8]

Across the bleak moorland where rabbits scamper, harriers hover on the air currents and sheep bleat miserably, time lies almost at a standstill and the centuries-old standing stones hold themselves erect as the heather swirls and the pines bend. Like sore thumbs, the monoliths demand attention and infuriate archaeologists with their mute disdain for the grovelling on hands and knees of those who would prod at the ground around them for burial remains. They will not give up their secrets to the uninitiated. Silent and sullen, stable, stationary, solitary, perhaps a little sinister to those without any semblance of sincerity, they stick up stark against a grey horizon of glowering thunderclouds.

In lowland fields their companions are the cattle, who rub against them, and any weary crow who finds one a convenient stop-over point between woods. Children believe those who say they are arrows fired from the Devil's bow, or that they are the evidence of a churlish giant whose fun was in hurling stones. To the mystified archaeologist these enigmatic menhirs attract notions of indefinable religious cults: a primitive civilization's unbridled superstitious nature and unswayable dependence on mollifying an awesome supernatural cosmogony of demons and terrifying forces requiring placating; savages at worship around these crude phallic symbols, representative of a deity; or monstrous memorials to a dead chieftain.

Their abundance makes it little easier to find a simple solution to their meaning. They are fairly common on moorlands, and also occur in some lowland districts. Known by the names monoliths, menhirs and standing stones, they are sometimes associated with stone circles.

Others have been incorporated into walls. Sometimes, as on Dartmoor and Bodmin Moor, they are arranged near together in a double row. The most remarkable monoliths are the Three Arrows, near Boroughbridge, Yorkshire, where the tallest is 22½ feet above ground level. Grahame Clark suggests they may have once belonged to a double alignment;[8] Leland, who visited the site between 1535 and 1543, said a similar one stood six to eight feet away from the central one; Camden, writing at the time of Elizabeth I, stated that there were two middle stones, one having been displaced in the hope of finding money.

The archaeological fraternity is certainly baffled. Are they sole vestiges of megalithic tombs, alignments or circles? In certain cases we can be certain that a monolith is the remnant of a circle. For though it was thought to be disastrous to remove circles, there is a tradition that it was customary to leave one stone as an act of propitiation. I have seen a field adjacent to Melgum stone circles, Aberdeenshire, with a single monolith in it, but patches of darker and taller grass in a circular form around it, suggesting that there was once a major circle.

O.G.S. Crawford believed most British standing stones belong to the Dark Ages, around A.D. 400-800, or that they were not originally isolated, but formed part of some monument whose other parts have been removed.[9] I do not believe them to be associated with post-Christian times, though in fairly modern times farmers have set up in their pastures stones for cattle to rub against to relieve their irritations, as we ourselves scratch away the humble itch. Such stones serve as strong pillars which the beasts cannot topple. Stones from the megalithic era will give cattle the added pleasure of being stimulated by the ley power held by the menhir. So unless one knows for certain that such a stone has been erected recently, and can therefore be safely ignored, it should be checked for alignments; particularly to determine whether it is placed where two or more leys cross.

Where a stone is found to have fluting, do not be satisfied with the naive explanation that this is the result of uneven weathering. The vertical grooves fascinated Alfred Watkins, who argued correctly that they were artificially cut. He drew attention to the Queen Stone, near Symonds Yat, on the Wye, which has grooves from five to seven inches deep and only two to two-and-a-half inches wide, and suddenly ceasing near the base. The fluting, being on all four sides, disproves the theory that stratification was a contributing cause, as that would create grooves on only two sides. The significance of the grooves is unknown, but they may denote the strength of current.

Alfred Watkins also noted the frequency with which menhirs were placed near to mounds. He assumed that because mounds, in forty cases in Herefordshire, adjoin churches, it was likely that the churches were built on the site of a monolith as the mounds remained unchanged.

He was intrigued that a monolith's top surface often indicated by its edge or backbone the direction of its ley.

Cup and ring marks on megalithic stones have never been explained satisfactorily by mainstream archaeology, and it is to Alfred Watkins that we owe a debt of gratitude for making this puzzle a little clearer. When Robin Hood's Stone, one with grooves, was moved at Allerton, Liverpool, he found that the ten cup hollows remaining underground formed six alignments of three points each. He believed that they were a ley map.[59] It was the stone in Tillington churchyard, Herefordshire, with four cup marks on its upper surface that provided the evidence he sought. Drawing diagonals between the marks and taking a northern bearing from the point of intersection, which he assumed to represent the stone's position itself, he found they pointed out two well-marked leys crossing at the stone. Others examined seemed to confirm his intuitive discovery.

These cup and ring marks form groups of small round and oval cavities and serpentine bands. Those on glaciated rock surfaces in Central Park, New York, are almost identical to Scottish ones. Peter Rawstone, a South African artist, held an exhibition of rubbings of such marks from megaliths in Ireland. He believed them to be abstract, rather than representational. The painter Paul Klee had been greatly influenced by similar carvings he saw on megalithic tombs in Brittany. Rawstone turned down an offer from a linoleum manufacturing company which wanted to use the designs, the artist having been offended by Lascaux cave paintings having appeared on waste-paper baskets.

General Forlong in his 1906 work, the second volume of *Faiths of Man*, mentioned an altar stone on Iona allegedly having round stones in cup marks, which the pious pilgrim turned around. 'The world', apparently, 'will end when the stone is worn through.'

The dolmen of Rocenaud, France, has cup marks which are grouped to resemble the Pleiades. Early this century it was believed by local folk that they were made by St Roch when he laid on the stone after arriving from Ireland. The peasants would knock in the holes with a flint when they wanted the wind to change. Frances M. Gostling, in *Bretons at Home*, published in 1909, tells a tale of how a rainy south-west wind was so provided just for her benefit.

Guy Underwood stated that standing stones are generally positioned over important blind springs.[55]

Barrows

> '*Is it just coincidence that their mounds — long barrows and discs — should bear such a strong resemblance to the cigar-shaped and disc-shaped objects in the sky?*' — *Brinsley le Poer Trench.*[53]

Past, present and future forces lie in flux in the heather-clad barrows of the moorlands, the grass-canopied tumuli of the lowlands, the domain of fairies, goblins and gnomes, where etheric energy accumulates in mounds resembling the various types of flying saucer, and placed to mirror the stars of constellations.

Barrows by their sheer numbers are indicative of importance. Round barrows are the most numerous, and today number around 20,000. Destruction by farming makes it likely that the original number was probably far in excess of this figure. At one time there were fourteen on the crests of hills surrounding Avebury. There are now five. Ploughing destroyed many; stones were removed from walls; the Victorians ransacked several a day and without thought for their complex structure in their greed for the gold popularly supposed to be within. In fact very little in the nature of gold objects has been found in barrows, though a gold cup found in 1818 near the Cheesewring was used by George IV as a shaving mug for a time.

This is not the type of work which requires detailed analysis of the extraordinary variety in both the structure and contents of tumuli. A few factors, however, are worthy of consideration as they would seem to provide a degree of explanation as to why tumuli can be counted as one of the most important types of structure in the ley system.

Long barrows were introduced in Neolithic times, and are mounds of earth or lumps of chalk mostly from about 100 to 300 feet long, and 30 to 100 feet wide. Their height was between 4 and 12 feet. About 200 survive. Their alignment is normally east-west, facing the rising and setting points of the sun. The east end was broader and higher, and the primary burial would be in the western end. Most have a ditch along each of the long sides, sometimes joined up in a curve.

According to Guy Underwood the site of a long barrow requires one or more blind springs, the majority having a powerful blind spring in the centre of the highest part.[55]

Round barrows are regarded as the standard tomb of the Bronze Age, and generally contained a burial. It is interesting to note that the mound was often built in layers of different soils, or had an inner mound of turf. Generally speaking they have a flat circular top and are 15 to 50 feet wide, and about 20 feet high. A.M. Hocart described the round barrow as a 'ritual representation of the universe'.

Chambered passage barrows are similar in size to long barrows, often include 15,000 tons or more of stones covered over, with a chamber and passage, and are mostly distributed in highland areas. Important examples are New Grange, Ireland; Stony Littleton, Somerset; and West Kennet, Wiltshire.

In using tumuli as ley points, a number of mare's nests need to be taken into account. There would seem to be no reason for including Roman or Saxon barrows, ornamental mounds on which trees were planted in eighteenth-century parks, and glacial moraines.

There is a great deal of folklore attached to barrows, later peoples having named them after heroes and invaders, gods and the Devil, elementals and giants. A line of research which could prove fruitful is the large amount of lore associating barrows with the supernatural.

Major F.C. Tyler thought that originally burials were made at sites already known to be sacred, but warned that later the capacity for detecting this sanctity could have been lost, and a custom arose of making a mound over a burial without any reference to the quality of sanctity.[54]

A very different view was held by F.R. Watts, who, describing the amount of effort required to construct tumuli, wrote: 'Obviously this was not a pleasant pastime, neither was it carried out in honour of the individual whose bones lie beneath ... indeed there is every reason to assume that the remains are those of a human sacrifice, made to consecrate the site.'[113] I find it hard to believe that this would be part of the megalithic civilization's creed, and would associate it with a later period, if in fact it was practised in this country at all.

What is significant, however, is the fact that barrows contain burials: that death and the ley system are inseparably linked. Arthur Shuttlewood reports that etheric energy is released from soil, particularly from the soil of tumuli, graveyards, plague pits or battlefields, where it builds up and the subtle energies are released periodically for good or ill. Energy cannot be destroyed, only can change from one form to another. David C. Holton, who has studied this psychism with relation to tumuli in the Warminster area, believes it to give a new understanding to the bizarre happenings in this flying saucer-haunted district.[46] I will develop this line of research in a later section.

My favourite story relating to a barrow burial is the one John Foster Forbes tells, connected with the discovery of a giant clothed in a gold corslet beneath a tumulus at Mold, Flintshire. Apparently a woman living nearby dreamed repeatedly of a giant in full armour standing above the tumulus, and her persistence in believing the mound to contain a great burial led to the excavation which proved her right.[15]

On a practical level, Alfred Watkins[59] has drawn attention to many examples of mound alignments in Herefordshire, and readers may seek for them in their own districts.

Dolmens

'Irish people ... thought of them as the bed of the magic love of Diarmuid and Grania.' – Geoffrey Grigson.[21]

The sun burns fiercely across the grouse moor as bees weave intricate patterns of flight between heather plants. Noon, and the wary lizard basks on the carpet of lichen clinging to the heavy capstone of the dolmen, supported by the trusty strength of its pillars. A merlin swoops down from the blinding sunlight; the lizard darts into a crevice, and peeps into the cool dark shadow cast beneath the rough capstone.

According to O.G.S. Crawford, the free-standing dolmen is a myth.[9] Gordon Childe thought them 'the most stubborn remnants of more complex structures'. Farmers found their main stones too heavy, so only took the small ones which had formed the basis of what had been a burial chamber or cairn. Early drawings with small stones scattered around were produced as exhibits A, B, C... to prove the case. Archaeologists do not allow poetic licence with the pen and pencil in the foreground. But Guy Underwood stated categorically that dolmens were never covered by soil, as were barrows. In barrows the stones touch. In dolmens there are gaps of two to three feet.[55]

H.J. Massingham has made an interesting observation on one particular dolmen, which is pertinent to our inquiry.[36] He reported that there were once twenty-four of them in Anglesey. From one of these, according to local people, there was a belief that ghost hounds with scarlet ears emerged. He noted that the old flag of England was red and white, but was previously the emblem of St George killing the dragon. Shades of the dragon pulse.

Dolmens, according to Guy Underwood, mark blind springs of considerable importance.

False Hills

> 'But many puzzles still remain. For example, here at Silbury, the converging lines of probability are once again beginning to point towards the induction and control of energies and vibrations of which we are scarcely aware and which are not yet fully understood.' – Andrew Davidson.[82]

Silbury, like its nationwide brothers, is a surprise in the

landscape. The feature is seemingly in disharmony with its surroundings. Isolated and odd. John Aubrey surmounted it in royal company. Charles II accompanied him, and with them was Charles's brother, later James II. James was fascinated by the snails which then infested the mound, and wondered whether they might be edible. Snails apart, Silbury is the largest artificial hill of prehistoric date in Western Europe, being about 125 feet high, about 550 feet across at its base, and is partially upon a natural knoll of chalk.

Archaeologists have attempted to probe Silbury's secrets, but have withdrawn mystified. However, though the solution to Silbury's mysteries remains unsolved, a few points can be stressed in an effort to get a clearer understanding of Silbury and its smaller counterparts.

These false hills, as I shall call them, for I would include several examples of such features not accredited by orthodox archaeology to the megalith builders, are always conical. They look dramatic, far beyond the scope of hills sculptured only by nature's powers of erosion or glacial deposition. The cone is a great source of energy. Herein lies the crux of the matter. Silbury, and almost certainly all the others, is built of varying layers of material over some form of chamber. Perhaps when built there was a moat of water around the mound all the year round. Let this be only a hint and a foretaste of a consideration of the part played by such false hills in the ley system.

Silbury, far from being unique, is only the most impressive of its breed. Many of the so-called Norman motte and bailey castle sites are truly prehistoric. Examples of large ancient mounds can be found in E.O. Gordon's *Prehistoric London*,[20] and there are many others — castle mound, Cambridge; Freeborough Hill, North Riding; and Short Cake Hill, near Hartlepool, County Durham.

Before, however, leaving these mounds, the words of two psychometrists can be given. Olive Pixley was convinced that Silbury had been erected by those who wished to disintegrate very evil magnetic influences which had been induced and established at its centre. This would seem to echo the curious statement made by Major F.C. Tyler, who believed there to have been a stone circle beneath: 'A burial-place, truly, but not for a human interment.'[54]

A similar reading to Miss Pixley's was given by Iris Campbell at the Bass of Inverurie, Aberdeenshire (which I have found to be a major ley centre), who stated that the mound was built to 'frustrate and dissipate' an evil earth magnetism. She read that Druids later cast spells of redeeming influences over such mounds. She postulated that they contained no burials, because what was once a feature of these places 'was indeed most real and potent, but all the same invisible'.[15]

Camps

'The physical facts of their distribution seem to put out of court any idea that the sites on which they stand were originally selected for defensive reasons.' — Major F.C. Tyler.[54]

Camps figure prominently in the ley system. Alfred Watkins's hypothesis was that two or more mounds of the Neolithic era were later extended to create the camps as enclosures during a later period, when the inhabitants became exposed to raiding and warfare. The alignments would seem to bear this out as every camp seems to have several leys over it, usually coming across the earthworks, not the centre.

Alfred Watkins also found them to align in groups of three or more with alignments on either side slightly converging upon a mound or church. This was particularly apparent on Salisbury Plain. He was surprised and perplexed, but suspected some relationship with the sun, a traditional Welsh phrase for sunset being 'the sun goes down behind his camps'.[60]

That earthworks occupied sites originally used as places of sun worship was Tyler's hypothesis, and he attributed the building of churches inside certain earthworks as perhaps a fulfilment of Pope Gregory's injunction to use pagan sites.[54]

Mark Stones

> *'In theory it is difficult to distinguish a mark-stone from other casual stones, but not in practice, for a mark-stone was always selected to appear different, either in shape, size, or kind of stone from other stones about in the district.'* — *Alfred Watkins.*[60]

Mark stones the size of footballs surrounded by grass, broken glass and discarded cigarette packets, scratched with the initials of lovers, peeing points on dogs' territorial boundaries, mystifying remnants of dying folklore and garbled superstition; mark stones too large to be removed, enigmatic environmental oddities, regarded by the ignorant as meteorites and by the miseducated as glacial erratics.

I find them a source of wonder and inspiration, and they were F.R. Watts's favourite ley points. He sought lovingly for them in the Cotswolds and farther afield, recording and photographing and aligning them. He was a master at Charlbury School, and many examples were noted and depicted in the pages of the school's magazine.

Both he and Alfred Watkins were of the opinion that they simply marked the direction of the Old Straight Track. Another believer in this explanation was M.C. Carr-Gomm, who related how the word 'mark' (sometimes spelt 'merke' or 'merch') signified a boundary or landmark throughout the Middle Ages, and drew attention to the verbal similarity of mark or merch to market or mercate, the marchant or merchant, and the god Mercury whose symbol was an upright stone. We may safely state that they generally mark a ley power point, where the quicksilver deity's power lies, and that later they become associated with merchants and market places.

There was an ancient law in Wales which made it an offence to remove these stones. F.R. Watts expressed concern and annoyance that anyone caught damaging a barrow was liable to a fine of £100, yet, deplorably, anyone breaking or removing a mark stone could do so with impunity.[113]

M.C. Carr-Gomm believed that the ledges and grooves cut on the stones, which are generally a few feet in height, were moulded so that a traveller could kneel or lie and get a bearing when looking through the groove to another mark stone on the skyline. He gives as an example the Heathstone, about three miles south-east of Chagford, Devon, from which can be seen Castor Rock. At Pitlochry, in Scotland, he found another where the stone had been deliberately cut to allow a traveller room to place his whole body so as to align his sight in the direction of the fords over the river. However, though this sounds perfectly feasible and a commonsense reasoning from the facts, I would suggest a separate purpose, especially in the Pitlochry instance, though not refusing to regard Carr-Gomm's reasoning as false. Ley point stones can be used for charging one's body, and this may be the primary reason for their being cut. Alfred Watkins called these sighting stones.

Examples of mark stones can be found where walls have been built to avoid them, ones built into walls, ones surrounded by cobblestones, in fields, by roadsides, and at road junctions.

Alfred Watkins believed them to be the prototypes of market crosses, wayside crosses and churchyard crosses, as leys pass through all these. In churchyards he also found ancient, rough, unworked stones at the bases of crosses, and other ancient stones which had been chipped into crude representations of crosses.

It would be unsafe to consider post-Roman crosses as ley points, but when marking leys it is worth noting if such crosses do stand upon leys. It would then prove likely that such stones stand where there was previously a far more ancient cross.

Alfred Watkins suggested that the Stone of Scone, on which the monarchs of England are crowned, was formerly a mark stone. The mark stone at Kingston-upon-Thames is famous as the coronation-stone of Saxon kings.

Ponds

'A dew pond on the height unfed that never fails.' – Rudyard Kipling.

As the golden sun parched the grass brown and the sky remained clear blue day after day after day, rivers fell and streams became trickles and becks ran dry, but the dew ponds remained full. As the drought continued, other ponds became caked with mud. Frogs hopped and newts wriggled across unfamiliar country and the sticklebacks lay gasping. Mysterious waters, the dewponds, the Southern England chalk district's mist ponds rippled in the breeze; the fog ponds of uplands limestone Derbyshire reflected the sun. Round, shallow, artificial hilltop pools with their mystique of constant renewal.

We may presume that a number of these are prehistoric, though others have been created in recent times by craftsmen. Some authorities have attributed them to craters left by small meteorites, but this does not explain their almost invariable capacity to remain full during the most severe drought. Neolithic stones have been recovered from the bottom of certain dew ponds, which supports the contention that it was in this period that they were first created.

The technicalities of their creation need not concern us. It can be stated simply that the principle does not involve magic. However, Guy Underwood has claimed that they mark blind springs, so some form of geomancy must have been involved in their siting.[55]

Geraldine Mellor, writing in *The Home Owner* for January 1964, reports that a Derbyshire farmer told her that early one morning he saw water in a.dew pond ruffled as though rain was falling, yet the sky was clear. Perhaps it was a manifestation of ley power. No one to my knowledge has checked to see whether dew ponds are ley points, but it seems certain, if they are sited on blind springs.

As for other ponds, those in villages and farms are generally regarded as being unlikely to pre-date Saxon or mediaeval times. But this would seem untenable, for Alfred Watkins found that practically all such ponds have leys running through them. What is inexplicable is that he produced evidence of roads passing through them. In *Early British Trackways* he depicts a causeway of stones with well-defined edges running through a pond at the foot of

Holmer Hill. People would not wade through them, surely. So we must look for another purpose, something seemingly associated with the ley current.

Islands in ponds or lakes may be supposedly created when ponds were being cleaned, but leys have so often been proven to pass through them that these almost rank as ley points.

I would suggest that there may be some significance in the material in Crawford's *Archaeology in the Field* with regard to ponds. He relates that in an area which is usually dry he saw a spring pond at Cold Henley, near Marlborough, full of water. The name 'Cold' will be explained more fully in the consideration of place names. Another spring pond quoted by him is called Ceolbrithtes Seath, near Everley — Ceol may equal Cold. He also says that the Saxon word 'Sol' defines a muddy place, yet 'Sol' means the sun today; the sun being, of course, an important factor with regard to leys. He cites 'heortsol' ('hart's soil' to him) as an example, and others. These should be checked for leys. Other pond names are pol, flash and plash.

Mare's nests in this category include former clay and gravel pits which have been allowed to fill with water. The Forestry Commission, in 1970, blasted instant duck ponds on the North Yorkshire Moors to provide homes for birds, amphibians, fish and insects. With a shortage of water on the moors to provide a refuge for wildlife, this was the Commission's contribution to European Conservation Year. Using 500 lb. of explosive, a pond 70 by 30 feet could be created in a few hours at a cost of £20 to £30.

John Michell has shown the exceptional incidence of moats in East Anglia falling into alignments.[40] He suggests that maybe they indicate the passage of water lines, artificially straightened, which would account for the high proportion of neglected moats retaining their water. These are Middle Ages features, but often align with churches, and the sites may, therefore, be of greater antiquity. Alfred Watkins regarded them as unsafe ley points, however.

In Scotland and Ireland wide lakes have artificial islets at ley centres. Also he found that causeways across lakes coincide with leys. In Scotland the artificial islands are called crannogs.

In passing, it is worth noting that Alfred Watkins suggested that prehistoric man actually may have not only ridden but walked through ponds. I do not think that walking through them gives our ancestors much credit for intelligence, but for its humorous quality, I will quote Watkins: 'I saw where a pool of water, a couple of yards across, had been formed in a walking way by the stopping of a drain. A girl of ten came up, inspected it with much interest, and with plenty of room to go round, she deliberately walked through, with the water over her boots.'[59]

Sacred Waters

'Do not relieve yourself into springs.' — Hesiod.

Fidgety caddis, *Stenophylax stellafus*, the megalithic variety carrying around itself a case made of particles of gravel, hiding in the nooks and crannies of rocks. Whirligig beetles swimming rapidly in endless gyrations on the still water of a late summer lake. Scoop up a screech beetle and it will announce its presence by a loud squeak. A great diving beetle winging into the night on a secret odyssey for food, only to mistake a wet road for a stretch of water, and become crushed by an articulated lorry. Ferocious pike hunting fish, frogs or furry voles.

Starwort on sacred lakes. Sanctity and sticklebacks. The forces of nature in harmony in each lake, pond, stream and river. Yet some are sacred, some are not. We are told personal and tribal prosperity depended on the goodwill of the water deities to whom votive offerings were thrown. Rivers, lakes and even village ponds can be sacred waters. Shrines were sometimes built at the source of a river. Yet the question remains: why are some stretches of water sacred, and others not?

Legends are always significant and could give us some data as to what caused some waters to be regarded as sanctified. These legends should be checked against proven leys and comparisons made between the legends and powers possessed by leys.

Certain holy wells supposedly cure love sickness or skin diseases, and enhance fertility, the cure invoked by the gift of metal or piece of clothing material, placed by substitution in the beneficient power of the well's spirit. Alfred Watkins found a ley going to, or passing, all the examples he checked.[58] Sixty-two of the 1,179 wells in Wales are associated with megaliths. Many wells are dedicated to St Helen, a confusion with Elen, the Celtic goddess of roads and armies.

Before leaving the relationship between leys, legends and life-giving water, readers may be interested in a few notes about a series of prophetic streams, whose predictions – or coincidences – are intriguing. In East Yorkshire are streams fed by springs which flow intermittently. These gypseys, as they are known in the Wolds, flow over chalk, which permits the formation of extensive underground reservoirs and natural conduits which produce the widespread gypseys, probably on the siphon principle, in an area devoid of ordinary springs.

These springs, sometimes called Woe Waters when in full spate, appeared in accentuated form immediately before the Restoration, the landing of William of Orange and the two world wars of this century. Largest of all, the Gypsey Race, ran strongly after a gap of several years before. The phenomenon is also believed to have predicted local events such as major seastorms and the fall of a great meteorite at Wold Newton in 1795.

In connection with prehistory it is worth remarking that the 22-mile Gypsey Race is associated by legend with the Rud Stone, a tall monolith in the ancient churchyard of Rudston. The tradition is that it was erected as thanks for the sun's warmth and for a spring which swells the Gypsey Race below. For its slenderness and great height this monolith is unique, and it would seem more than coincidence that it and the Gypsey Race are in such close proximity.

Rocking Stones

'The grim and hideous forms [of Brimham Rocks]

defy all descrimination and definition.' — J.R. Wahlbron.

As a child I spent one carefree, joyous Sunday afternoon playing hide-and-seek among the curious rocks on Brimham Moor, in Yorkshire. Peeping from behind weird pillars of millstone grit, seeking among the puzzling blocks with their perforations and indentations. Where stones of a dozen tons weight vibrate at a touch.

These rocks are examples of where man intervened to complement nature, and a raspberry to archaeologists who prefer to believe them to be natural and creations of weathering. Rocking stones, or logan stones, which are balanced and capable of being rocked, are the most spectacular types of rocks where man's hand can be seen at work.

Brimham Rocks, the Cheesewring on Bodmin Moor, and Dartmoor tors, reveal evidence of the megalithic culture taking upon itself the task of taking subtle liberties with nature. John Michell has described the Cheesewring,[40] and Guy Underwood investigated the tors,[55] so I shall concentrate on Brimham.

In 1792 William Lord Grantley, who owned the land on which the rocks stand, began charging tourists to see the formations and inflicted a guide upon them. Dr Borlase had advocated in his *Antiquities of Cornwall*, in 1758, that Druids were responsible for fashioning a number of rocking stones. The Revd John Watson wrote in 1773 about the stones at Brimham, and attributed their peculiarities to the Druids. In 1787, Major Hayman Rooke also wrote of them, and credited them to the Druids. Grantley's guides were ready to give the stones names such as Druids' Head, Druids' Altar and the Idol Rock, and cash in on the interest in Druids.

Rocking stones occur in at least four separate places at Brimham. In one place a group of four rocking stones together exists, and I believe all four move at the present time. Watson believed their motion to be spiritual — 'fit emblems to represent the external existence of the supreme being'.

But Brimham's oddest stone is the Idol Rock. It is 19 feet high, 46 feet around at its broadest part, and yet is joined to bedrock by a conical column tapering upwards from a minimum diameter of about one foot.

In places there are passages between the rocks, some a few feet wide and several yards long. There are also basins cut in some, one large enough for a person to sit in.

John Michell has found that several alignments in Cornwall terminate on the coast at rocking stones, and states that tradition associates them with the invocation of fertility. He also believes they played an important role in the generation and transmission of ley power.[46]

Few rocking stones are still capable of movement. The one above Treen, in West Cornwall, having been levered into the sea, was retrieved by block and tackle and put back into place, but the delicate balance was lost and no longer would it rock.

Notches

'On looking at a calendar that happened to be hanging in our home, I noticed that it showed a good photograph of a hill notch. . . . As I had a map of that particular area – Porlock, in Somerset – I decided to see if there was a ley aligned on the notch. . . . I found the hill with the notch to be Bossington Hill. And the line from the notch through the point in Porlock where the photographer had been standing was certainly a ley. . . .' – Jimmy Goddard.[86]

If we accept that leys are in reality much more than mere trackways, then Alfred Watkins's explanation regarding notches lacks conviction. Alfred Watkins wrote:

Where a mountain ridge stood in the path of a ley, the surveyor, instead of building a tump on the ridge as a sighting point, often cut a trench at the right angle and in the path of the ley. This shows as a notch against the sky and makes a most efficient sighting point from below. Each notch can be seen on the line of sight, and disappears when a quarter of a mile right or left. They are sometimes emphasised (as at Trewyn Camp) by an earthwork thrown up on one side.[59]

Surely a traveller would not choose a straight track up a mountain, but would find a valley for himself to save his strength and avoid the risk of injury.

Notches therefore either denote the point on the horizon where the ley power flows and/or denote the position of sunrise or sunset on a particular day.

Alfred Watkins provided a category of ley points which he called sighting cuttings. These occurred where the ley passed over a bank in lower ground, and he also noted cuttings at most fords, allowing the water to be seen from above, and he believed they acted as sighting points.

Old Roads

'In many cases a modern road or track swerves more or less from a straight ley, but comes back to it, and the points at which it comes back are almost always cross-roads of tracks or a meeting point of tracks; this is noticeable in all the plans.' – Alfred Watkins.[59]

The weekend motorist driving through the Yorkshire Dales follows the twisting lanes which fail to relate to the topography, winding across flat stretches between drystone walls where yellow-hammers watch. The driver's petrol is running low, his wife urges him to stop so she can pick honeysuckle though the road is too narrow, and the children in the back grow restless of collecting car numbers. They want to bathe in a stream, the wife wants a cup of tea and the driver thirsts for a pint of bitter. Clouds are gathering and rain threatens. 'The sun's shining over there. Go that way.' The long and winding road twists on.

Guy Underwood had an explanation for the winding nature of roads. First tracks would be made by animals following geodetic lines. Man would see these tracks and adopt them.

As stressed earlier, geodetic lines twist and turn; leys are straight. It has also been stated that leys pass through bogs and over precipices, and in many cases would be impractical as trackways. Yet there is much evidence to prove that in certain cases leys were used by travellers. Possibly they became used increasingly by travellers when the knowledge of the power became lost or was used only by a priestly elite. As trackways, Alfred Watkins found them to be as little as four feet wide, though usually six to seven feet. Excavations revealed cases of them being 'surfaced', one recorded as having one foot of gravel. Watkins wrote: 'Until the sewer-cutting discoveries just detailed there was no inform-ation as to the surface of the ancient tracks; it is possible that – except in soft places – many were not stoned. There is need for spade investigation in the matter.'[59] And there still is.

Watkins, having wholeheartedly established to his own satisfaction that leys were trackways, developed his thesis to divide them to some extent into routes used by traders of various kinds. He associated the names *white, wick* and *wich* with salt pedlars' leys; *red* with potters' routes; *knap* with the flint trade. Archaeologists reckon there is no evidence for Neolithic trackways, yet somehow products of the Cumber-land axe factories reached Wessex. However, finds of objects have established the existence of Bronze Age trade routes. We may assume that where practicable leys were used as trackways, though this was not their original or primary purpose.

R. Hippisley Cox attempted to construct a map of prehistoric trackways in Britain, and this has been treated with caution at best.

For most people it was the Romans we should 'thank' for our straight roads. It seems, however, that the Romans merely chose to resurface many leys which were in fact used as tracks. A great deal of work needs to be done to reappraise Roman roads in this light. Barbara Crump has investigated the Fosse Way (Bath-Exeter) and found sufficient evidence to refute the notion that the Romans were its original builders. Her survey establishes the fact that the Fosse Way is composed of many short straight stretches of leys, which cause its deviations. She detailed in an article in *The Ley Hunter*,[81] various sections, many of which extend as leys in either direction for great distances. Of the Romans, she wrote:

> Perhaps we have the Romans to thank for making some of these sites more permanent through incorporating them into their road-ways, though it is probably truer to say that they did more harm than good by over-riding them with their strong negative influences of war, and unconsciously bringing the final stages of man's material- ism.

In prehistoric legend, King Cole's daughter Elen is associ- ated with road-building, as is King Dunwal Molmutius (of *circa* 500 B.C.), and his eldest son Belinus, who completed the road-building programme begun by his father. Molmutius produced a law which stated that a man on a road, river, or in a place of worship was under the protection of God, and anyone who interfered with this law of the King's highway was a criminal. Molmutius, according to Celtic lore, was a 'restorer and protector of the ancient sanctuaries and of the highways that led to them'

Hill Figures

'The White Horse, in symbology, represents Mind.'
– Brinsley le Poer Trench.[53]

Thomas Taylor, a schoolmaster, so history tells us, had the idea to create a white horse hill figure on the western slopes of the Hambleton Hills. In 1857 John Hodgson, with the help of thirty men, cut Yorkshire's only hill figure. It still remains, visible for many miles around, situated above Low Kilburn, 314 feet long, 228 feet high, and with an eye space which can accommodate twenty people. It requires six tons of lime to keep it white. Of course it is not prehistoric, but I have heard that reconnaissance has revealed another horse above it, now overgrown. Did the schoolmaster hear a legend of an earlier figure and wish to re-establish it, or did he intuitively recall the earlier figure from the recesses of his mind's collective unconscious?

However, a number of hill figures can be ascribed to prehistoric origin. In the chalk above Cerne Abbas, in Dorset, is a giant, 180 feet high and 44 feet broad. His huge phallus reveals a generative aspect at variance with the threatening club he holds. Further phallic symbolism is found with the earthen ring above, which was for a long time the site of the maypole. John Foster Forbes called him part sun god and part war god, the upper part exemplifying the latter, and the lower part the former. Geoffrey Grigson thought the figure might have been 'the obscene jest of a ribald free-thinking eighteenth-century nobleman making fun of antiquaries,' adding, 'though it is now a little shakily interpreted as a Romano-British cult figure of Hercules of the second-century'.[21] I am inclined to attribute it to the megalithic period.

The first series of *The Ley Hunter* had as a trademark, on the front cover, the outline of the Long Man of Wilmington. This 240 feet high Sussex giant was believed by Alfred Watkins to be a representation of the dodman – the name he gave to those he believed to have surveyed Britain and marked the leys. The old name for the common snail, with its twin horns like the Long Man's 'staves', was dodman. 'Dod' is also a frequent name on leys. But it has been argued that the purpose of leys was primarily to mark ley power, and that trackway use became a later function. This in no way explains the Long Man in these terms, unless, perhaps, the 'staves' are rods used in geomantic divination. H.J. Massingham gives a more interesting origin for him, that he was believed to be a representation of Mercury, the deity of the leys.

Upon the Berkshire Downs bounds the Uffington Dragon. This puzzling figure is usually referred to as Uffington White Horse, though it is unlike any horse, and is, I believe, representative of the dragon and all that fabulous beast symbolizes. It is a prominent feature in its landscape and is 365 feet long (is the length to be equated with the number of days in a year?). It may well be Neolithic, and to those who regard it as being of the Iron Age because it bears a strong resemblance to horses on various coins of that period, it can be suggested that the coins may have been based on this older figure. Above it is the camp Uffington Castle, and below this on one side of the hill are The Dragon's Stairs, and beyond lies Dragon Hill, where Uther Pendragon is supposedly buried.

There are three further hill figures with a claim to antiquity, but no longer visible. The present Westbury White Horse was cut in 1778, but it was preceded by an elongated figure. Until 1798 a Red Horse existed above Tysoe, Warwickshire. At Wandlebury, Cambridgeshire, the late T.C. Lethbridge[29] discovered the Gog-Magog figures, since allowed to become overgrown once more.

The first attempt to link the white horses into the framework of our study was made by Doug Chaundy, who published a preliminary report in *Enigmas of the Plain*, a duplicated booklet.[72] In fully developed form his researches were published in Arthur Shuttlewood's book *Warnings From Flying Friends*.[46] Doug Chaundy noted that white horses at Cherhill, Alton Barnes and Pewsey are not only aligned, but the outermost ones are equidistant from the centre one. When Cherhill and Pewsey were joined to the Uffington Dragon an isosceles triangle was formed, with Broad Hinton White Horse lying on a line between Cherhill and Uffington. Westbury and Manton (Marlborough) White Horses also fit into a coherent pattern with the others. Lines extended from the triangles created by the white horses arrived at specific points visited by UFOs, almost all actual landing locations, and also such places as Glastonbury Tor, Butleigh (Glastonbury Zodiac centre) and the Prescelly Hills. According to the pattern of other white horses, the one at Manton appears misplaced, but its present location was critical for the locations listed by Doug Chaundy. In the letter to Arthur Shuttlewood, printed in the book, Doug Chaundy states that these white horses are the only ones in Wiltshire not left to deteriorate.

This is all very strange. The Westbury example replaces an older figure, Uffington is ancient, yet the others are all comparatively modern. But what if, as seems the case with Low Kilburn White Horse, all replaced older white horses?

This would then explain the pattern, but would leave the postulated link with UFOs a deep mystery or coincidence.

Modern Man this century took a great interest in hill figures, for during the 1939-45 War they were covered with turf so as not to enable enemy aircraft to find their bearings by them. Happily all were restored to their former glory after hostilities ceased.

Castles

'Every castle in this district [Herefordshire] has a ley passing over it.' – Alfred Watkins.[58]

The castles which interested Alfred Watkins originated in a tump upon which a keep was built many centuries afterwards. The word castle has, however, been applied to many mounds where no building ever existed. These we may for simplicity's sake regard as the miniatures of the false hill discussed earlier. When the word 'castle' is part of a place name, it signifies the presence of a mound. Castle mounds were by an earlier generation of archaeologists attributed to the Saxons, and more recently to the Normans.

Alfred Watkins stated that the Normans built their motte and bailey castles upon pre-existing prehistoric mounds, which were sufficiently common for their requirements, though in some cases it seems they enlarged them. Records relating to examples such as Worcester, Duffield, Warrington, Arkholme and Penwortham provide evidence of the discovery in the mounds of articles of prehistoric date. Those who attribute the castle wholly to Norman workmanship are 'most woefully in error', and Watkins castigates archaeologists for 'closing their eyes' to the local records which afford proof to the contrary.[60]

His evidence provides us with a' large safety margin for assuming that castle keeps on mounds are ley points.

Christian Edifices

'through many a dark hour

I've been thinking 'bout this
that Jesus Christ was
betrayed by a kiss
but I can't think for you
you'll have to decide
whether Judas Iscariot
had God on his side.'
  — Bob Dylan

Pre-Reformation parish churches can be counted as ley points as there is documentary evidence that orders were given that pagan sites were to be adopted for Christian churches. Alfred Watkins and his predecessors have built up a huge amount of data regarding churches built on or near mounds, monoliths, stone circles, or within earthworks. On almost any six-inch map, alignments of up to six old churches can be found. Alignments of these have also been recorded in such cities as Oxford, Cambridge, Bristol and London.

There are instances of the mark stone, which decided the site of a church, being found embedded in the foundations upon demolition. Alfred Watkins suggested that here was the origin of the custom of laying a foundation stone.

He also found that in many cases a ley passed through a church tower only, and was perplexed that the ley did not skirt the church, his 'trackway' therefore being blocked, though in a few cases passageways do go through churches.

One of the major questions concerning churches is the date at which they would no longer be built on leys. Alfred Watkins stated that ley hunters could safely presume that churches built far into the Middle Ages would be on leys. I would accept all those built before the Reformation. Basically the Reformation put an end to church building for almost two centuries, until the growth of towns made new parishes and churches necessary.

Nevertheless a number of modern churches have been built not only on leys, but at points where they cross. Major F.C. Tyler was surprised to find the seemingly modern church of Redlynch in a private park — on a ley.

While staying with Jimmy Goddard, he took me to see St

Augustine's Church, behind his home in Addlestone, Surrey. He subsequently wrote about it in an article in *The Ley Hunter*:[89]

> One of them is St Augustine's Church, a twentieth-century building near the foot of Woburn Hill. . . . The church is brick-built and very obviously modern, having been built just before the last war. There is no surviving evidence of a former church or other structure on the site, yet on entering it I felt the same humming in my head that I have experienced at some ley centres. Mapwork revealed that it is in fact the centre of several leys, a mystery which is deepened by two other features of the church. One is that it is aligned precisely east, which is unusual for a modern church, but not inexplicable. What is more interesting is that the base angles of the roof are 52°, almost identical to those of the Great Pyramid. (The pyramid angles are in fact just under 52°, almost exactly the same as the angle which is one-seventh of the circle $51\frac{3}{7}°$. However, it is impossible for me to be accurate to measurements smaller than a degree, as measurement has to be made against the brickwork line holding the protractor in mid-air.) It may well be that the angle is critical for some purpose concerning the ley power. Also, the walls of the church are so low compared with the height of the roof that, approaching it from the east over the little bridge from the Weybridge road, it almost gives the impression of being a pyramid. Indeed, there may well be more to be found from the structure, but it would need the mathematical ability of a Keith Critchlow to find it. Do we see the work of unseen planners here?

Many churchyards are circular, and even archaeologists are willing to believe that these probably mark the sites of former stone circles. Walter Johnson's *Byways of British Archaeology* gives examples of churches within earthworks. Also R.A. Courtney's *The Hill and the Circle*, privately printed in 1912 in Penzance, gives examples of churches dedicated to St Michael in Cornwall and Brittany being built within earthworks.

Today, old churches are regarded by many as architectural curiosities rather than places of worship. Too often they are locked against thieves who seek the silver from the altar, satanists who seek communion wafers for their rites, and vagrants who seek shelter. Of old churches, John Michell wrote: 'While our older churches are still capable of use as precise instruments for spiritual invocation, many of those built in modern times are nothing more than empty halls.'[40]

As with old churches, ancient chapels, abbeys, priories, friarages and Gothic cathedrals would all seem to stand upon leys. John Michell has propounded that these religious edifices were sited by divination, and has provided examples of legends to support his claim.[40]

Another investigator into Christian places of worship whose dimensions relate directly to the megalithic period is Professor Lyle B. Borst, the United States astro-physicist. His researches into the relationship between these edifices, their plans based upon megalithic sanctuaries over which they stand, and alignment with various stars, can best be discussed in a separate section, but it can be noted that the cathedrals he adduces to stand upon megalithic sites include Canterbury, Wells, Lincoln and Winchester.

E.O. Gordon, commenting on Winchester, wrote: 'That Winchester Cathedral was erected on the site of a druidic circle is practically certain from the fact that several druidic stones were at one time to be seen in the Close.'[20]

Trees

> *'It is not a theory, but an observation built up that Scotch firs are almost certain signs either of the line of an ancient track, or more particularly its sighting points.' — Alfred Watkins.*[58]

Trees form ley points. Despite the fact that any tree planted in Neolithic times would have died and disappeared long ago, generations of trees would grow at the same point. Hawthorn planted to encircle a single tree or clump could act as a barrier to keep within the circle seeds from the tree or trees, and thus perpetuate the mark point.

Alfred Watkins noted that trees were often to be found at points where leys cross, and that where a ley came upon a natural hill, a single tree at the summit marked the point. He believed a pole was sometimes used in the same way as a tree, and became in more recent times a maypole.[58]

As for avenues of trees, all the ones Alfred Watkins tested had leys down their centres. He also found long, straight strips of woodland sure signs of a ley, and discovered that the word 'park' probably formerly indicated woodland connected with leys.

Orthodox authorities. state that Neolithic Britain was almost certainly wetter than the present day. However, the number of mark stones in lowland areas, the mounds, ponds and other ley points, so clearly indicate that afforestation was even sparser than at present. Watkins suggested today's number of trees to be a cause of the decay of the ley system, and the notion that ancient Britain was one dense forest is 'a glib statement'.[58]

The Scots pine is the tree most characteristic of leys, with its height making it particularly noticeable. All single trees of seeming significance should be checked as ley points, and also named historic trees, especially gospel oaks.

Scots firs often mark ley points, though K.J. Bonser, in *The Drovers* (Macmillan, 1971) has stated that 'farmers willing to put up herds for the night sometimes planted clumps of three to five Scots firs close to their farmhouse at a high point visible from afar,' This sounds unlikely due to the time it would take such a clump to grow, but may indicate certain persons' knowledge of leys for travel or the beneficial effect upon beasts of ley points.

In Addlestone, Surrey, is the Crouch Oak, presumably so named because of its crouching position with one of its branches pointing out almost horizontally. It is reputed to be more than 800 years old and is still alive. The local Oddfellows' Masonic lodge has significantly named its lodge Oak of Addlestone after it. The oak had to be railed off in the last century as it was being killed by people stripping off its bark, which was believed to have aphrodisiac qualities. Queen Elizabeth I is reputed to have picnicked under it. Jimmy Goddard discovered that the oak is on a ley via Crouch Oak Lane, leading to Chertsey Abbey.

In Rogation week a procession around a parish's boundaries would be undertaken and under a gospel oak the parson would say or sing the gospels to bless the crops and the land.

Tony Wedd has also been attracted to trees' significance in the ley system. In 1949 he first read *The Old Straight Track*, and with, its details fresh in his mind he walked across Parliament Hill and on towards Ken Wood. He spotted a lone Scots pine more than ten feet higher than surrounding beeches. A solitary tumulus lay nearby, topped by another lone Scots pine encircled by thorns. When he returned home he plotted them on a map, and they fell on a ley going through Westminster Abbey.

In 1960 Tony Wedd began to relate UFO sightings to pines, especially where the spacecraft hovers over the clumps.[115] In 1963 he made a special trip to France to visit places where UFOs on orthotenies, quoted in Aimé Michel's book,[38] visibly altered course and at the moment of doing so executed a falling-leaf manoeuvre. He wrote:

> I visited Meursagnes first, in Burgundy, and just about where M. and Mm. Vitre had observed their UFO, and alerted nearby farmers, I found a group of three pine trees. Strike one! At Frasne, disappointed, I found nothing — until I reread my Michel, and realized that actually the UFO had been seen south and west of Dompierre. Useful negative check; you cannot find pine trees just by going out looking for them! Travelling on to Le Tertre I found a little knoll by the roadside, with a little shrine set at its edge, and a tree clump including both *Pinus nigra* and *Pinus sylvestris*: Holy Ground, beloved by the gods. (Maybe some angels died at Meurs-anges?) Strike two! Next I visited the Rhine bank between Niffer and Kembs and saw nothing in the twilight, so turned into the woods to camp. In the morning I found myself in a forest thick with Scots pines! Too thick to make out any one particular mark point, so I could only allot myself two-and-a-half points out of three. Maybe that's not conclusive for anyone but me. But I returned home satisfied that leys and orthotenies had some very promising points of similarity.

While at Stonehenge in 1967, Tony Wedd noted that Rox Hill Clump on the skyline to the south, though mostly of beech, also carries ash, elm, elder, yew, box, hornbeam, holly, ivy, sycamore, privet, may and willow. He suspected it to be an old Celtic grove planted with the thirteen trees of the tree calendar, which were also the names of the Beth-Luis-Nion alphabet letters.

In *The Ley Hunter*, Tony Wedd returned to the subject of trees, and one in particular:

But there is one tree yet to be described, with which I have a personal connection: a curly sycamore, standing just beyond the wall of what used to be my garden at Tye Cross [Chiddingstone in Kent]. On May 21, 1960, a friend called Mary Long came to visit us, and from her own extra-sensory perception found her way to the sycamore, and pointed out that there was a vortex in its spiral bark form. That night she received a communication from Attalita which referred to the healing power of the bark of the tree; named a ley which I had already plotted; and described an interesting pattern of healing centres in the neighbourhood.

Looking out from the first floor windows of Chiddingstone Castle, you can see a clump of pine trees breaking the skyline of the Sevenoaks Range beyond. I discovered that they drew the eye to One Tree Hill, and that from this clump, at Chested, one looked back over the top of Chiddingstone Castle to the clump at Mark Beech, beyond. The ley extends to Forest Row, via the church at Holtye in the south-west, and to Oldbury Camp via a church at Stone Street in the north-east. Eventually it reaches the Thames at Cliffe.

The core of Attalita's message, however, was this: that I should work around the clock from this 6°N. of N.E. alignment, and find on each of the twelve alignments so obtained, a centre of healing power. But this was too much! It was so extraordinarily geometrical, for a layout in the landscape, and it drew such emphasis to my own particular dunghill. I was most reluctant to accept it.

Yet the fact is that the chalybeate spring at Tunbridge Wells lies exactly upon one of these lines, and so does the Spa Hotel, which is six miles as the crow flies. On the next alignment lies an interesting pine clump at Burrswood, a healing centre established by Dorothy Kerin, and the main spring of this place flows out from the grotto among these trees, five miles off. And five miles off on the other leg of the next alignment still, the one 9°E. of N., lies Spring Hill, a magical spot in Whitley Forest, where the River Darent flows out so strongly that a mill lay only just 200 yards away, until burnt down recently. This alignment passes through the striking clump of Scots pines that stands untouched close to the Sevenoaks bypass.

The coincidences start to pile up. There is a clump of pines at Outridge Farm on the 21°W. of N. alignment, and the line joins Weardale Manor, another magical spot on Toys Hill, to the high point at Keston Common, 497 feet, touching the boundary of

Caesar's Camp. A clump beside the Hartfield-Withyham road marks the most interesting ley of all (Spring Hill in the other direction) as it passes through what the old tithe maps clearly call The Clump, now only a few pines lost among the modern planting, by Highfields, in the woods close by. Here there is an old cruciform cave cut out in the rocks, partly caved in, but said to be Mithraic in its layout: a southern transept which conceals five lamp-holes, four square and one circular . . .

In one of my own communications, I understood that the twelve sorts of healing water had twelve specific uses. . . .[116]

Alfred Watkins's study of trees led him to deduce that all places called 'The Grove' which he checked were on leys.[58] The location of Iron Age Druid groves is difficult, and no one has yet discovered the whereabouts in Southern Scotland of the great woodland sanctuary, Medionemeton.

When following leys on foot, one should keep one's eyes peeled for a solitary tree or significant looking clumps, and check if these are on leys, particularly if the variety of tree is not common in the locality.

Underground Passages

'Legends of underground passages between ancient sites, such as churches, castles, abbeys and camps are amongst the curiosities of archaeology. . . . It has never been my fortune to verify one, and other archaeologists have had the same experience.' — Alfred Watkins.[59]

Alfred Watkins believed that the tradition of underground passages connects with leys. He explained that there is evidence to support the theory that where one finds underground passage legends, these hidden lines follow leys, the notion being that such subterranean passages are a folk memory of leys.

Persistent traditions of such passageways exist in my own district, particularly between coastal caves and churches a few miles inland. The most interesting case, however, is one which alleges the existence of a passage connecting the ancient parish churches of Billingham and Norton, in

Teesside. Between these high churches is a lowland area prone to flooding, named Billingham Bottoms, which makes a subterranean tunnel an impossibility. But the two churches are connected – by a ley. Starting from Billingham it continues beyond the Norton church to Redmarshall Church, Castle Hill at Bishopton and on to Walworth Castle.

Faces and Symbols

'... the angel putting new dime into this adoption machine as out squirts a symbol squawking & freezing & crashing. ...' – Bob Dylan (Tarantula).

A cheery little stone lies at the end of a lane in Gildersome, West Riding. A wall has been built with a kink in its alignment to avoid the stone as narrowly as possible. Though recently damaged, since prehistoric times it must have lain there, for though only the size of a football it is covered with striking faces of men and beasts.

Iris Campbell produced a psychometric reading from a photograph of the stone:

The face appears to be composed of three eyes and a nose. The presence of the Third Eye represents spiritual vision. .... The stone is part of a megalithic group not now used for generating spiritual power, but at one time those who officiated at the festivals could draw elemental powers from the earth on which it stood. I think it was used more for prophecy than for healing, but at different times of the year it may have been the centre of differing ceremonies. Whichever way the stone is turned that face looks at you. So does the Third and All-seeing Eye, perceiving without deviation that which is before its attention.

Others have noticed faces of men, elementals and animals on stones. Frank Lockwood wrote of examples in Derbyshire,[77] and Mollie Carey has spent many years studying faces at Stonehenge and Avebury. The Helestone at Stonehenge is a particularly magnificent example of a fish or serpent. Mrs Carey is of the opinion that traces of colour still adhere to some megaliths. A popular representation is of elephants!

Many interestingly worked stones can be found, large or

small, such as one of the remaining uprights at Duddo stone circle, Northumberland, which has the appearance of a pair of clasped hands.

Symbols on stones are also worth looking for and attempting to interpret. One of the most significant is the swastika.

John Foster Forbes, writing during the Second World War, commented with some insight:

> The swastika is the Sun in true motion; only the motion must be true and not reversed as it purposefully has been done by a Fallen God of Central Europe who still believes he can set the world right by reversing the motion of the wheel. If the wheel, which this mistaken individual is now straining to its utmost capacity, has a spring in it, I venture to think that its reactionary motion, when it is released in order to recover its true direction, will be simply tremendous in its effect.[14]

Many writers have considered the symbolism of the swastika. George Hunt Williamson's is probably the most extraordinary. He postulated that the four points of the swastika represent 'the Four Great Primary Forces', which are static magnetic field, electro-static field, electro-magnetic wave and resonating electro-magnetic field. He believes that the symbol was brought to Earth by extra-terrestrials.[62]

Place Names

> '... for when once we have said in public that a certain name has a certain derivation, it is like drawing a tooth to acknowledge some other derivation.' – Alfred Watkins.[60]

In relating ley points to place names, only probabilities and possibilities can be put forward. The traps are many and it may prove to be a fact that Alfred Watkins erred on the generous side. A great many names on maps do betray a prehistoric origin. Leys and their mark points pre-date towns, hamlets and homesteads, but such places frequently bear traces of their origin. The following names should therefore be treated with great caution, but are worthy of con-sideration.

Ley: A common suffix. It is now used in rural districts as denoting a meadow. In North-East Scotland 'ley' comes from the Gaelic *leis*, and means leeward or sunny side. The word ley, however, in many cases cannot denote a meadow or a sunny side, and a full explanation of this and why ley is a particularly apt choice of name for the alignments was given by Alfred Watkins.[59]

Ton: A common suffix. According to Alfred Watkins it may have originated as a mark stone on a ley becoming the nucleus of a hamlet or town.

Bury: A suffix or alone. Watkins believed it to indicate a mound. Variations are borough, burgh, berry, barrow, low, how, howe, haw, cop, knap, knoll, knowe, ball, tump, toot and tout.

Broom, Brom and *Bram:* Watkins found them common on leys, but attached to no particular mark point.

Og: A prefix. John Foster Forbes found the term 'og' in place names in close proximity to stone circles with solar connections. He instanced two adjacent hamlets, Ogbury St George and Ogbury St Mary, noting the masculine/feminine duality. He noted that a circle with a central dot is the cypher for the Sun God, or 'the Great and all-seeing eye'.[15]

Wick or *Wich:* Watkins believed these, generally suffixes, were designated to places on 'salt routes'. Another theory is that they refer to a group of buildings, often a dairy farm. A 'wick' on the coast (i.e. Runswick Bay) may be from the Old Norse *vik*, for creek or bay.

Stock or *Stoke:* Suffix or prefix, could mean holy place connected with church, monastery or saint.

Don: May mean a hill.

Cold or *Cole:* Several investigators, notably K.H. Koop, have produced material relating Coldharbour or Cole(h)arbour to the ley system. Koop found that they are usually found on forward slopes of hill ranges and that the majority have no buildings. He also noted that even until today folk memory regarded it as best to keep these sites clear. However, housing developments in the Home Counties have broken the taboo (Ewell, Surrey; Hayes, Middlesex). Also Coldharbours have often been found at the junction or boundary of three parishes. They usually provide fine views. Coldharbour, of which there are supposedly 500 examples, has been suggested as an Anglicization of the old Celtic *cuil-lair-boreadh: lair* – place; *cuil* – sacred cell; *boreadh* – birth or springing up (of the sun). I would be so bold as to suggest that the true meaning can be taken to be a place where the sacred fertilizing ley power springs up.

Alfred Watkins has explained that many names common to ley points antedate the written word, which is accepted as the starting point for philologists, and that caution must be exercised in associating place names for the purpose of seeking leys. However, names can be helpful, but Watkins's notes are well worth reading for confirmation.[59]

Part 3

MAN AND THE HEAVENS

10. Look Up

'Just as the sky over a modern city is occulted by smoke and industrial throwaway, its proper atmosphere, so that antique science based on the inspection of the sky becomes mythologized, and hence a fossilized, hence a despised, science, rather than an open possibility.' — Robert Kelly.

Before we can suitably discuss the properties inherent in the ley system or ones which evidence so far collected suggests to be manifested by it — such as effects upon fertility, gravity, other dimensions, communications, electro-magnetism, the spirituality of man and inspiration — it is advisable that note be taken of fields of research which play a vital part in coming to a closer understanding of leys.

So far this book has dealt with down-to-earth matters of the mark points laid down by man to make plain the courses of alignments where a subtle energy manifests. Now we must look skywards as did early man; look into the depths of space and consider the physical effects of stars upon Earth and the changes the motions of the heavens have on the destinies of men, and look also to those enigmatic lights in the sky we mockingly call 'flying saucers'.

After consideration of these aspects of our quest we may give thought to the way in which man has utilized the ley system.

The stars watch Pageos A making its interminable orbit, the full moon looks on as dogs bay, the Pleiades skip merrily behind fleeting clouds, the full moon shines on the troubled asylum, Betelgeuse is high above the Post Office Tower, the hunter's moon lights the scene for the poacher tickling the trout which are neither the lord's, the gamekeeper's, nor anyone's but nature's, Spica winks at the rippling cornfield, the harvest moon aids the prowling barn owl gliding over Essex, the drunk sees two of Epsilon Eridani, the miser turns over his coinage under the new moon's grin, lovers embrace in Venus's glory, Mars is visible on both sides of the Iron Curtain, Mercury's motions made insignificant by the quick-silver speed of the last train returning courting couples to Heaton, Walkergate and North Shields, Bellatrix lost in the glare as the traffic lights change from green to amber to red for stop, nuclear submarines navigating under the Arctic ice cap without the Pole Star's help, stars populated by Ray Bradbury, Caster and Pollux brought closer by the river's ripples, the hedgehog who knows the car's headlights are not the sun and moon, the poet sees further than the Astronomer Royal, the hawkmoth chooses to fly to the candle and not the moon, witches dance naked in waning moonrays as astronauts stoop in protective clothing to collect moondust, the lighthouse switches off vampirically the beam as the sun emerges in the east.

Our ancestors found fascination in the stars, for they understood their effects upon the affairs of mankind, in whose sight each man was equal, and their laws affected both the highest and the most humble. Astrology, which is a science, does not differentiate between a king and a pauper. Astrology, which to the majority of people today is classified as charlatanism, superstition or at best highly dubious, is regarded by this writer as appointed to the destinies of people, nations and races, and a positive indication that the movements of the heavens have a direct bearing upon the actions and fortunes of the populace of Earth.

In this section I will attempt to relate scientific knowledge regarding the heavens to man's understanding and interpre-tation of the universe in terms of the ways in which he utilized his knowledge. That Megalithic Man did study the movements of heavenly bodies is not disputed by most orthodox archaeologists, but such people do not give early man credit for the great depth of his understanding and its application.

Naturally, having a settled agricultural basis, the megalithic civilization would require a practical grasp of the seasons, which would be deduced from the movements of celestial bodies. Pioneer work into prehistoric astronomy suggests that the observers studied the heavens in a sophisticated way.

Their observations must have been recorded and mastered skilfully, but was this simply a practical exercise, or did they speculate on what the objects they studied actually were? It seems they were particularly interested in the Sun, Moon and eclipses. They were interested in the positions of the heavenly bodies, but did they know what the Sun and Moon were? Did they think of. The Earth as being flat? Did they know that Mars, Mercury and Venus were planets?

In a book whose chief aim is to comprehend leys there is not room to speculate too deeply on Megalithic Man's comprehension of the heavens, but I believe it is fair to assume that he understood astrophysics to a degree. The Babylonians and Greeks seem to have discarded or never inherited this knowledge, for the Babylonians, though having largely solved the question of celestial forecasting, do not seem to have had an understanding of what the stars were. In Greece, Anaximander of Miletos theorized that the Earth is cylindrical, while Anaximenes of Miletos claimed that heavenly bodies did not move under the Earth but circled above it – the Sun's disappearance being explained by its having gone a long way from us and become hidden by higher parts of the Earth.

For the ley power to be manipulated it seems that a complex knowledge of astrophysics was necessary, and in addition to asking how this was utilized, we must ask how it was come by. Was mere observation sufficient? Did they have telescopic lenses? Did they have special vision? Did they travel astrally to distant stars? Did extra-terrestrials teach them cosmology, and were they taken to the planets, as such people as George Adamski, Dino Kraspedon and Buck Nelson claim to have been taken this century? We do not know.

Let us consider the words of John Michell:

> The skill of modern surveyors has now given us the groundplans laid out four thousand years ago together with the key to the whole antique science. Unfortunately there must be few today capable of using it. Kepler or Newton, had they had access to the plans and measurements of Stonehenge, could have discovered the full range of prehistoric astronomy and cosmology, and learnt the answers to many of the problems with which they and others of their contemporaries such as Brahe and Galileo were concerned.[40]

The heavens still withhold many secrets, and as far as Megalithic Man's having discovered them is concerned, we may never know. We do not now know for certain the cause of sunspots, the 'blue clearing' of Mars, certain aspects of solar eclipses, and the effects of cosmic disturbances on our weather, air, and physical and mental states.

Effects which are 'authenticated' as being caused by planetary influences may be slim or wide, according to one's approach and sources. Occultists will claim remarkable results regarding plantlife after following rules laid down by the positions of the Moon for tending them. Scientists will state that a single marine plant, and none on land, is affected by the Moon. What is agreed upon is that sunspots affect the weather, which in turn varies the fertility cycle in nature through its influences on rainfall. It can also be connected with a higher rate of suicide, unrest causing migrations or changes in political affiliation, and increased crime. Solar activity plays a major role in whether we breathe positive (harmful) ions or negative (beneficial) ions, which affect our health, and consequently our mental state.

Experiments have shown that the Moon influences a limited number of animals. But many scientists who have worked on women's menstrual cycles agreed that the Moon was not involved, nor was it influential in birth and death cycles, or influencing those who are mentally unbalanced, according to Michel Gauquelin.[17] Gauquelin does not seek to dispute the Moon's influence on tides.

In addition to solar considerations, lunar influences are also associated with stone circles, according to Iris Campbell. Her psychometric reading at Sun Honey by Echt led her to comment that Aberdeenshire's circles, which are now in an appalling state, were caused to be so dilapidated by those who used them and brought into play a great deal of 'the wrong magnetism which was due to exaggerated lunar influence, with the result that many of these sites became drenched in evil vibrations.'[15]

Guy Underwood claimed that lunar variations caused changes in certain types of secondary geodetic lines.[55]

Cosmic rays are assorted particles coming from the Sun

and stars. They are so dense in the high atmosphere that when black mice in a balloon twenty miles high were exposed to them for a few hours they turned white. Many of these particles are known to be the nuclei of heavy elements, including gold, lead and the rare earths. Some have been measured to have vast energy – many quintillion volts. Cosmic rays, according to occultists, have an off-shoot of rays named after colours. Depending on the time of day, and a person's position according to latitude and longitude, he is subjected to these, and the effect is related to his astrological make-up. How we may tie this in to our study I will leave to others better qualified. Did Megalithic Man harness cosmic rays? Were they concentrated, stored and channelled at stone circles? In passing, however, it may be worthwhile to remember that the blue ray is supposed to come under Hermes, and in Ancient Egypt and Chaldea it was known as the Magician's Ray.

From such speculations it is timely to fleetingly consider three aspects of prehistoric activity which can still be examined, and which make plain three separate means by which early man identified himself with the stars: the orientation of stone circles, the placing of tumuli in the shapes of constellations, and terrestrial zodiacs.

11. Calendars in Stone

Let me say at once that ley hunters should approach this subject with the understanding that it · is a complex and difficult one, that map observations, owing to the many factors involved, are quite insufficient, except as a rough help to actual sighting trials on the spot, which are indispensable; that star alignments are best left out for the present, that the sunrise angle differs with the latitude, and also with the elevation of the horizon caused by local conditions, and that very careful correction should be made for the varying magnetic difference.' – Alfred Watkins.[60]

Hail to the rays of the Sun.

The first grain of truth relating to the stone circle solar orientation theory was provided by William Stukeley, who in 1740 pointed out that Stonehenge's main axis was aligned to midsummer sunrise.

It seems that the first man to discover alignments to both sunrise and sunset over a number of stones at certain stone circles was A.L. Lewis, whose results are scattered in the transactions of various societies. His observations were made at the close of the last century. The same results were obtained by Magnus Spence, working in the Orkneys. This pioneer work was followed up by Sir Norman Lockyer, the Astronomer Royal, in the early part of this century.

Also in 1909, Edward Milles Nelson wrote, after completing extensive fieldwork on the subject:

> With respect to the astronomical significance of stone circles it is very doubtful if there was any beyond the laying out of the prime vertical, and the indication of the Sun's solstitial amplitudes ... it is extremely doubtful if there is any astronomical cult to be investigated, apart from the solar amplitudes ...[42]

Yet Rupert Gleadow has stated: 'Two thousand years ago there may have been half a dozen men who could locate the equinox, but there is no reason to think there was anyone at all in 1,000 B.C.'[18]

But observers have found accurate alignments to the spot at which the sun rose or set at the equinoxes, solstices and half-quarter days. In all there are eight days in the year at which observations might have been made at either, or both, sunrise and sunset. Archaeologists, despite Lockyer's professional integrity, blandly dismissed such evidence. Sixty years later the matter is not entirely resolved.

In the years 1920-22, Admiral Boyle Somerville confirmed previous results at circles in Scotland and Ireland.

Alfred Watkins understood the significance of such alignments and found them not only indisputable, but providing additional evidence for the existence of leys. His conjecture was that extensions of such lines would afford information of calendrical dates to not only the people in the immediate environs of a stone circle but to populations in districts across many miles of country. He found supporting evidence of two churches oriented on a sunset observation, together with significant place names.

A later reference to the subject occurred in a letter in the 8 June, 1945 issue of *Country Life*, in which Ludovic MacLellan Mann states:

> These alignments radiate for stretches of miles from apparently important prehistoric stations, and closely agree with alignments directed towards the rising and setting points of the sun at the equinoxes and solstices, March 21, September 23, December 22 and June 22. A line for the stellar equinox of February 26 is found to occur very frequently.
>
> The ancient (Neolithic and Bronze Age) lines differ almost imperceptibly from the modern direction because of nutation and precession. The direction of most of these lines betrays a Neolithic origin. They may differ slightly in the same district according to the varying heights of the observing stations and the horizon.

He refers to careful spacing of sub-stations, and adds that the stations often bear the name Coldharbour. Mann also notes that Beggar's Bush, from the Celtic *Beachdair-boisg*, is the name of other stations to be found on solar alignments. The observer is the *beachdair*, the first flash of light of the rising sun being the *boisg*. Variations include Bisley, Baslow, Busby, Baschurch, Pasley, etc. There is the Boscawen-un circle in Cornwall, where *bos* means flash and *caomhainn* or *camhanauch* means dawn.

Fresh impetus for work on solving the mystery of the stone circles was provided by Prof. Gerald Hawkins, an American astronomer, who published work on astronomical observations at Stonehenge in *Nature* during 1963-64, and enlarged upon these in his book *Stonehenge Decoded*.

It is not easy to make an accurate assessment of the value of Hawkins's researches, or those of Hoyle, Thom and others on the subject. However, an exceptionally lucid and objective account on the subject appeared in the Spring 1970 *Journal* of the Institution of Post Office Electrical Engineers (N.E. Region) by K.F. Wood, of Lincoln.

The paper, 'Circles, Clocks, Calendars and Computers', covers the debate fully, and Mr Wood writes that in an *Antiquity* review of Hawkins's book, Prof. Richard Atkinson charges Hawkins with using unreliable data, illogical arguments and unsound mathematics. In *Nature*, Hawkins's book was described by Atkinson as 'tendentious, arrogant, slipshod and unconvincing'. Prof. Fred Hoyle, the Cambridge cosmologist, came up with a new set of astronomical results, and speculated that the discovery of smelting after the building of Stonehenge I brought about a cultural inversion. The full understanding of Stonehenge was lost by the time of period II, and had not been fully regained by period III. Others entered the debate, and then Prof. Alexander Thom, retired Emeritus Professor of Engineering Science at Oxford, published results which were far more acceptable to many archaeologists.

Thom's work is extremely complex, and his study of more than 450 stone circles resulted in the contentions that Neolithic Man used a standard unit of length, his circles were set out with an accuracy approaching 1 in 1,000, were usually based on right-angled triangles, and that they had astronomical alignments and functions. Full site data and mathematical calculations can be found in his two books.[50,51]

For *The Listener*, Prof. Atkinson took another look at Thom's first book and commented:

> It has all the characteristics of a well-constructed parcel-bomb. The non-commital title, the carefully tabulated measurements, the inevitably mathematical treatment of the data, all combine to provide a tough but apparently dull package; but it is one which conceals a core of explosive power, capable of damaging severely a number of received ideas about the prehistory of Britain and about the beginnings of scientific thought and practice.[65]

He then gave Thom's conclusions a fair paraphrasing, attacked 'ill-considered fantasies about alignments at Stonehenge, or the supposed Megalithic foundation of Canterbury Cathedral', called for archaeologists to learn the necessary mathematics to appreciate Thom's work, and ended by saying we must question the axiom that urban living caused man to make systematic observations, measurements, and develop mathematics and geometry as functions of civilization. He wrote: 'It is about time, perhaps, to remember that barbarians too had brains.' Barbarians indeed!

Thom was the subject of a BBC-2 documentary, 'Cracking the Stone Age Code', and a piece of him, 'A Time-bomb under Archaeology', was published as a preview in the *Radio Times* (31 October, 1970), in which Dr Glyn Daniel attacked the 'lunatic fringe' again. He mentioned it in the programme too, saying Thom 'is not part of this'. Despite such sudden fame, Thom had to work for thirty years before he had the required evidence to prove to at least a section of archaeologists that he was correct. For the programme, the BBC sent him to Carnac to test his theories there and an article on this was published by Thom in *The Listener* of 31 December, 1970, entitled 'The Megaliths of Carnac'.

Less kind treatment has been handed out to another academic, Prof. Lyle B. Borst, of New York State University. Borst, an astro-physicist, was in Greece doing research to determine whether the Spartans could make steel (he found they could), and he and his wife played truant to visit the temples of Hera at Argos. Here allegedly a vestal virgin allowed the first temple to burn down and so a second one was built. Borst noted that the two were not aligned, and being an astronomer he found that the second temple's alignment corresponded to the rising position at the vernal equinox of the red star Spica, one of those observed by Megalithic Man. It was a year later that while in Britain, visiting Canterbury Cathedral, he noted the axis of the building is bent in two places. Briefly, he surmised that the cathedral was aligned to the rising point of Betelgeuse, and that the deviation implied an original series of stellar observations between 2,300 and 1,500 B.C.

By associating Canterbury Cathedral's layout with Thom's work, Borst deduced a plan similar to that of Stonehenge, Woodhenge, Arminghall and other lesser-known circles of Thom's Type I. Similar geometry was found at Wells, Winchester, Gloucester and Norwich. He identified Lincoln as Thom's Type II. At Wing church, Buckinghamshire, with its slightly irregular polygonal apse, he concluded that it stood where once there was a wood henge, like Arminghall, in 2,500 B.C. with an orientation to Bellatrix. Thus Wing church would be the oldest continuously used religious site in Britain. It was, in fact, scheduled to be razed for the site of London's third airport until recently.

A fascinating article on Borst's work is 'Megalithic Mathematics' by Ian Rodger, published in *The Listener* of 27 November, 1969. Articles by Borst have appeared in Britain in *Science* (Nos. 163-6), *Nature* (No. 224) and *The Ley Hunter* (No. 11), in which he identified a megalithic plan beneath the Houses of Parliament.

Dr Glyn Daniel was critical of the attention paid to Borst's work by *Nature, Science,* and a BBC Third Programme talk, and called his work 'highly personalized and deplorable astro-archaeology'. Borst's work is perhaps more open to criticism and less strong than Thom's.

Along the same lines, John Michell published an article which sought to prove beyond any doubt the validity of leys by using astronomical alignments as evidence.[97] Alfred Watkins pointed out that the same ley phenomena are studied by both ley hunters and scientists concerned with the astronomical significance of stone circles.[60]

But while the astronomers such as Lockyer and Thom use large scale

plans of a small area and concern themselves only with short
alignments in the immediate vicinity of a circle, which indicate a
significant astronomical declination, followers of Watkins have come
to the further realization that these same alignments may often be
extended over many miles of country to other prehistoric points,
forming a long distance ley. If this can be shown to be in fact the
case, the existence of leys is put beyond doubt, for the possibility of
prehistoric stones falling by chance exactly on those very lines,
which have already been independently established as prehistoric
astronomical lines, is too remote to be considered, [wrote John
Michell].[97]

Michell chose for his survey West Cornwall's Penwith
peninsula, for the stone circles there had been earlier
analysed by Sir Norman Lockyer for their astronomical
properties.[30]

To avoid any possible dispute, the only sites taken into consideration in this survey were those of undeniably prehistoric provenance,
stone circles, standing stones and dolmens. These stones are each
represented on the map by a small dot. A three-foot steel ruler was
used to plot their alignments, allowing no visible margin of error.
The maps used were prepared by Stamford's of Long Acre.[97]

The alignments plotted by Michell had been found by
Lockyer to have astronomical significance.

Lockyer took a bearing from the centre of a stone circle to an
outlying stone in order to calculate whether it might have been
erected to mark the rising point of the sun or of one of the six
notable time-keeping or warning stars on a day corresponding to one
of the chief festivals of the May year in about 2,000 B.C. He used
only one of the 25 inch or 6 inch map and did not concern himself
with the possibility that the same line might be extended over other
prehistoric stones not visible from the circle.

Michell extended Lockyer's observation lines from two
circles and found them to align with many other prehistoric
stones, and concluded: 'In this survey the evidence is at least
as good as that accepted by archaeologists for astronomical
indicators, since in the first four examples the lines were not
arbitrarily selected, but represent extensions of lines already
noticed by Lockyer as having astronomical significance.'[97]

Many stones not marked on the maps used also fell on the
alignments, and Michell's words on the subject should be
heeded:

Prof. Thom, the authority on Megalithic astronomy, writes that even insignificant boulders about the countryside should be recorded before being removed, if this has to be, for he finds that many such were placed as markers on astronomical lines. In exactly the same way, Alfred Watkins observed that smaller stones, often featuring in local folklore, stand on leys. There are also many uncut boulders, which are now generally regarded as ancient, artificial structures. Of these the author of a popular textbook on geology writes, 'In many places great rocks can be found which are quite alien to the district, and these occur as the result of glacial action. We know this because no other agency could have placed them where they are.' On such tenuous assumptions many of our great sciences are based.

The important question concerns stone circles. It has always been assumed by those who investigated their astronomical properties that they were simply built as observatories. Yet this theory fails to explain the existence of great stones, continuing the astronomical lines far across the country. Obviously some further principle is involved of which we are still ignorant, yet which was so highly regarded by men of the ancient civilization, that they devoted their entire resources and technology to the construction of a worldwide system of aligned megalithic instruments . . .[97]

Michell also made a pertinent point on the subject when, discussing Thom's work, he stated:

The lines of stones that produce and determine the circle's formation are set to point out these astronomical points in such a way that the astronomical bodies themselves create the figures on which the circles are based. The celestial movements are thereby reduced to a system of geometry and mathematics illustrating the basic universal laws and the patterns of life itself.[40]

The objections to astronomical observations being within Megalithic Man's capability have included the assertion that prehistoric man could not write, so consequently could not make the necessary records on which to base his alignments, or calculate eclipses or the Moon's small perturbation. However, Alexander Marshack, a research associate at Harvard's Peabody Museum of Archaeology and Ethnology, spent seven years studying more than 1,000 bits of bone, rock and ivory engraved by Cromagnon Man in Western Europe, dating from as far back as 32,000 years ago, and decided that the complex, symbolic rows of dots and zigzags appear to have lunar notations, sets of symbols that uncannily accord with the phases of the Moon. Marshack stressed in *The Guardian* of 13 February, 1971 that he cannot 'prove' this. What it certainly means, he asserts, is evidence of 'pre-writing and pre-arithmetic'.

Before leaving the subject of stone circles, readers may be interested to learn that an anonymous contributor to *The Ley Hunter* (No. 6) gave a comprehensive account of how one of the circles at Stanton Drew can be detected as a calendar based on the planet Venus.

12. Ethno-Astronomy

'There can be little doubt that life could be made much richer, and our temperaments far more vital and equilibrated were we to observe the times and seasons in a way that all primitive faiths that are in close touch with nature observe them.' — Dion Fortune.[16]

The simplest way to describe what ethno-astronomy is may be by direct comparison with astrology. The differences may not seem particularly important or useful, but nevertheless there are differences and the two subjects can best be discussed separately.

In ethno-astronomy stars are used as route maps by travellers on land or by navigators at sea. In ethno-astronomy the stars are utilized by man. In astrology the stars themselves guide man's destiny rather than he guide himself by their positions at a given moment. In astrology their biomagnetic play on his soma rules his actions.

In ethno-astronomy position in a landscape was important for a man, and Red Indians laid villages out to such a principle. A map of the sites of individual huts would be geometrized by the heavens, as would the villages of various groups within a tribe. In astrology position is less important, though it is so at the moment of birth and the stars at that moment.

Ethno-astronomy led Red Indians to migrate *en bloc*, and as they changed their latitude and longitude then the astrological conditions for each would change separately.

Ethno-astronomy creates the Earth's shape and continental drift, it marks by the stars' courses the twists of major rivers, islands, bays and peninsulas. Its changes are slow and sure. Astrology's changes can be sudden but within a framework, causing volcanoes and the basic geology.

To put this into basics:

Astronomy is concerned with measuring the constituents and movements of the heavenly bodies.

Ethno-Astronomy is noting the physical effects of heavenly bodies upon the Earth, and living one's life within such a scheme on an esoteric level, and utilizing for travel the positions of heavenly bodies for direction-finding on an exoteric level.

Astrology is the science or art of interpreting the influence of heavenly bodies on individuals and determining the path their lives will take.

Prehistoric man's interest in the stars is reflected in the positioning of tumuli in parts of the North Riding. The first person to draw attention to this was Robert Knox, who, in an 1855 work, noted the pattern of conspicuous howes near Ugthorpe which form Charles's Wain. Frank Elgee, in *Early Man in North-East Yorkshire* (1930), suggests that the arrangements were intentional, though he notes that his studies to find more often revealed likely arrangements, but crowding of small barrows could make designs accidental. However, a few groups of larger barrows show it distinctly. He gave several examples and noted that in some places the figures never seem to have been completed. On the top of the escarpment above Carlton-in-Cleveland there are six barrows so arranged that if another were added it would form the figure of The Plough. Six barrows between Bransdale and Farndale also suggest The Plough.

J.R. Mortimer, in *Forty Years' Researches* (1905), had shown that the Bronze Age folk of the Yorkshire Wolds arranged some of their larger howes in the form of constellations, notably The Plough or Charles's Wain, and more rarely The Chair in Cassiopeia. He quoted an example of Huggate Wold where not only are the seven brightest stars of the Wain represented, but also two neighbouring stars and the adjacent solitary star Cor Caroli.

Coincidences? Star worship? Cult of the departed? Why these constellations.

As for the United States, Alice C. Fletcher, writing in the first few years of this century, reported that the four bands of the Pawnee Indians then still placed their villages with a shrine named after a star in which sacred relics were kept and each village being named after the shrine, in fixed positions corresponding to the stars, so the villages on the Earth reflected the picture of the stars in the heavens.

The bands were organized by the stars whose powers made them into families and villages and taught them how to live. Their earth lodges had circular floors symbolizing the Earth and a dome-shaped roof symbolizing the arching sky, and the four posts were suggested to be the four stars in the body of Ursa Major. For them, apparently, Ursa Major represented four men carrying a sick or dead man. The Field Museum of Natural History, Chicago, has a Pawnee star map at least 300 years old which shows that the Pawnees recognized the constellations as we do, the main stars and their magnitude; it shows careful observation and study. They even recorded some double stars. Being so old, the map informs us that their knowledge of astronomy owed nothing to the white man and was impressive.

2. Tre-Fedw mound, Herefordshire, is situated on a ley between Pandy and Llanvihangel. (*Alfred Watkins*)

3. Chun Quoit, an impressive dolmen at Morvah, near Penzance, Cornwall. (*Central Office of Information*)

13. Astrology

'A sympathy leads the body and sky to communicate and transmutes the movements of the planets to the adventures of man.' – Michael Foucault.

On the first day of the 1971 postal strike the horoscope for Pisces printed in a North of England newspaper began: 'You will receive a letter . . .' So much for newspaper astrology.

It takes a great number of years and much study to become a competent astrologer, and the reading of a horoscope is a fairly complex and lengthy business. In a work such as this I can only briefly cover the subject, but I would stress two points: that I believe firmly in astrology as a practical reality, and that an elementary knowledge of the subject is extremely helpful when researching the terrestrial zodiacs in our countryside.

Astrology, like ley hunting, is a heretical study as far as orthodox science is concerned. Al H. Morrison, president of the Astrologers' Guild of America, said in an interview in *Friends* (No. 19): 'Astrology is not a primary science like nuclear physics or astronomy. Astrology is more an art of correlation between astronomic fact and our experience here. Astrology is a secondary discipline.' He added:

> You can actually see, with your bare eyes, planetary patterns in the weather picture. When it gets that obvious it's like the tides following the Moon. It has N.A.S.A. people practising astrology. They don't call it astrology, they merely call it the correlation of astronomic fact. For a while they had a science named 'astrogeophysics', until I pointed out by registered letter that this was a synonym for astrology, and they promptly scrapped all their printed stationery to rename it 'astrophysics and geophysics'.

Spring: the Sun's path climbed higher into the sky day by day; day by day the crops climbed higher and higher to ripeness. Autumn: the Sun's path fell lower in the sky day by day; day by day the crops died back further and further. The Moon waxed and waned; tides high, tides low. The happenings in the heavens had their correspondences on Earth. The harmonies were studied, correlated, astrology was born from primitive man's labour.

This was early in mankind's history, when, I believe, all men were peace-loving equals. Yet it would be noted that though each would be socially equal, some men would be taller, or stronger, or more handsome, or cleverer, or more skilful, or luckier. These unequal divisions would not be regarded as chance occurrences, for nothing happens without reason, everything being within a framework of cause and effect.

Prehistoric man would have sought to identify the causes of these anomalies, and most writers on the origins of astrology have formed the opinion that to the heavenly bodies he attributed god-like powers ordering men's destinies and requiring propitiation. Assumptions such as these have gained widespread acceptance; yet the existence of huge, detailed terrestrial zodiacs in Albion makes it plain that early man was not so superstitious as to regard stars as gods, but that he evolved a systematic and sophisticated interpretation of cosmic forces in which the beasts of the zodiac and later gods were symbols and not hypothetical actualities.

It is difficult not to conclude that astrology was born in Albion and not Chaldea, and that zodiacs were first noted in the landscape by Megalithic Man, who added details. It is also apparent that leys which are also solar alignments; that stone circles shown by Thom and others to be observatories; that the Sun's effect on ley energy; together with terrestrial zodiacs; reveal that prehistoric man studied both astrology and astronomy, perhaps without pigeon-holing both as separated studies. Astrology was born under a good sign.

Today we seem to be on the threshold of a return to a linkage between these disciplines as astrology seeks to reaffirm its scientific basis. In the book *Astrology and Science*, Michel Gauquelin made plain the differences between astronomers and astrologers. He pointed out that the two types of experts are in conflict, with the astronomers refusing point-blank to accept that the stars may have some influence upon man's destiny, and the astrologers believing it to be so without the necessity for absolute proof. The feud may be over, however, as a new school of scientists have broken the vicious circle. Gauquelin's words sound ominously like those which could apply to the ley hunter's predicament: 'They will have to fight to get their discoveries accepted, but their ideas will one day triumph. So the problem of the stars' influence which has been considered insoluble up till now is at a turning point at the present time, heading in a new and more promising direction.'[17]

Science has attempted to discredit astrology many times: Copernicus proving the Earth's rotation around the Sun; Watson and Crick explaining DNA with its genetic code programming our fates; Sigmund Freud's psychoanalytic observations on our motives; deoxyribonucleic acid and psychoanalysis stating that a man's future was within him at conception, in his genes and deepest recesses of his mind.

Yet other scientists have striven to find links between man and the cosmos: Prof. Fred Hoyle's defence that we are 'stuff of the universe'; Oparin's conclusion that life was created through the luminous and ultra-violet energy from the Sun reacting with water; Stanley L. Miller's success in confirming that the Sun did create life upon Earth, are assurances that the cosmos does play a significant role in our lives.

The question of cosmic cycles, from the creation to disintegration of galaxies, to the sadly short lifespan of the gentle mayfly, are not researched by scientists in a bid to defend astrology, but as an attempt to take the mystery out of astrology and provide rational, scientific explanations for life.

The simplest cycle is that of day and night, and man's sense of time is tied up inexorably with a dark night sky. As Prof. Fred T. Haddock commented: 'The fact that you have a night sky, a black sky, is the most important fact of our existence. This is Olber's Paradox.'

No wonder our ancestors were so fascinated by the night sky — and its opposite, the sunlight of day.

Michel Gauquelin, nevertheless, after his monumental

inquiry, concluded that 'to predict the future by consulting the stars is to delude the world, or at least to delude oneself', adding that 'ravings about astrology are regularly symptomatic of certain mental illnesses'.

Be that as it may, I believe the foundations of astrology to be sound.

A scientific explanation for the astrological birth chart based upon magnetic fields has been suggested. Marc Petros, in *International Times*, No. 22, stated: 'Our Earth receives light from the stars, therefore, since no body will radiate energy unless there be another body within range to receive that energy, it follows that there must be an attraction between the Earth and the stars.' The Sun's energy makes the Earth, by induction, a magnet. The Moon and the Earth are charged with the same kind of electricity on their respective hemispheres facing the Sun, so the side of the Moon facing the Earth is charged with electricity of an opposite kind to that of the Earth. The magnetic field is then further complicated when other planets happen to be in various aspect to the Sun at the same time, the planets also being inductively charged by the Sun. As the planets move, the magnetic field alters.

So what happens at the moment of birth?

The crux of the matter is the conjunctions when the baby takes its *first breath*. Marc Petros stated:

> Until that moment the baby had no separate existence. It was merely a collection of living cells forming a physical part of its mother. But at the moment of taking its first breath self animation enters the child. At that moment the lines of force of the resultant magnetic field of the sun, moon and stars run through the baby where they fix and determine the relative positions of the electrons and protons in the atoms of the child's flesh, blood and bones for the duration of its life. Which is why the child behaves in a characteristic manner throughout life. Temperament, personality, and individuality being the impelling cause. This is why certain aspects of the planets and signs appear to affect him.
>
> The actuating medium being the type of magnetic field created by existing configurations.

Whatever we may think of astrology — art?, science?, superstition? — scientists of standing, such as Lockyer,

Thom, Hawkins and Hoyle, have proved beyond dispute that prehistoric man in Britain was a skilled forecaster of cosmic phenomena and knowledgeable about all the visible motions of heavenly bodies. However, we must consider whether all his methods were purely computational, complex arithmetic following ingenious rules. Did he, in fact, know what the planets actually are? Could he explain not how, but why, the bodies he observed moved as they did?

Could prehistoric man have had optical aids? Neolithic telescopes? Might some form of crystal have been placed in tubes such as those which penetrate rocks at Brimham, in Yorkshire? Several of these are almost horizontal and up to eighteen feet long. Further examples exist at Hitchingstone and Earl's Crag near Keighley. At Brimham two such were once called the Little Cannon and Great Cannon. One writer believed them to be 'oracular stones', supposing that a Druid hid on one side invisible to the populace and delivered oracles via the hollow tube. The little Cannon was also called the Druid's Telescope.

Lewis Spence could not find sufficient evidence that the zodiac had its inception in Atlantis, so he pointed to Egypt. I would point to Albion. Natal astrology is the branch which is understood – or rather misunderstood – by most people. But astrology is more than an individual thing for there is mundane astrology, which deals with nations and peoples, and which is more our concern. Albion is Aries in the world scheme. Research has shown that it is likely that England and Wales can be divided into twelve, Arbor Low being the centre, with each segment containing a primary zodiac and a number of secondary zodiacs. These are the terrestrial zodiacs.

14. Terrestrial Zodiacs

'She was pottering around the Glastonbury area when she was struck with a thought that may yet turn out to be as profound as Newton's observation of the falling apple or the Duke of Edinburgh's recurring obsession with his ebbing bathwater. She had stumbled upon an outline of a zodiacal sign.' – Geoffrey Moorhouse.[98]

Not only did Mrs Katherine E. Maltwood stumble upon the outline of a zodiacal sign, but a complete representation of the astrological signs laid out in Somerset. Since then much has been published on the subject of this zodiac, The Somerset Giants, and it has captured the imagination as no other zodiac has, largely through its conjectured connection with Arthurian legend.

John Michell wrote:

> Roaming the countryside where every episode in the history of the Holy Grail has its physical location, Mrs Maltwood was haunted by the feeling of imminent revelation. One summer afternoon, standing on a low hill and looking out across the plain towards the distant ramparts of Camelot, she saw both physically and intuitively the elusive secret.[40]

It was during the 1920s, and Mrs Maltwood checked on Ordnance Survey maps the realities of her vision. Spread before her she noted the winding River Cary between Charlton Mackrell and Somerton outlining the underside of a great lion, the contour of the head, back, tail and paws being defined by roads and footpaths. The remainder of the figures followed. She published two books, pamphlets, commissioned an aerial survey, and the resultant photographs were published as a supplement to one of her books.

Yet Katherine Maltwood was not the first person in historic time to notify the public of the zodiac's existence, for Dr John Dee, writing during the reign of Queen Elizabeth I, wrote of the figures in clear fashion. Also Dr

Dee's friend Edward Kelly claimed to have discovered at Glastonbury the powder for alchemical transmutations.

Several confirmed zodiacs have now been publicized in Britain. Lewis Edwards wrote in great detail of a zodiac engraved in the Welsh landscape around Ffarmers; Mary Caine discovered another around Kingston-upon-Thames; there is a vesica piscis-shaped zodiac around Nuthampstead, Hertfordshire; Yorkshire has a zodiac at Holderness; North-West Durham has its Stanley zodiac.

My own researches have led me to suspect at least three other zodiacs in County Durham alone. Other suggested sites have included Glasgow, Edinburgh, Banbury and the Wirral. With the resurgence of interest in leys, zodiacal research has been given a new lease of life, and a great many more zodiacs can be expected to come to light as our partnership with the ancient wisdom becomes closer.

Zodiacal figures may be found separately.[90] And is it pure chance that the bowl-shaped Howe of Cromar in Aberdeenshire 'bears a remarkable resemblance to the effigy of a human head, with the face turned to the right?'[43]

The Nuthampstead zodiac is both interesting in its own right and in comparison with other examples. Nigel Pennick discovered the landscape figures on the boundaries of Essex, Hertfordshire and Cambridgeshire on 18 October, 1969. Within ten miles of the zodiac's centre are seven camps, an initiatory maze at Saffron Walden, and what Pennick described as 'the greatest ancient monument of its kind in the world' — the Gog-Magog figures at Wandlebury, discovered by the late Tom Lethbridge.

Perhaps the most important feature of the Nuthampstead zodiac is its vesica piscis shape, as opposed to the basic circle. However, the figures are similar to those around Glastonbury, whereas those in the 'Welsh Temple of the Stars' differ in many respects. Pennick has also pointed out that where in the Glastonbury zodiac the Fosse Way cuts the circle, in the corresponding area in the Nuthampstead zodiac lies Beards Lane, another 'Roman' road.

Pennick wrote: 'It appears then that the lines of cosmic power [Earth rays postulated by Von Pohl] somehow produce such phenomena as the zodiacs at their intersections, whether by conscious efforts of the ancients or by a more esoteric influence, it is so far impossible to say.'[101]

That terrestrial zodiacs are completely artificial seems extrèmely improbable as they are formed too greatly by contour lines; but roads, rivers, ponds and mounds can be manmade, wholly or partially. Quite probably a geometrical plan lies at the core of the mystery.

Mary Caine has refined some of Katherine Maltwood's Glastonbury figures, written extensively on the zodiac, surveyed it from the air, made a film of it, and her husband has held an exhibition of paintings of the figures. As an introduction to one of her articles, published in *Gandalf's Garden*, an anonymous writer introduces her piece:

> It can be seen only from about five miles high in the sky. Why? For whom were these gigantic figures created? And by whom? Was the whole countryside laid out as a mystical path of initiation by Ancient Sumerians or forgotten travellers of Elder Days? Or could it be that at the intersections of the strange lines of psychic power, which appear to criss-cross our planet, certain forces accumulate and cause the landscape to arrange itself into meaningful designs, in much the same way as snowflakes and all other natural phenomena geometrically construct themselves? Such a cosmic concentration of energies could also have the property of subconsciously moulding the minds of the men who worked the land, causing them to create the Zodiac without being aware of it, since life on this earth is, in general, controlled by the subtle influence of the planets. Could the Zodiac be an immense symbolic landing stage marked out for the guidance of unearthly airborne objects, which even today still appear to use Glastonbury as a landmark? Was its existence known to the enlightened Sage Merlin, and its hidden meaning the esoteric answer to the real significance of King Arthur's Round Table?[69]

A puzzle indeed. Arthur, Avalon, Jesus Christ and his uncle, Atlanteans, Sumerians, extra-terrestrials the mystique of Glastonbury is strong, yet it is far from unique. Stranger zodiacs exist.

There is a great temptation to believe that cosmic influences are at work everywhere, eternally moulding the landscape and causing mankind to live according to a great plan. Such a conclusion is inevitable. Consett steelworks is in the sector of Stanley zodiac under the dominion of Mars. Coincidence? Study, experience, intuition have led me to discount coincidence in such cases. Unseen planners guide our actions. But more to the point than who created the zodiacs is what created them. If non-human actions did not play a major part in the creation of the figures, then it would have been extremely time-consuming for prehistoric man to create the figures. Being so much representations of the heavens, it would seem natural to assume that the planets and stars played a part in the zodiacs' formation. This, of course, not only puts we who are seeking the truth of ancient skills and wisdom into a position of greater alienation from orthodox archaeologists, but consequently involves us in a similar headlong collision course with orthodox geographical studies.

As for dating the period when man added details to the zodiacs, it is probable that this was a part of the same scheme whereby leys were marked and megalithic monuments erected. Lewis Edwards postulated that the Ffarmers zodiac was marked around 4,000 B.C.

Edwards also mentioned leys within the zodiac, and he wrote of its markers: 'Their mathematical knowledge and the organization required to construct such a temple [of the zodiac], shows a very high social and intellectual develop-ment, and contradicts the usual assumption regarding the primitive, social structure of the early inhabitants of Britain.'[8][3]

Discussing the figures, he added: 'The Zodiacal signs may be regarded as symbols of the spiritual powers guarding the Temple. They were not the centre of its worship. This we find in the centre sanctuary, where daily, men worshipped God and where on High Festivals people from far and near gathered to pay homage unto Him.'

As can be seen, not everyone is in agreement on the subject, and in the tabulated notes below it will be seen that in the case of Glastonbury not all authorities agree as to the outlines or the legendary associations. I have attempted a synthesis of opinions, but I doubt if any expert will agree with all the points made.

We must not be too hasty in altering our landscape, for the stars have spent billions of years shaping it with mountains, hills, valleys, streams, becks . . . and zodiacs. Nature chooses where its plants should grow and we drown them with artificial reservoirs. Nature provides rivers for the fish and we pollute them with chemical effluent. Nature provides sunlight and rain for vegetation and we provide smog and insecticides, against all the rules of harmony. Man looked to Nuthampstead as a site for a new massive airport where a small aerodrome stood, but the site was not auspicious, and neither was Wing with its ancient church.

Terrestrial zodiacs provide us with one of the most fascinating categories of esoteric prehistoric study, with connections in astronomy, astrology, geography, archaeology and folklore. A great deal more research is required.

GLASTONBURY	FFARMERS	NUTHAMPSTEAD
AQUARIUS Eagle or phoenix. The Tor is its head and Abbey its tail. Denotes rebirth.	Squirrel. Situated at Hill of the Sacred Place near Llanfair Clydogan.	Eagle. One tumulus for its eye and another at 475 feet above sea level in a way corresponds with Glastonbury Tor.
CAPRICORN Unicorn. Horn is formed by great earthwork, Job's Coffin or Golden Coffin.	Unicorn. Tip of horn at Pass of the Front of the Horn.	Leaping goat. Its outstretched hind legs encompass Ickleton.
SAGITTARIUS Archer on horse. Stars of Hercules fall on the rider. In a 3-mile arc.	Man on horse with lance.	Man on horse. Hercules's horse stumbling as at Glastonbury. In a 2½ mile arc.
SCORPIO Scorpion. Is stinging horse of Sagittarius, causing it to stumble and unseat its rider.	Scorpion and eagle. Sting outside circle and represented by wood in constellation Serpens. Points to another wood giving eagle's outline.	Scorpion. Around Arkesden, ending near Duddenhoe.
LIBRA K.E. Maltwood and Elizabeth Leader could find no scales as astrologically these only evolved from Scorpio's claws in Roman times. The dove at Barton St David covers The Plough.	No identifiable figure, but Lewis Edwards marked an outline similar to a figure eight.	Sector has continuation of large scorpion, but a dove is found at Scales Park.

	GLASTONBURY	FFARMERS	NUTHAMPSTEAD
V I R G O	Large figure of woman and sheaf. Mary Caine calls her Virgin, Mother and Black Witch, the three-phased Moon; pregnant with tumulus for nipple.	Woman. Hills form her body and triangle of roads forms sheaf.	Figure similar to Glastonbury of woman and sheaf. Lies around Brent Pelham.
L E O	Lion. Three miles long, starting from Somerton.	Lion. Proudly erect; rivers give identical leg outline to Glastonbury. Below Leo in the sky is Hydra, and though in the zodiac there is a Pass of the Back of the Serpent, Edwards did not disover an outline.	Lion. Figure too far south for a circular zodiac, and makes the design appear akin to a vesica piscis, probably centred upon Cross Leys.
C A N C E R	Figure absent. Leo takes space.	Figure absent.	Figure absent, Leo taking all sector.
G E M I N I	Here is a boat (Argo Navis) and man with raised arm (Orion). Of these two constellations the former is not visible in Britain! Is there one figure or more? Mary Caine suggests a meditating monk-like figure. Elizabeth Leader believes this to be a griffin.	Man's head and arms; also boat (Argo Navis and Orion).	Man with flexed elbow. It terminates on Ermine Street.

	GLASTONBURY	FFARMERS	NUTHAMPSTEAD
T A U R U S	Bull's head. Horns are two manmade ridges at Marshal's Elm. Pleiades are over the earthworks on the shoulder. The star Aldebaran is the bell beneath its neck.	Bull's head.	Bull's head and foot. Nose terminates at Cave Gate.
A R I E S	A crouching ram. Stars start at Street and continue down its chest.	Ram.	Crouching ram looking over its shoulder as at Glastonbury. Road named The Joint is its back. Forepaw is Ashgrove and inside it is Periwinkle Hill.
P I S C E S	Two fish and whale at Wallyer's Bridge. Mrs Maltwood was fascinated when Tony Wedd suggested a figure within the whale.	Two fish. Figures marked by two woods, each with a camp.	Two fish. One at Little Chishill and the other south of Royston.
E X T E R N A L F I G U R E S	Great Dog of Langport.	Woods shaped like a leopard, an extinct water fowl and a raven-like bird.	

15. Alchemy

'The alchemists claimed that manipulation of matter in their crucibles could provide what the moderns would call radiation, or a field of force. This radiation would transmute all the cells in the operator's body and turn him into a truly "awakened" man – a man who would be alive, both here and on the "other side".' – Louis Pauwels and Jacques Bergier.[44]

Ley hunters are alchemists. In common with the alchemists of old, today's seeker after the ancient wisdom of prehistoric times finds his study affecting his mind or soul. His condition is changed.

But why should a work of prehistory concern itself with a denigrated pursuit – largely mediaeval – regarded by the public as a confidence trick, which either led to the swindling of princes or madness for the alchemist? What sense may be made from the almost undecipherable writings of the alchemists?

Some answers can most easily be given by direct quotation from *The Dawn of Magic*, by Louis Pauwels and Jacques Bergier:

Alchemy . . . could be one of the most important relics of a science, a technology, and a philosophy belonging to a civilization that has disappeared.

We are tempted to believe that alchemy contains the fragments of a science that has been lost, fragments that, in the absence of their context, we find it difficult to understand or to make use of.

The real aim of the alchemist's activities, which are perhaps the remains of a very old science belonging to a civilization long extinct, is the transformation of the alchemist himself, his accession to a higher state of consciousness.

It may be that spiritual energy plays a part in the physical and chemical operations of the alchemist. It may be that a certain method of acquiring, concentrating and directing this spiritual energy is essential to the success of the alchemists' work.

One distinguished alchemist wrote under the name of Fulcanelli. It has been suggested that his work had allowed him to achieve a state of longevity. He wrote two books around 1920, one of which, *Le Mystère des Cathédrales*, is a dissertation on the age-old custom of transmitting through architecture the message of alchemy, which seemingly dates back to the time of the stone circles. According to Pauwels and Bergier, Fulcanelli believed that the connecting link with vanished civilisations was alchemy. They wrote:

> Of course no archaeologist or historian of high repute will admit civilizations have existed in the past more advanced than ours in science and techniques. But advanced techniques and scientific knowledge simplify enormously the machinery, and traces of what they accomplished perhaps staring us in the face without our being able to recognise them for what they are . . . So long as archaeology is only practised by archaeologists we shall never know if the 'mists of antiquity' were luminous or obscure.

Bergier believed that he met Fulcanelli in 1937, and was told: 'Certain geometrical arrangements of highly purified materials are enough to release atomic forces without having recourse to either electricity or vacuum techniques', and Fulcanelli quoted Frederick Soddy — 'I believe that there have been civilizations in the past that were familiar with atomic energy, and that by misusing it they were totally destroyed.' Shades of Atlantis. Does the geometry of leys conceal great secrets? As for atomic power, what of the vitrified stones of prehistory?

Marjorie Craddock discussed the subject of beacons and power in standing stones with John G. Williams, and wrote:

> Mr Williams is considering a theory that 'powers' far stronger than mere information went along these routes. For one thing some of the stones have distinct burn marks greater than any which could have been produced by an ordinary fire, since the actual stone shows signs of having been melted. One of these is below Llangynidr Bridge on the Usk. Did prehistoric man know of nuclear energy?

Fulcanelli then told Bergier:

> The secret of alchemy is this: there is a way of manipulating matter and energy so as to produce what modern scientists call 'a field of

force'. This field acts on the observer and puts him in a privileged position *vis-à-vis* the Universe. From this position he has access to the realities which are ordinarily hidden from us by time and space, matter and energy. This is what we call 'The Great Work'.'

And 'The essential thing is not the transmutation of metals, but that of the experimenter himself. It's an ancient secret that few men rediscover once in a century.'

It is when we consider the alchemist's actual operations that we find recurring certain scientific ideas which ley hunters are attempting to apply to their study, including cosmic rays and terrestrial magnetism.

Just as certain laboratory experiments, which should always provide exactly the same result each time, can be affected by the positions of heavenly bodies, it seems that the correct conjunctions of stars were vital in alchemy, and this would explain the many repetitions of the same experiment, a practice which so baffled modern scientists until recently.

'The alchemist will repeat this operation thousands of times . . . Perhaps he is waiting for the moment when all the most favourable conditions will be fulfilled, cosmic rays, terrestrial magnetism, etc,' wrote Pauwels and Bergier.

The alchemist awaits the correct cosmic conditions, as perhaps prehistoric man studied the stars to find the auspicious moment for planting, reaping, travelling or making love. At a later stage in the operations, in the alchemist's luminous metal would appear a reflection in miniature of constellations or the Milky Way. Pauwels and Bergier believed that the Great Work, when completed, leads to the alchemist's transformation — 'fusion with the Supreme Being', 'concentration on a fixed spiritual goal' and 'junction with other centres of intelligence across cosmic spaces'. Radiations from the crucible put him into a new state, prolong his life, raise his intelligence and powers of perception. This is a higher degree of consciousness, a foundation of Rosicrucianism. The authors offer us something else, maybe of use in our study, that the keys to the secrets of matter are to be found in Saturn, according to old alchemical texts.

Radiations which affect the alchemist and raise him to an

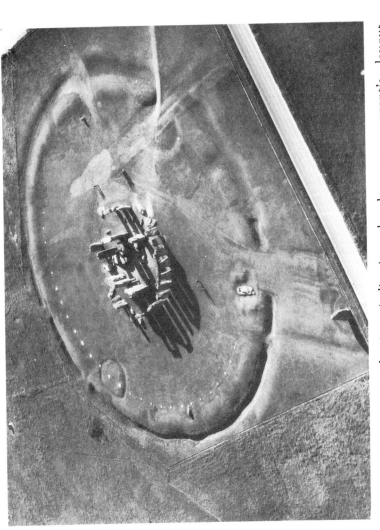

4.   Stonehenge. Aerial view indicating the henge monument's layout. *(Cambridge University Collection: copyright reserved)*

5. Stonehenge at its most dramatic. A perfect study in light and shade captures the magnificence of Britain's best-known prehistoric monument. (*Department of the Environment*)

'awakened state' may have an affinity with, or be the same as, those in leys. People such as Alfred Watkins, Katherine Maltwood, and other such visionaries, find themselves in remarkable positions *vis-à-vis* the spiritual reality of leys and zodiacs.

Mrs Mary Ann Atwood wrote a pamphlet entitled 'Early Magnetism and its Higher Relations to Humanity as veiled in the Poets and the Prophets'. Published posthumously, C.A. Burland believes it to have been the result of 'some kind of sudden realization of the link between past and present, accompanied by a vision of light; the kind of experience which the mystics call illumination'.[6] It was she who went on to write *A Suggestive Enquiry into the Hermetic Mystery*, which she and her father attempted to buy-in when she realized that the knowledge in it could be dangerous for those who passed along the secret path too quickly. The book was, however, republished in 1960, 110 years after the pair's attempt to have every copy destroyed.

But to view the subject in a scientific way. An experiment by Professor Giogio Piccardi proved that place, time and cosmic influences — as in astrology — have their part to play in chemical operations. He proved that oxycloral bismuth, in an open tube, reacted at varying speeds according to short-length variations related to sudden solar eruptions, powerful magnetic disturbances and large collections of cosmic rays; eleven year variations related to sunspots; annual variations, where speeds increased in March and September, related to the Earth's movement (a spiral trajectory).

It is as Michel Gauquelin stated:

> Until this date it was believed that identical experiments, carried out under strict laboratory conditions, always had to produce identical results. But this remains true only of solids, systems which cannot be broken down. In the case of liquids, whose structure is eminently fragile, no precaution taken in the laboratory can stop it: water, blood and all the colloids are broken down by cosmic effects. Because of these, the best designed experiments, if they are carried out at different times, will yield variable results'.[17]

Of course there was a scientific basis at the heart of the process, but until we know every secret of the universal laws

we cannot but regard alchemy as anything but a spiritual
pursuit. C.A. Burland described the alchemist's 'journey of
exploration' as 'not so much a chemical process as a search
for the inner meaning of the whole material universe. The
quest brought its own satisfaction.'[6]

According to G.R.S. Mead, 'there were apparently four
phases of transmutation – physical, psychical, vital and
spiritual, in the high sense of the last term'.[37] The
alchemist's quest was difficult, fraught with dangers to the
body, mind and life, and though agreeing that in the pursuit
of knowledge risks must be taken if progress is to be made,
Mead charged the alchemists with the responsibility of having
by their camouflage techniques increased the danger to those
who were inexperienced, yet worthy. He was convinced of a
'supra-physical, vital and psychical side to alchemy – a scale
of ascent leading finally to man's perfection in spiritual
reality'.

The processes in their furnaces, alembics and other
paraphernalia only intensify and hasten changes in the body
and psychical faculties for the alchemist; the symbols and
colours are the unseen life of body and mind. The alembic
represented the physical body of man and the carefully
controlled fire was warily watched to hatch his spiritual self
from the 'philosophic egg of his subtle nature', alchemy being
'the purification and reorganizing of man's physical
apparatus'.[37]

Whether Hermes was the art's revelator and patron – and
there seems to be no real evidence for this – it cannot be too
strongly affirmed that Hermes is inextricably bound up in the
mystery of leys, as will be shown in a later section.
Nevertheless it is good and appropriate for alchemy to be
attributed to this distinguished god.

Another aspect of alchemy is that view that its operators
sought to speed up nature's processes, bringing about in a
relatively short time the changes in mineral growth which
nature only accomplishes throughout many aeons, and until
the eighteenth century, scientists believed that when metals
were removed from the earth, the veins grew again by
subterranean regeneration. Though discredited, this theory

may not be as ridiculous as it seems, for those who believe in elementals have a classification for such helpers who work in the mineral kingdom, and when considered in conjunction with the alchemists' statements about salamanders it suggests the slim feasibility that the alchemists' Great Work was aided by ultra-dimensional helpers.

Science has a limited objective, and each scientist seeks only to add a minute portion to knowledge; if it has a use, then technology will as likely as not find an evil application for it. Alchemists sought not to create innumerable new chemical substances, yet the archaeologist seeks to catalogue the booty of his mole-like operations. Alchemists of yester-year gave the gold which they allegedly made to cure the sick, feed the starving and clothe the penniless. But they were not foremost philanthropists, for their work was a solitary affair, and their results were not set out in weighty scientific journals.. They pursued their quest with little or no care for the operations of other seekers. They ranged over a wide spectrum of interests, mostly those ignored by the public, such as philosophy and astrology.

The alchemist aimed at the unification of nature, for he appreciated nature intuitively, knowing that a living spirit interpenetrated everything.

This is not science, but is philosophy, and is truth. The philosophy behind alchemy will be further discussed in a consideration of the doctrine of pneuma.

As for journeys along leys, they are not so much a search for prehistoric stones as a quest for spiritual significance vibrating from the beginnings of time through the golden megalithic age to the present and ahead into the future, where we must follow in the hopes of attaining knowledge about the inner meaning to life and man's place in the scheme of cosmic creation. If leys cannot satisfy this yearning, then fulfilment may perhaps be found in other esoteric branches of knowledge – astrology, alchemy – but leys would seem to hold the purest wisdom and trace the straightest course. Alchemy was a long quest with dangers of explosions; astrology can reveal what the astrologer would rather not know. Leys are no exception, and in seeking the skills of the Ancients, the follower must exercise caution and intelligence, lest he be tempted from the straight and narrow.

16. The Straight Track in the Sky

'I think the leys are a most important part of the flying saucer saga.' – Brinsley le Poer Trench (letter to The Ley Hunter, *No. 2).*

Once upon a time a small boy stayed for his summer holidays with distant relatives at a house in the scenic village of Redmire in Yorkshire's Wensleydale, where time passes so slow. He had a den at the bottom of the garden, beyond the nettles, where newts were hoarded in a glass tank. He wandered the lands gooseberrying, collecting flowers to be pressed and stuck into albums, roamed the countryside for feathers, dammed miller's thumbs in pools and watched the trout jumping at dusk. He walked across the moors where the aluminium scrap of a crashed aircraft was stored in a cave, where a hermit lived until recently in another cave, where puffballs grew to enormous sizes and where Mary Queen of Scots made a bid for freedom. From the morning ramble he would descend Scarth Nick with his parents, to sip lemonade through a liquorice straw in the King's Head before lunch. In the afternoon it was a trip down to the river, past the ancient mound upon which Oliver Cromwell's Roundheads mounted a cannon to bombard Castle Bolton, over stiles, by the field where rabbits scampered, to the gently flowing waters cascading musically over falls.

Yet one morning, while in the garden of the house where he was staying, the boy looked south towards Pen Hill and saw a discoid golden craft manoeuvring over that prehistoric mound. Shining in brilliant sunlight, it made an impression so unforgettable as to be imprinted upon his mind from that moment onwards.

Years later the small boy read books about flying saucers, eventually heard of leys, began publishing a magazine on the two subjects and subsequently wrote this book. That day at

Redmire my future path was marked.

Since then I have been back to drowsy Redmire many times. I found a dolmen on the moors, behind which is a curious depression and in front of which is a large circle where fine turf grows in deference to the long wiry grass and heather all around. I have seen shamrock by a wall which was pointed out to the residents by a passing gypsy; later, in 1969, only nettles were in the spot, yet in 1970 here was four-leaved, five-leaved and six-leaved clover. A local inhabitant told me of a 'prehistoric circle' near the village, and when I investigated it I found rows of short, stocky pieces of quartz forming alignments between a gate and the bridge over which had once been the tracks of the Northallerton to Hawes railway line. Since then the quartz has vanished.

The mound over which the UFO appeared is flat-topped, covered with short grass except for a small circular patch on the top, and in one corner of the field close by is a solitary juniper tree. It was Philip Heselton who pointed out to me that Redmire is on one of the dragon lines referred to earlier.

This was not, however, the last UFO to be spotted by me. Apart from a wide variety of inexplicable lights in the sky of varying colours and sizes, one evening I saw two cigar-shaped, grey craft – called mothercraft or motherships by some ufologists – passing above Hartlepool, moving slowly southwards together. These two could have been physical 'nuts and bolts' UFOs, but the Redmire craft may have been entirely different, and I am tempted to believe that it was more symbolic, spiritual or extra-dimensional.

It is outside the scope of this book to make a lengthy study of the UFO phenomenon, but a definite connection between UFOs and leys has been postulated, and would seem to be a reasonable one. Apart from anything else, the current interest in leys has benefited greatly from a link with ufologists.

Tony Wedd, a prominent ufologist, was responsible for connecting UFOs and leys early in the 1960s. His own words, as published in 'Skyways and Landmarks', a publication of the Star Fellowship, explain how the hypothesis was born:

Suppose Major Gagarin or Commander Sheppard had returned from

Space with unmistakable evidence of other people's activity there, would we have altered our lives, stopped making atom bombs or killing people on the roads or producing horrid advertising or contriving an inflation squeeze? Of course not.

If we had wanted to change, we would have listened to information already given us. Only if the Space People tried to force themselves on us would we begin to take heed of them: for instance by a further dose of inflation, while missile lorries hurtle murderously along country roads in Army exercises, and radio broadcasters explain how we must be prepared to face 'enormous changes'.

A Golden Age of peace and justice cannot be thrust upon us. So the Space People prefer to make contact with isolated individuals, here and there, and give them a picture of how things might be . . . if we were willing.

If the voyage described by Buck Nelson to Mars, the Moon and Venus was a real experience, some of our pioneer astronauts are going to have to climb down a bit. But even if it were not, such a person would doubtless provide a means of relaying the sort of information the Space People are trying to get over to us; we might miss some useful information in rejecting the whole story. For instance he explains that the space ships travel along magnetic currents, and that each of these is named and numbered. He also says: 'The Space People tell me that the places where magnetic currents cross is comparable to a crossroads sign'.

Now an analysis of flying saucer sightings in France during a particular 'flap' in 1954 shows that the space ships do appear to travel along certain well-defined lanes; and that they pause at one of these 'crossroads' and execute a 'falling leaf' manoeuvre before setting course along another lane. One could argue that the lanes are the paths to and from a mother ship or carrier craft, and Aimé Michel shows that this was in fact so on many occasions. But to follow a straight line, and then turn off at a sharp angle and follow another one doesn't make sense unless what Buck Nelson says is true.

Now notice the word 'sign' since the sentence would be complete without it. Places must mean places on the Earth; if we can locate them, we may be able to observe these 'signs' for ourselves, some objects in the landscape or among the hedgerows that we have hitherto overlooked.

Since flying saucers have been visiting the Earth throughout recorded history, such crossroads signs would have to be prehistoric. With the publication in 1925 of Watkins's book on *The Old Straight*

Track, people have in fact become aware that there are landmarks across the country, lying along quite straight alignments, and a society now exists to plot them. And indeed the types of marks dealt with are in fact the prehistoric ones. So far, however, there has been no suggestion that these marks are the crossroads signs mentioned by Buck Nelson. But three sightings investigated in Kent in August 1960 strongly point to this conclusion: the clue was provided by existing place-names.

The sighting of a UFO at Keston on 16 August was reported to Gavin Gibbons, author of books on space ships, and thence to the Kent Area Investigator of the International UFO Observer Corps. Another at Mark Beech, by Mrs Everest, reached the same investigator via the London UFO Research Organisation. This was a pulsating white light, moving silently in a northerly direction. It returned to Keston on the 26th, where it was seen at 0045 hours by Mrs Clark and her mother, travelling roughly east to west. And this was close to a district called Keston Mark. The two marks align on Beacon Hill, Crowborough, which may be of some significance, though only the Mark Beech sighting suggests that the UFO was following this alignment.

Mark Beech is a striking hilltop halfway between the line of the Sevenoaks range and that of Ashdown Forest. The Ordnance Survey has set up a triangulation station there, and this location is the site of a clump of mixed trees, including Scots pine. It is not a significant beech clump, such as some of those on the South Downs: the pines seem to be more important.

On another feature, some four miles roughly to the south, stands a striking clump of Scots pines on Lyewood Common. This is repeated in a hilltop clump six miles in the other direction, close to Kent Hatch, on the edge of Crockham Hill Common. There is an exact alignment between the three points. A less perfect clump, again mixed, but with several pines included, can be seen at Chippens Farm, Hever, some mile and a half on the northerly side. Thus it can be seen that Mark Beech hilltop clump lies on a line of four definite marks: the line rises to Gillridge Farm at the Ashdown Forest end, but may well continue considerably farther than local investigations have so far extended.

Another striking mark is that at Gill's Lap on Ashdown Forest, and if this lies on the line through Westminster Abbey (located where there was formerly a thorn clump – so the old legend tells us) and the tumulus on Hampstead Heath, which has both pines and thorns, we get an alignment roughly parallel with the one already described. Another parallel would link the pines on Limpsfield Common with those at Chandler's Farm near Holtye. Number three would be the Mark Beech line already given. Number four would align Keston Mark with a Scots pine clump above Burrswood, Groombridge, via Scots pine clumps at Valence and Outridge Farm, near Westerham. Number five would run from Hanging Bank on the Sevenoaks range through Ford Place near Penshurst, which has a prominent pine. Number six could be located, perhaps, by a clump close to Rusthall Common, and number seven by the town centres, say, of Sevenoaks and Tunbridge Wells.

Now if these are the lines of 'magnetic currents' which Buck Nelson refers to, we can see the point of their being 'named and numbered'. The name would indicate the general direction, which in this case is the azimuth angle 21°W.

Line number four passes through Chiddingstone, and was one of six alignments mentioned in a communication received from a friend who has contact with the Space People. They told her; she said, that there was a magnetic centre at Chiddingstone, and that twelve others could be located by plotting these six alignments, starting with that which lies 6°N. of N.E. It is possible that one of these is located at Burrswood, which is already established as a notable centre of healing. No progress has been made with the others; but one remarkable fact has emerged: all recently reported UFO sightings lie on one or other of these lines; not only the three already mentioned, but one at Little Hawkwell in 1959 and one at Shoreham in 1961.

If Mark Beech hilltop does in fact act as a 'crossroads sign', it is possible that one of the routes crossing the one on the 21°W alignment is the 6°N. of N.E. alignment, which the Space People referred to. In fact the marks along this line had been observed before the communication about it came along.

Standing at Chested, a mile away, one can see that the castle at Chiddingstone aligns on Mark Beech, and there is a good clump of pines above Wilderness Farm between the two. Looking in the other direction one would have observed Chested aligning on One Tree Hill, except that the entire hilltop is now timbered over. The name is, however, a sure indication that it may once have served as a mark. So on this alignment also, Mark Beech hilltop aligns with three other marks.

The clump on Crockham Hill Common and the clump near Westerham seem to echo this alignment. So does a line through the Chippens Farm, Hever, clump, and a scatter of pine trees near Bough Beech, which reaches the Sevenoaks range at Bayleys Hill. Working from Gill's Lap in the same direction, the line strikes the fourth line at Stone Cross, which also sounds significant.

It is believed that the Mark Beech – One Tree Hill alignment coincides with an old track, and plans are in hand to excavate part of this and determine at what date it may have been made.

To conclude: there is a possibility that the UFOs use certain landmarks to navigate by, and that certain alignments of these marks would follow from the theory propounded by Aimé Michel that UFOs travel along straight lines, even when they make a change in direction. If we take a hint from Buck Nelson's story, we may find not only the 'star' systems referred to by Aimé Michel, but parallel systems also.

For further speculation, we have a pattern here of 'magnetic currents'. Is it possible that they will lead us to locate the 'magnetic centres' referred to by Dino Kraspedon in *My Contact With Flying Saucers?*

Aimé Michel's theory of orthoteny was based on his study of the wave of UFO reports which appeared in the French newspapers during the latter half of 1954, and the patterns which emerged. Before the publication of his book *Mysterieux Objets Celestes* in 1958, only generalizations had been made regarding UFO patterns, and his book made a considerable impact. Michel offered verifiable facts that during any 24-hour period during the 1954 wave, sightings appeared to be located upon straight lines crossing France.

Stephen Smith, former British Unidentified Flying Objects Research Association Director of Research, wrote a lucid article on the subject of orthoteny for *The Ley Hunter*, giving developments of thought regarding the orthotenic hypothesis.

Explaining the basis of Michel's findings, he wrote:

These alignments formed star shaped networks when the sightings included vertical cylindrical objects associated with diffuse clouds (cloud-cigars); and also, when the intersection of alignments was a sighting point, the object there was reported as displaying the well-known 'falling dead leaf' manoeuvre. Michel also noted, to the benefit of his future detractors, that the sightings along an alignment, though precisely located in time and place, were not of the same object nor were they arranged chronologically along the alignment . . . there were no indications that the UFOs were traversing an alignment from end to end. [108]

Spirited arguments favouring or attacking orthoteny have been propounded since 1958, but interest in the subject is now at a low ebb. A false trial? Ufologists have certainly given the subject the cold shoulder during recent years, and Smith commented: 'On the other hand, there would seem to be a lingering alliance for orthoteny among the ley hunters and this is a situation that could bear examination.' He concluded: 'Orthoteny has died a death and no reasoned argument has yet been put forward for linking orthoteny and leys,' and he questioned the validity of the statistical significance of both.

On 7 November, 1970, BUFORA organized a symposium on leys and orthoteny, at which Jimmy Goddard, Philip Heselton, John Michell and I were asked to present our case for a relationship existing between leys and orthotenies. The general opinion was that the evidence was so far unsatisfactory, and that until a full correlation between leys and UFO sightings could be made no definite answer could be given.

What is a fact is that at one point in Warminster thirteen leys converge, and this district is the scene of abundant UFO activity. A correlation certainly exists between ley centres and ufocals (areas of above average UFO activity).

If we are to consider that there is a link between UFOs and leys, then we must consider a number of questions – What are UFOs? Where do they come from? What is their attraction to leys?

No attempt is being made here to give an all-inclusive view of the UFO enigma, but the following hypotheses for the identity of UFOs is included for individual consideration.

1. *Extra-terrestrial origin.* The thesis is that other heavenly bodies support life and that their technology has advanced to such a stage whereby their inhabitants can and have explored space in UFOs. This is the simplest and most popular theory. A multitude of locations for these extra-terrestrials has been postulated.

2. *Terrestrial origin.* The craft may be based in the jungles of Brazil or in the deserted wastes of Antarctica, but piloted by extra-terrestrial colonists. A flamboyant concept is that of

a hollow earth, with holes at the poles from which emerge spacecraft. A novel slant is that the craft were designed and built in South America by former Nazi scientists.

3. *Extra-dimensional origin.* We shall deal fully with leys in relation to the etheric dimension later in this work, and one theory is that UFOs are piloted by 'etherians', whose disc craft exist in the fourth dimension, with the 3D world as its counterpart. Associated theories postulate an alternate reality and time travel.

4. *Natural phenomena.* Favoured by debunkers who believe UFOs are the result of observers' inability to identify celestial objects, aircraft, flying geese, swamp gas, temperature inversions, optical effects, etc.

5. *Unnatural phenomena.* The hypothesis that UFOs could be living entities existing in space.

As for the attraction of UFOs to leys, the four broad hypotheses are:

(*a*) That UFOs navigate by them.

(*b*) That UFOs utilize ley power for propulsion.

(*c*) That UFOs utilize ley power to defeat gravity.

(*d*) That UFOs are drawing our attention to leys.

Apart from this, there is the possibility that UFOs, in respect to leys, may be of two broadly dissimilar creations. That there may be actual spacecraft, and that there may be lights resulting from energy released along the alignments. The reader may consider the following comments.

Unidentified objects appear to use these connecting lines [leys] and also seem to appear at certain times. I know there are extraterrestrial beings who have a far wider knowledge of the forces surrounding the earth than any man on earth, but don't jump to the conclusion that all that passes between the centres has a 'man from space' within, for a sudden outpouring of energy flowing above the level of the earth would show shape and colour on occasions. This phenomena could give rise to the dragons of old. (*Frank Lockwood*[75])

A contactee informs me that navigation by the old leys is difficult nowadays for a flying saucer, because the leys are in a poor shape. Railway lines are far easier, which I, as a former R.A.F. pilot, can well appreciate. (*Tony Wedd*[114])

I was told [by a spacewoman] that thousands of years ago, when the

leys were first laid down, there were a number of settlements on
them, among which were a number of space people who had settled
on Earth. It is true that the spacecraft did follow the leys, not
because of any magnetic power which they emitted, but simply
because the spaceship crew hoped to contact their own people as
they travelled along them ... I can assure you that spacecraft are
physical and that the people are as human and as solid as we are.
(Philip Rodgers[105])
The magnetic forces which are radiating outwards from these areas
around our countryside, always present and having immense
potential in energy, act as a buoyancy stabiliser that prevents
spacecraft from being drawn within our gravity pull and density ...
It is only when such machines are in contact with stratas of magnetic
force areas upon our planet Earth, that they can make themselves
visible to us. (Arthur Shuttlewood[107])

Those are four viewpoints, and there are other matters to
consider too. Because I consider that UFOs are of different
categories, it is by no means simple to choose one theory and
reject the others. Manned spacecraft would find it difficult to
navigate from ley points, though they could 'lock on' to a ley
current, yet such power is not constant during any 24-hour
period, and would subsequently affect utilization of it for
propulsion or gravity techniques. Energy balls released by an
outpouring would similarly be restricted to periods of ley
current activity. But perhaps spacecraft operate independent
of ley current and choose to make themselves seen along leys
in order to draw attention to the magic lines so we might
investigate and utilize the power within them. The discoverer
of Stanley zodiac had the landscape figures revealed to him
by a bright ball of light in the sky.

Philip Rodgers referred to extra-terrestrials living among
earthmen in the past, and a comprehensive literature now
exists relating the gods of legend to extra-terrestrial origin. It
is not therefore my intention to duplicate, appraise or
condemn such writers, but it is necessary to consider one
factor here. Did spacemen play any role in educating early
man to mark and utilize leys? Old records refer tantalizingly
to winged messengers, fiery wheels, space chariots, flying
dragons and angels. Are these references to UFOs and their
occupants? It is indeed tempting to draw correspondences

between the crystal fortresses of Celtic legend and today's UFOs. As with UFOs these had no observable openings and they revolved. Lewis Spence gave several such examples, including the glass house or castle on the island of Bardsey, to which Merlin took the thirteen treasures of Britain.[48] Both Merlin and Arthur are connected in legend to glass vessels – Algernon Herbert, in *Britannia After the Romans*, referred to an old Welsh poem describing Arthur as a 'swiftly moving lamp'. Though there is a revolving fortress of Caer Pedryvan and the revolving castle of Saudon Og, it is Arthurian lore which proves the most interesting, his being so intimately connected with the skies and the Great Bear. This oblique reference of Spence's is charged with mystery and fascination: 'Gildas seems to allude to the existence of pagan rites in Britain when he attacks the Cambrian prince, Cuneglasse, alluding to him, as he does, as "the guider of the chariot which is the receptacle of the bear".'[48]

Before John Michell wrote of the dragon pulse and it became obvious that the Sun was an activating force for leys, Mrs Mollie Carey wrote of Stonehenge's link with Atlanteans and extra-terrestrials, of whom she commented: 'They like us to know that they "travel the road of the Serpent along the Highways of the Suns".'[70] She believes figures of spacemen can be discerned on the trilithons of the monument. Brinsley le Poer Trench is another writer who has postulated that the megaliths were built by Atlanteans, with a likelihood that extra-terrestrials intervened at some stage. I have also been told that a very sincere man, now dead, spent a night at Arbor Low stone circle, where he awakened to be told by 'ghosts' of Atlanteans that it had been created by them, and they explained to him its purpose and dimensions.

Yet Stonehenge particularly calls for our attention. In discussing the fact that in his experience UFOs rarely touch the ground, Arthur Shuttlewood wrote in *BUFORA Journal* of an occurrence at Stonehenge, where a spacecraft 'blacked out entirely in the autumn of 1968, before becoming a ring of fire that evidently shot from the stones themselves, whereupon the UFO fled upward from our curious approach'.

This suggests that the UFO could have been simply energy. John A. Keel believes that UFOs are only seen under certain circumstances, and that it may be that only certain people can see them at all. By scientific standards therefore UFOs do not exist as solid objects, and are not 'real'. This makes an extra-terrestrial theory unlikely, and puts their being in an extra-dimensional state more viable, and also suggests the possibility that they can operate beyond our time co-ordinates.

An author who has looked at the UFO phenomenon in depth in the context of leys is John Michell. He wrote:

> I think most of us realise that the phenomena of UFOs and prehistoric alignments are in some way related. After all, it was the reports of UFO sightings that led to the present re-examination of the ley system. Alfred Watkins was years ahead of his time, and had it not been for Jimmy Goddard and a few others, who some years ago first suggested an association between leys and UFO paths, his work would have remained neglected. But unfortunately the association is very hard to prove. The ley system stretches all across the country, set out with the accuracy of a modern surveyor. The precision of alignments between individual standing stones can only really be appreciated on maps of the six inch scale. On the other hand, very few UFO reports contain any exact information on the location and direction of sighted objects. In general, UFOs, and also migrating birds, do appear to follow certain lines of exceptional magnetic properties such as geological faults. The Earth's magnetic field, and thus everything within it, is directly influenced by the Sun, Moon and the planets, and this may well explain the prehistoric practice of astronomy in connection with leys and alignments. The legends of dragons as manifestations of cosmic energy indicate that the phenomenon of UFOs was known to the prehistoric astronomers as it still is to primitive people, and that its nature was once far better understood than it is now. That is why I believe that the most rewarding approach to the problem of UFOs may be through the study of prehistoric science and philosophy.

Today, ufology is still far from reaching agreement on the nature of its subject matter, and John A. Keel may be correct in his hypothesis that the phenomenon itself is responsible for creating confusion and diversions, with its multitude of variously-guised ufonauts and their multifarious points of origin; its intergalactic craft from which fall loose nuts and bolts; its messages of hope for humanity and its horrific warnings; healing of ailments and death from radiation. We are confused, but what of prehistoric man;

We can see that his tumuli are based on the two present-day basic UFO forms, but this may not necessarily have followed from sightings of such craft and been a 'cargo cult' exercise. It is conceivable that these burial mounds release energy from which forms such as UFOs are manipulated by some super intelligence alongside us on Earth. It is possible that, if we accept Keel's energy hypothesis (to be treated more fully later), Neolithic man had discovered the phenomenon's source and was utilizing the same source; also that eventually it led him astray by introducing him to metallurgy, finance and other corrupt practices, which put him on the road from innocence to corruption, and he fairly rapidly became materialistically minded and the truth was lost.

Certain people claim that they have received, telepathically, messages from entities, whom they generally believe to be ufonauts. John A. Keel believes that the UFO phenomenon is primarily electromagnetic in origin. He also reckons that it possesses the capability of adjusting beams of such energy to any given frequency, and messages by such a means could, feasibly, be picked up by the 30 per cent of individuals with the faculties to receive them. Some communications may be helpful to receivers, others may not.

In general, such people, sometimes without having been told by the entities whether they are ufonauts, have decided that they have been contacted by extra-terrestrials. John A. Keel states that specific kinds of people become involved in ufology and are manipulated by the phenomenon, just as it manipulates matter. He feels that investigation of people's experiences is more important than the study of sightings. Are the people contacted being duped into believing the phenomenon is extra-terrestrial, when in fact it is ultra-terrestrial — here, now?

Regarding the choice of people to receive transmissions, Dr Meade Layne, who published privately *The Coming of the*

Guardians in 1955, suggested that those chosen might be less affected by supersonic frequencies, and expressed his ideas in occult terminology, calling his ultra-terrestrials Etherians.

Part 4

ESOTERIC LEY HUNTING

17. Physics / Metaphysics

'And now to explain why these stones are magnetic. The majority of them have been erected with
the smaller end in the ground; and on placing a
hand upon them, one receives the astonishing
sensation that they vibrate, and with very little
effort could be pushed over. This extraordinary
illusion may be limited to only those persons who
are susceptible to the hidden forces of nature —
such as water-diviners, crystal-gazers and the like
— amongst whom I am happy to number myself.
Yet many who are unaware that they have any
psychic qualities have recognized and noticed this
curious vibration when touching the stones of
Carnac.' — Brigadier-General William Sitwell.[47]

Those who have pursued the truth behind the ley system
have come to several conclusions, none of which seems to be
all-embracing and applicable to the totality of the known
properties and theories regarding leys. Having exorcised, I
hope, the notion that leys were laid primarily to mark
trackways, much further explanation of the purpose of the
network is required.

Basically two theories to explain the nature of leys have
been propounded. The first, and most popular, is that leys
and their monuments mark and/or manipulate electromagnetic currents. The second, and lesser known, theory is
that they mark paths of etheric energy — matter on a higher
psychic plane than that perceived by our basic senses.

As previously stated, the aim of this book is to present to
the reader a comprehensive and integrated review of ideas
and theories postulated to reveal both the reality of leys and
to determine their nature, purpose and application. Therefore, having given a detailed explanation of what a ley looks
like to the observer who is interested in topological features,
the writer will here attempt to delve deeper into the subject,

and demonstrate how we may come to fully comprehend the esoteric significance of leys. Just as a road is useless without cars, a runway without aircraft or railway lines without locomotives, leys can only be regarded as odd brainchildren of prehistoric camp and country planning officials unless we probe the motives which led to the marking of such a system, the great reverence shown towards the lines and their uses.

I have attempted in this book to provide the researcher with all the known facts, stated clearly and objectively, but in this section I cannot avoid the temptation to suggest a number of lines of research which I hope will bear out subjectively intuitive theories on the ley system. No attempt is made to conceal others' ideas, however, and in fact my bias should be fairly acceptable – purely theoretically – to all, as it attempts to amalgamate the two basic theories within a single framework.

No pretence is made here to scientific expertise. I am almost totally ignorant of basic physics and in making such an admittance I hope that my candidness will overrule any immediate urge to therefore dismiss my views. If the reader be a scientist, let him be reminded that the scientist's attitude should always be one of openmindedness.

In a subject as complex as this, in which research has been carried out for so short a time, and for so little of this into the esoteric aspects, it is to be expected that investigations are far from complete. It is obvious that there are a multitude of facets to leys, each worthy of investigation, and until we have all the data at our fingertips we cannot formulate a cast-iron, all-embracing theory which will provide us with all the answers and the entire truth. We must note all the distinguishing features of leys and observe all the manifestations of power, the information must be analysed and attempts made to relate it to various scientific fields, noting the regularities and correspondences of the features and the power's attributes. An overall understanding of the features of leys and the power is required before we may safely state categorically the nature of the system and its part in the cosmic scheme.

We must inevitably agree with Mircea Eliade, who writes in

Patterns of Comparative Religion that 'the stones were used as instruments . . . they were not adored, but made use of '; the stones being either 'the signs of a spiritual reality beyond themselves' or 'the instruments of a sacred power of which they are merely containers'. They can be symbols and instruments at the same time.

If we are to treat ley hunting as a science, then we must follow certain rules. Despite the fact that such an approach has been undertaken by many researchers, the results have been scorned. Even if we were to find all the answers to the puzzle we might still find ourselves derided. Admittedly not everything in this book is scientific, but in a quest such as ours we may be forgiven for taking such liberties if it brings us nearer to the answers. Alfred Watkins's vision was not scientific, but he used it to lead him to proofs of the ley system which were scientific.

Certain aspects of the ley system are of a scientific nature and others are spiritual. Therefore it is not surprising that investigators favouring one or other line of research tend to approach the study in divergent ways: those with a scientific bent tend to be hypercritical and cautious in presenting their evidence, whereas those with an intuitive flair and who lack training as scientists can be over-hasty in making assumptions which may not fit all the facts. Both produce useful evidence, one species of investigator being criticized from 'plodding along', the other for 'woolly-mindedness'. In a subject as complex as this there is room for both types of researcher and both modes of approach. Each is dependent on the other.

Stephen Toulmin and June Goodfield wrote: 'The progress of science always involves a delicate balance between critical observation and speculative theorizing – between careful, piecemeal investigation of particular problems and imaginative general interpretation of the results obtained.' And: 'Other things being equal, the wider the implications of an investigation, the more important it is.'[52] The writers state that there are two kinds of advance in science which, when they come off, are particularly striking. One is when several different branches of science have developed along independent lines and they can be brought into harmony within a general framework. In finding the complete nature of ley power we must probe various branches of science for the full answer. The other striking advance is whereby the advance has repercussions outside the boundaries of science, producing radical changes in the ordinary man's view of the world. The answer to the reality of ley power should shake our attitude towards architecture, behaviour of animals, myths and legends, UFOs, our prehistoric ancestors, religion and human consciousness.

Earlier in this book an argument was put forward to prove that prehistoric man aligned his works within a geometrical framework. This in itself is a concept far beyond the comprehension of many people. This section aims to indicate that this feat was accomplished for practical and spiritual reasons and involved a form of energy whose nature is still far from being entirely clear.

Brinsley le Poer Trench is a highly respected researcher, who has not only spent a great many years investigating UFOs, but also man's environment and history. He supports the view that prehistoric technology was exceptionally advanced. In one of his books he wrote:

> The idea of improving such an august body as our sun may sound arrogant in the extreme, yet hasn't it always been the pressing duty of man to refine and improve the raw nature of his planet in order to survive upon it? And as he succeeds in having 'dominion over' his Earth he always sees more that should be attended to which gradually, but naturally, extends outwards to 'source level' projects – the taming of the raw current beneath his feet and the taming of the raw generator above his head. To bring stability and harmony into his entire environment is precisely why man is here.
>
> The time has come to speak out because it is increasingly clear that many observed ley features are wholly inexplicable on utilitarian considerations and must be related to magical beliefs.

Allen Watkins believes, as I had independently come to realize, that the classic elements of earth, air, water and fire play a part in the ley framework. But in my opinion the 'fifth element', ether, is way ahead of these in importance. In this section on esotericism and leys, the reader will also be given the opportunity to consider the validity of looking into dragonlore, fairylore, giantlore, gods and goddesses, saints, sacred centres, inspiration and the Aquarian Age on the esoteric level, and go beyond the physical truth of leys as mathematical and geometrical realities to a deeper level of electromagnetism, properties of quartz, levitation, orgone energy, the life force, fertility, ESP, communication, sound and dematerialization.

The reader is asked now to leave behind the exoteric, provable reality of the alignments being beyond statistical probability, and using the word esoteric in its broadest sense, consider the truths behind leys which are still beyond provability, and lie half in the realm of science and half in the domain of the occult. An attempt is made by the writer to divide these facets of the study into the 'scientific' and the 'spiritual' for simplicity's sake, but it must be stressed that his purpose is *not* to make any *strict* definition between the two. The division is probably an arbitrary one in the factuality, usability and functioning of leys.

Before presenting the reader with known or suspected properties of leys, I shall include sections on dragons and giants, whose significance is best made plain at this point.

18. The Dragon Pulse

'It does help to clear our heads, swimming derelict in the ocean of human aspirations and fears and incoherent inventions, to know that all the dragons were really one and the same dragon.' – H.J. Massingham.[36]

Dragonlore is as complex as the leys themselves, and the facets of it are as inexplicable as the interwoven enigmas of ley hunting. The term 'dragon' envelops a singly-named, fabled, fabulous beast in a multitude of forms, many of which are far removed from the dragon of children's fairy stories. Whatever outward form our dragon or serpent takes, we must consider it as a symbol of ley power or the strange lights seen crossing our skies by night. In the single concept of the dragon we will find recurrent links with leys and UFOs; lines above upon which unworldly forms move between the heavens and the Earth.

Taken somewhat simply, our fables suggest three types of dragon:
(a) Royal ancestor dragons.
(b) Maiden-devouring dragons.
(c) Treasure-guarding dragons.

We can profitably interpret the dragons in two ways:
(a) Dragon equals ley power.
(b) Dragon equals UFO and/or occupant.

So we find that:
(a) The dragon can be ley power in symbolic form and this is the treasure.
(b) The dragon is the light in the sky. Perhaps it descends, perhaps its occupants emerge and take away victims as wives or concubines (maiden-devouring), or the occupants inter-breed with Earth people and their descendants become a royal line.

Of course, the matter is not as simple as this, and other points deserve attention. Firstly, however, analysis is required

into the continuing popularity of dragon legends in an age
when we know that the classically portrayed dragon does not
and probably never has existed. If we are to discount the idea
that race memory has retained within its annals of long past
history garbled recollections of dinosaurs, it could be inferred
that the dragon represents either a racial memory of an
esoteric truth about leys or UFO visitations and inter-
breeding, or that the dragon is an archetype of power in the
broadest sense. Even so we meet a problem straightaway —
why should dragon legend dwell morbidly to a greater extent
upon evil dragons than on beneficent, kindly dragons? Is the
dragon a personification of evil, death and destruction?

British legend literally crawls with tales of harmful
dragons, associated with evil, menace, darkness, violence and
reptilian coldness. The dragon/serpent also implies a wriggling
motion — not straightness, which is the foremost point
regarding leys. However, the wave motion which for a snake
is horizontal could be perpendicular for ley power.

Yet the serpent is also a symbol of many things connected
with leys and their suspected properties:
(a) The life force.
(b) Sperm.
(c) Wave form of energy.
(d) Creative energy.
(e) Regeneration.
(f) Immortality, eternity and time.
(g) The Great Creator.
(h) Galactic civilization.

Dragon legends are not only common to Britain, but can
be found in the mythology of every race. In a book such as
this, which attempts to concentrate upon Albion, it would,
however, be unforgivable not to pay even token attention to
the dragons of the Far East. There seems to be some common
origin to the dragon legend and one suggestion is that 'the
dragon reflects a time of which we have no record, a time
when the white race was engaged in a terrific struggle for
survival against the black race, who until then had been
masters of the world and whose emblem was the dragon'.[5]
This is one theory, but not perhaps a strong one. The author

from whose book this is taken goes on to note that the same attributes distinguish the dragon almost everywhere as essentially evil and breathing fire (perhaps a misconception arose between physical and spiritual fire). Yet the supernatural power of the Chinese and Japanese dragon differs from his Western counterpart for it was assumed to be directed towards good rather than evil. The fact that the Chinese dragon was regarded as a life-giver may correspond to the fact that but for a few rare lapses the Chinese have always been a peaceful people.

R. de Rohan Barondes regarded dragons as symbols of the cosmic forces contrasting good and evil, light and dark, peace and war, 'their manifold types simply stood for different forces of nature, and human behaviour. They may be of either sex: the male dragon being represented with phallic horns, while the female has a triangular protrusion similar to ears, and representing the pubic region.'[5]

In China, before the Communist regime came to power, the people believed that dragons inhabited every hill and mountain, and whenever a new house was to be built a Feng-shui geomancer was consulted to determine if the location was within range of friendly dragon spirits. Geomancers were also concerned with even the placing of trees, posts, or stones, and before the practice died out the siting of tombs was of primary importance.

Discussing Chinese geomancers, John Michell wrote:

> It was recognized that certain powerful currents, lines of magnetism, run invisible over the surface of the earth. The task of the geomancer was to detect these currents and interpret their influence on the land over which they passed. The magnetic force, known in China as the dragon current, is of two kinds, yin and yang, negative and positive, represented by the white tiger and the blue dragon.[40]

The geomancers understood the heavens' effect upon the landscape and made sure that this was retained or enhanced.

John Michell stated: 'The fleeting vision which Watkins experienced on the Bredwardine hills could be achieved at will by men who understood the secrets of terrestrial geometry.'[40]

Michell also believes that, as in China, there was a period in

Albion's history when every feature in the landscape was moulded to reflect a geometrically magic system. This is hardly beyond doubt.

Barondes, in his book on China, draws a distinction between the snake or serpent and the dragon, believing that the former preceded the latter. Probably there is no necessity to make a division, and his interpretation of the serpent's role in Genesis can be more profitably dealt with under a consideration of the Fall of Man, in a later section.

In a happier vein, the serpent, whether or not it wrongfully gained its immortality – symbolized by its annual shedding of skin – from its cunning behaviour in the Garden of Eden, this quality of self-rejuvenation has given the serpent its universal reputation as a healer. It became a prototype of the medical profession, whose symbol is the winged staff around which twine serpents – the caduceus.

The caduceus was carried by Mercury, and also symbolizes the adept who has power over the kundalini, a primordial power situated at the base of the spine, which in an unawakened state is represented by a serpent coiled dormant around a tree's base. It can be made to rise to man's seven spiritual centres (corresponding to seven vibratory states). It should also be stated that the dragon is often depicted as having seven heads. As for kundalini, one novel theory is that the operators of certain UFOs channel it for the craft's propulsion. Also there is the theory that the caduceus might be the instrument tapped upon stones to make them levitate.

Regarding another aspect of the serpent, there may be a link between a heretical early-Christian sect and leys. Gnosticism and Rosicrucianism seem to be the most interesting such groups concerned with this study, but there may be valuable information to be gleaned from research into the Ophitae or Ophiani, professed serpent worshippers.

Barondes also notes that the dragon admires precious stones and detests iron. Are the gems in reality the quartz of the ley stones, and the iron a remembrance of how metallurgy was a death knell to comprehension of leys?

From China we cross Asia ands Europe to Brittany, to Carnac, with its 10,000 stones – 300 of which are more than

15 feet high — winding for about eight miles like a serpent. Carnac means Cairn-Hac: *cairn* = mound or heap of stones; *hac* = serpent; i.e. Serpent's Hill. Then across the English Channel to Avebury, where the head of a giant serpent avenue of megaliths, detailed by William Stukeley, ended on Overton Hill, the southern promontory of the Hakpen Hills. On westwards to the chalk hill figure, the Uffington Dragon, the half dragon/half horse near Dragon Hill. Westwards again to Stanton Drew stone circles in Somerset, the megaliths of which according to legend were once serpents which were turned into stone. And crossing the country are John Michell's dragon lines, linking sites ascribed to encounters with serpents, dragons and huge worms, such as Serpent's Lane, Mordiford, near Hereford, a sunken road down which reputedly came the Green Dragon to drink at the junction of the Lugg and the Wye.

A great many dragon legends have been collected by John Michell and these can be found in his published work.[39,40,96] In his first book, Michell concludes that ophilatry, the worship of the sacred serpent, was an expression of the flying saucer cult, and that early man's erection of serpentine figures was an attempt to propitiate extra-terrestrial gods and their vehicles, acting as a 'cargo cult' to attract them to the Earth. By the time of writing his second book, Michell had come to regard dragonlore as illustrating the life-giving aspect of leys, though in his book he returned to the link between UFOs, dragons and leys, though making different interpretations, and his conclusions were more sound. For instance he stated: 'The places associated with the dragon legend, the nerve centres of seasonal fertility, appear always to coincide with sites of ancient sanctity.' Also, 'images such as that of the dragon have a precise though indefinable meaning. Symbols are only used when there is no literal expression of sufficient scope to comprehend the attributes and correspondences none of which can be analyzed in isolation'.[40]

Because John Michell has detailed many of the dragon legends, I shall limit myself to describing only one, that of the Sockburn Worm.

Sockburn is a small parish in County Durham within a curiously shaped piece of land around which the Tees twists its serpentine course, a loop of which creates what is commonly referred to as the Sockburn Peninsula.

William Wordsworth, staying for the summer of 1799 at Sockburn Farm, called it a 'pleasant green isle'. Wordsworth courted his future wife Mary in this enchanting spot and was joined by Samuel Taylor Coleridge, who had a passionate tryst with Mary's plump little sister Sara. Such a romantic setting would seem to be hardly likely to be the venue for a greater tale. For here generations of the Conyers family were lords of the manor and intimately connected with a legend and its ramifications.

The legend refers to a fiery, flying serpent, sometimes called a dragon, sometimes a wyvern, but most commonly the Sockburn Worm. Shortly before William the Conqueror landed to claim Albion's throne, this beast is reputed to have terrorized the neighbourhood. A document in the British Museum describes the monster thus:

> Sir John Conyers, Kt., slew that monstrous and poisonous vermin, wyvern, ask, or werme, wh. had overthrown and devoured many people in fight; for that the scent of the poison was so strong that no person might abyde it. And by the providence of the Almighty God, the said John Conyers, Kt., overthrew the sd. monster and slew it. But before he made this enterprise, having but one sonne, he went to the church of Sockburne in compleat armour and offered up his only son to the Holy Ghost. That place where this great serpent lay was called Graystone, and this John lyeth buried in Sockburn Church in compleat armour of the time before the Conquest.

This 'Graystone' still exists and can be seen in the field surrounding the present hall (the first hall was demolished and another took its place in 1833). The church remains in a ruined condition.

Leslie Marr, of Norfolk, wrote to me about the legend and recalled staying at Sockburn Hall before the last war, when his aunt lived there. He wrote:

> I remember the stone effigy and the knight in the old chapel, with pieces and 'worm' around his feet. Also the mounds and depression in the field to the south-east, which I was told was a Roman village. My aunt refused permission to various people who wanted to dig, as

she firmly believed that the 'little men' would come and get anyone who did so. She told me that two young men had dug somewhere else, in spite of having been warned by the little men, and had suffered the usual fate – death before the year was out. In fact pieces of carved stone *were* dug up (I remember seeing them in the chapel), when a ditch was dug to enclose the garden.

In a field there is a big stone under which the worm is supposed to be buried; a farmer tried to move it with dynamite, but only succeeded in cracking it.

A recent interpretation of the Sockburn legend puts forward a less romantic or mystical view of the worm than its being anything to do with UFOs or psychic energy, or simply fanciful fiction. Danish pirates raided the north-east coast, and would sail up the rivers such as the Tees in boats with high prows fashioned in the form of a serpent, and this insignia would be emblazoned upon the sails. Certainly the number of nearby villages with the Danish suffix 'by' would seem to indicate the presence of Danes in the district.

Perhaps we have here a legend being a jumbled and embellished recollection of Danish raids; but this fails to explain the Graystone.

Conyers slew the dragon – or Danes – with a curved sword, and this falchion is kept in Durham Cathedral. The falchion was presented to each newly-elected Bishop of Durham by the Lord of Sockburn until the early eighteenth century, and the ceremony took place in midstream at Neasham Ford (or on Croft Bridge if the river was too deep). The falchion was taken by the Bishop and immediately returned as a token of the family's fitness to guard the strategic peninsula.

No Conyers now acts as guardian at Sockburn, for the tale has a sad ending. The last of the Conyers, Sir Thomas, was a pauper in the workhouse in Chester-le-Street in 1810, aged 72, ill and friendless after his nephew, Sir George Conyers, had squandered his fortune and died leaving no issue. Sir Thomas had inherited the title, but no property. Robert Surtees, the Durham historian, heard of his plight and sought financial assistance for him through *The Gentleman's Magazine*. The plea was a success and the old man was taken to a private house. Two weeks later he was dead.

But the legend lives on, the Graystone still stands, and maybe those who choose to tamper with the power at Sockburn learn their mistake too late when they lie in the shadow of a gravestone.

19. Giants

'Megalithic, not celtic England, engendered the giants.' — H.J. Massingham.[36]

When H.J. Massingham wrote in a chapter on giants about 'a kingdom made with thoughts not hands', he may have been intuitively reflecting one of the greatest spiritual truths of all time, or he may have been being simply poetic.[36] His writings have solid archaeological bases, but he was, like Alfred Watkins, a brave and somewhat unorthodox thinker and researcher. In this essay, the lead given by Massingham and John Foster Forbes will be followed, and hopefully a comprehensive and thought-provoking account of the giants' place in ley study will emerge. As with dragonlore, in which we found both good and bad intermingled, we will here find a duality on the level right and wrong, and also as with the exoteric and esoteric idea of dragons as beasts or as manifestations of the ley current, we will consider giants as being of great physical stature and as entities of great stature either mentally or spiritually.

Firstly we will take Massingham's views on giantlore and then compare these with Forbes's, who was a similarly enlightened antiquary.

Massingham believed that the origin of giantlore lay in the Neolithic: 'What first arouses us is the suspicion that the giants were not invented by the Celts but were a distorted legacy bequeathed to them by the archaic civilization of the megaliths they supplanted.' He concluded that Geoffrey of Monmouth's tale of the giant Gogmagog referred to a definite historical event — the destruction of Bronze Age tribes by Celtic invaders.

Boulder-throwing contests are a feature of giantlore, and examples of such legends can be found throughout the country. Massingham made the point that such was not 'indiscriminate Aunt Sallyism', but that two giants were normally involved, each on a prominent hill (terminal ley points?) and the stones that they threw fell between these (as mark stones?), which were given such names as devil's quoits or giant's arrows.

A selection of legends from giantlore reported in *The Ley Hunter* by Janet Bord (*née* Gregory) will give the reader a taste of the typical forms in which these have reached us in the twentieth century A.D. She wrote:

St Michael's Mount in Cornwall was partly constructed by the giant Cormoran and his wife Cormelian out of gigantic blocks of granite, which Cormelian carried in her apron and deposited on the summit. One stone fell on the sand when Cormelian's apron-string broke, and is now her monument. A giant at Treryn near Land's End built a cliff fortress by using his magical powers and compelling it to rise from the sea. Another giant, Gorm, was one day wandering around with a shovelful of earth, wondering what to do with it. When he came to the edge of the Cotswolds, he stumbled and dropped the soil into the Avon Valley, thus forming Maes Knoll. At the same time, he constructed Wansdyke by digging his shovel deep into the Earth. The Wrekin, a hill 1,300 feet above sea level close to Shrewsbury, was said to have been formed unintentionally by a Welsh giant. He had quarrelled with the mayor of the town and was carrying a spade of earth with which to dam the River Severn and thereby flood Shrewsbury. But he didn't know his way and asked a passer-by, a cobbler who saw that mischief was afoot. The quick-thinking fellow quickly showed the giant the bag of tattered shoes he had to mend, and said that he had worn them all out since he left Shrewsbury, it was such a long way away. Upon which the giant, who was already tired by his journey, threw down the soil he was carrying. This became The Wrekin, and Wenlock Edge was formed where the giant wiped his boots.

The sea-giant, Wade, is connected with some big stones near Pickering in Yorkshire, called Wade's Causeway. He was building a highway for his wife to use on her daily journey across the moors to milk her cow, and she was carrying the stones in her apron. But the apron-string broke, and the stones fell in a heap. Note the similarity to the legend concerning St Michael's Mount. Another causeway, the Giant's Causeway, is formed of great boulders said to have been put there by the giants of Ireland and Scotland to make their visits across the sea to each other easier.

Two Scottish giants were shoemakers, and having only one set of tools between them, they used to throw them across the Dornoch Firth to each other. The 'Soutars of Cromarty', two large promontories, were their tools. Two giants in Shetland, Herman and Saxe, threw rocks at each other whenever they quarrelled. And in Lancashire, two giants on opposite banks of the River Rother were at loggerheads, and sometimes threw stones at each other.

Giants using rocks in various games is a recurring theme. The giants living on Trencrom Hill (an Iron Age fort) in South-West Cornwall were very fond of a game of bowls, for which purpose they used enormous rocks. One of these now stands isolated in a cottage garden at the foot of the hill, together with a National Trust notice naming it 'The Bowl Rock', and giving brief details of the legend. Tarquin, a giant from the Manchester area, was in the habit of playing quoits with a stone which was really the pedestal of an ancient cross. And in a game of quoits between the Welsh giants, the giant of Trichrug in Cardiganshire was supposed to have thrown one of the quoits across the sea to Ireland.

She concluded that such a superior race was 'perhaps not so much a race of gigantic stature, but of giant mental abilities, that is when compared with the ordinary people of the time'.

In North Yorkshire, conical Freeborough Hill is attributed to the work of a giant, and in the same district there is a legend with the twist that the 'combatants' were the Devil and a witch. Frank and Harriet Wragg Elgee wrote:

A witch story related by a native 25 years ago attempts to explain two conspicuous natural features two ·miles apart, on Pickering Moor; Blakey Topping, an isolated hill, and the Hole of Horcum, a deep basin-shaped valley. The local witch had sold her soul to the devil on the usual terms, but when he claimed it, she refused to give it up, and flew over the moors, with the devil in hot pursuit. Overtake her he could not, so he grabbed up a handful of earth and flung it at her. He missed his aim, and she escaped. The Hole of Horcum remains to prove where he tore up the earth and Blakey Topping where it fell to the ground.[12]

There is a Bronze Age settlement at Blakey Farm and between it and, the Hole of Horcum is a stone circle. The rough trackway leading from the Hole of Horcum to the circle is known as Old Wife's Way.

H.J. Massingham, a convinced diffusionist theorist, believed that giants made 'no sense other than the supernatural impersonations of the old mining kings of the archaic civilization, bequeathed to the warrior Celts in a demonic guise'.[36]

But the best work on giantlore was written by John Foster Forbes, and included psychometric readings from various prehistoric sites.[15] It is my contention that giantlore is one of the major keys to the ley mystery, and it is worth giving a fair degree of space here to Forbes's beliefs on this subject. If I am correct in my interpretation of the mystical phraseology in which he describes the evolution of mankind, there was first a race of people who were visited by another race who had attained god-like qualities and whose 'home indeed was among the stars of the universe'. In religious terms he described them as 'emissaries from God empowered to impart the divine wisdom'. They dwelt with or adjacent to the race they found on Earth for a long time until the Fall, which came about as the 'result of the machinations of "fallen Angels" from other Realms'.

Ufologists may choose to refine his arguments into the theory of visits by good and bad extra-terrestrials, but John Foster Forbes was an unashamed believer in the spread of civilization from Atlantis — a physical Atlantic continent of Atlantis — and he developed his theory as far as to propose that the Irish race, the Firbolgs, were probably of an exaggerated form, and the Formorians, another prehistoric Irish race, are described as 'begotten dwarfs . . . men with Goat's Heads'. He believed that such people had the power of 'shape shifting', even to taking on animal forms, among a vast collection of magical practices which changed from white to black as time went by. As for giants, he asserted that there is evidence to show that giants of enormous physical stature once existed, and that terrific contests took place between them.

A more modern theory is that the giants are the devas of occultism, the huge spiritual beings associated with mountains. There is a belief that devas contacted earlier civilizations and have retained an interest in humans. They aid humans' evolution, and they subtly influence by advice and inspiration certain humans who are responsive.[24]

20. Leys and the Physical Plane

There is now much evidence to support the contention that leys mark routes taken by energy currents, but upon the nature of this force there is not so much disagreement as almost total bafflement on the part of researchers. Personal experience, the findings of others and reading has convinced me of the reality of a ley power, but I feel that it would be foolish to be dogmatic about its nature.

Researchers have talked in vague terms of an electromagnetic force in the leys, but certain aspects of ley hunting have cast grave doubts upon so simple an explanation. Leys link sacred centres and no one is likely to propose that religions are based upon electromagnetism. Therefore it is clear that we must look beyond the physical field concept of ley power for the answer. Of course, it must be remembered that leys are basically connected with the identity and purpose of man and the human force field does have an electromagnetic nature.

From the mark stone at Hart, County Durham, I and several others have felt a tingling sensation of varying intensity. My wife received an unpleasant shock when touching it one evening. Such energy is felt by one of the basic five senses, but other effects have been brought about by other such stones, whose impact has been more subtle and felt on the psychic or spiritual plane.

Electromagnetism

'Electromagnetism seems to be one of those ubiquitous underlying abstractions that can be

defined only in terms of its behaviour.' — *Guy Murchie.*[41]

All energies are of an electromagnetic nature; all solid matter in our environment is composed of energy; our eyes perceive only a tiny proportion of the electromagnetic spectrum; and electromagnetic waves of many different frequencies exist on our planet and throughout space.

The speculation that electromagnetism is the basis of ley energy does not make it any easier for us to neatly package the current into scientifically acceptable theories or make it easily understandable.

John A. Keel has stated the belief that the UFO phenomenon — closely allied to leys — is primarily electromagnetic in origin and that the phenomenon is usually invisible because it consists basically of energy, as opposed to earthly matters. He contends that a great intelligence guides it and has concentrated itself into areas of magnetic faults throughout history. Alien forms such as UFOs and a wide range of entities are its forms, created by different patterns of frequency. UFO data, he believes, confirms this hypothesis, and conclusive proof is lacking only because we lack the necessary technology to prove it.[25]

Electrons and energy particles form atoms; atoms and molecules form larger structures, not touching. Occultists and scientists know this, and that it means reality is illusion.

The manipulation of energy by chemical and physical processes has been the work of man for centuries, whether it be prehistory's Beltane blazes, the alchemists' alembics, or technologists' Hiroshimatic disintegration of humans.

Man's approach to energy has depended upon his idea of what reality constitutes. We touch something, see it, smell it, hear it; we know it exists. We also know that many equally real things, such as radio waves, exist but are invisible, for in this instance it is the radio which allows us to know so. But what of other forms of energy beyond our five senses and technology? Are they real or an illusion? What of energies of a different frequency coexisting in time and space with us? Keel's researches point to this coexistence, and he calls for us to come to terms with ' "it" or "them" or the Great Whatzit in the sky'.

This book is about the 'Great Whatzit', its manifestations and in particular how we may come to understand it today, particularly through early man's similar comprehension of reality as illusion; and his efforts to come to terms with the hidden powers of his environment, which seemingly sent thunder and lightning to scare him, snow to freeze his flesh, but sunshine to warm him and encourage growth. Orthodox archaeology claims `prehistoric peoples were ignorant and superstitious, but the evidence accumulated in this volume clearly points to their comprehension not only of meteorological phenomena, but astronomical, astrological, spiritual and paraphysical forces and energies which played a part in their lives.

Contemporary singer/poet James Taylor told a *Rolling Stone* interviewer: 'I think fear, or pain or some kind of discomfort is the major motivation for almost all endeavour.' Fear, another word for ignorance, led early man to analyse his environment and take steps to learn everything pertaining to his existence, and find ways of making it more comfortable and exercise as great a degree of control over it as possible. The vibrations of leys and rays from outer space were put to use and became the marked system across the land, and a calendar for mapping out times for agricultural labours and a multitude of other pursuits of a more recreative character. The other planes of existence were explored through consciousness expansion and named Ultima Thule, Atlantis, Avalon, Hyperborea, the Underworld, Valhalla.

Accepting that ley power exists and has an electromagnetic basis, we must consider polarity, flow, and its manipulation. For it to flow there must be a negative pole and a positive pole. Andrew Davidson and others have dowsed the power, and Davidson has stated that most standing stones and the Stonehenge uprights have seven power centres each.[88] This power, if tapped correctly, can cause a person to be thrown from the stone. John G. Williams has described the power as a spiral-like force building up through the body and propelling the investigator away from the stone. Davidson has found that each stone is predominantly positive or negative, and oppositely charged to its neighbour, and that polarity changes with regard to the Moon. Davidson discovered that when dowsing by pendulum at the time of a polarity change, the pendulum slowly stops, then gains momentum in the opposite direction. The whole process takes seven minutes.

As for leys themselves, it will be postulated that they form a matrix of the Earth and were formed as our planet cooled. However, the transmission of ley power presents difficulties in definition. Did it flow naturally, did it depend upon cosmic influences drawing it from the ground and leading it from site to site, or did man intervene to increase the flow, regulate it and perhaps extend or realign it? That planetary influences play a part is quite probable and also that this was a motivating factor in early man's great interest in heavenly bodies.

I would postulate that prehistoric man not only marked the energy patterns – leys – but manipulated the power beyond concentrating and storing it. Electricity can be either direct current or alternating current. With direct current transmission a point is reached where the flow 'collapses' and returns to source. Nikola Tesla discovered that if 'boosters' were provided at 'collapse' points in a circuit then the current would continue. It may therefore be that the stones and other prehistoric monuments acted as 'boosters' in some way.

The Earth has a magnetic field and through investigation of the palaeomagnetic properties of rocks it has been shown that in 500 A.D. this field was 50 per cent stronger than it is today. The rate of decrease is supposedly getting quicker. Consequently it may be that the Earth's magnetic field was very much greater at the time of the megalith building, and that leys were greatly more active in those days. My experience is that today ley power intensity is far from uniform, either in time or place, and, of course, on a different level, only some can sense its presence at all.

St Elmo's Fire

'Safe comes the ship to haven,
Through billows and through gales,

If once the great Twin Brethren
Sit shining on the sails.' — Macaulay *('Lays of*
Ancient Rome').

St Elmo's Fire may well be a false lead. Masts of ships
particularly, but also mountain peaks, under favourable
conditions when exposed to intense fields of a thundercloud,
will provide a glow discharge which can be very conspicuous.
This is St Elmo's Fire. Any conductor, not necessarily of a
pointed nature or of a great height, can act as a discharger.

It is difficult to accept that menhirs and trees of the ley
system were laid to create point discharges, but by their very
nature they can do so. But other factors must be considered,
for St Elmo's Fire is associated with Castor and Pollux, the
patron deities of seamen and voyagers, and also of the
electricity which played around the sails and masts of ships.
John Michell associated Castor and Pollux with Saint George
and Saint Michael, two aspects of the same principle, and he
related them to the same archetype. Michell called St Elmo's
Fire 'a current of etherical electricity over which the Greeks
seem to have retained some control even into historical
times'.[40]

Gravity

'Gravitic anomalies are very much disliked in
academic circles because there is no valid explan-
·ation for them.' — Egerton Sykes.[109]

Any electromagnetic field has a coexistent gravitational field.
This leads one to consider whether the special nature of the
leys' electromagnetism is reflected in a special gravitational
nature. Michael Faraday discovered that the magnetic properties of the atmosphere are altered by the Sun's passage,
and he deduced that heated oxygen in air compensates for
the difference in the magnetic power of the atmosphere by
creating currents or winds, having their origin in magnetic
balance, and restoring balance.

So we should consider how the Sun, in addition to altering

the atmosphere's magnetic properties, alters the nature of stones and ley current, and also gravity affecting such. The megalith builders' great interest in eclipses may be connected with this.

Science states that gravity cannot be refracted, nor can such waves be led along conductors like electrical waves. But if electromagnetism, which is transmitted along leys, has a coexistent gravity field then it must be possible. Can gravity also be focused, knowing that there are in the world a number of gravity distortion areas?

These areas of gravitic anomaly are baffling, and though space scientists would dearly love to create the anti-gravity field so beloved of science fiction writers, there has as yet been no scientific explanation. North America has seven examples, France has one, Italy one and Britain four. These may not, of course, be the total, but Britain's known examples are near Ranmore Common, Surrey, on a road coming from Dorking; one near Long Mynd, Shropshire, where a stream runs uphill; The Electric Brae, Ayrshire, on the A719 road; and a stream by the B797 road in Ayrshire also runs uphill. Egerton Sykes has suggested that 'the basic cause may well lie in a nearby meteorite of sufficient size to cause this effect'.[109] Philip Heselton, who knows the Ranmore Common road, suggests that the effect may be merely an optical illusion, as he has noticed identical effects elsewhere when climbing hills, but he is unable to ascertain how this is caused. Egerton Sykes notes that polarized glasses will partially remove the distortion. Nausea is also caused by the sudden change in gravitic fields at an angle of 15 to 25 degrees. Philip Heselton notes that Ranmore Common church is a major ley centre and that there are several alignments in the vicinity of Long Mynd.

Before discussing the manipulation of stones by levitation, a few words on personal levitation. Around 200 saints have had the ability to levitate; witches too. If one's vibratory rate is altered to allow levitation, are leys a particularly good medium for this? Arthur Shuttlewood reported that three women separately spoke of a floating sensation when crossing a footpath across a cornfield near Battlesbury, Warminster.[46] Were they on a ley?

But what of levitation of materials? Man has reached the Moon by using brute force in a heavy vehicle burning huge amounts of fuel. It is pertinent to ask whether a similar process of brute force was utilized to build Stonehenge; vast numbers of men hauling stones weighing many tons on wooden rollers over many miles. No, hardly. It must have been by levitation as Merlin is supposed by tradition to have engineered.

There is a compelling and strong tradition of great weights being levitated. Iris Campbell, in her psychometric reading at the Bass of Inverurie, stated that hypnotized sacrificial victims had their entrails removed and from these a 'double magnetism' was drawn which increased their killers' own hypnotic power and enabled them to lift great weights and move or even hurl them at will.[1 5]

The Mahatma Dhut Kuhl stated in *A Treatise on Cosmic Fire*:

> The laws governing the erection of large buildings and the handling of great weights will some day be understood in terms of sound. The cycle returns, and in days to come will be seen the reappearance of the faculty of the Lemurians and the Atlanteans to raise great masses . . . Mental comprehension of the method will be developed. They were raised through the ability of the early builders to create a vacuum through sound.

Early Irish races such as the Firbolgs and Tuatha de Danaan are connected with legends of flight, as too are prehistoric races the world over. Brinsley le Poer Trench goes so far as to write of the Atlanteans that they 'undoubtedly . . . had space ships and were in communication with other planets'.[5 3]

I think it quite feasible that Stonehenge was built with the aid of levitation, but am sceptical of other forms of prehistoric flight, with the exception of astral travel.

Nikola Tesla

> 'Nikola Tesla literally gave the world light.' —
> Brinsley le Poer Trench.[5 3]

Nikola Tesla is one of the world's great unknowns. He was

born in 1856 in what is now Yugoslavia. As a boy he sought ways to harness natural energy, was a quick-witted scholar, learned eight languages fluently and worked so hard that he suffered some ill health. He dedicated himself to electrical engineering and never married. He invented many things, but his discovery of alternating current is our chief concern. Brinsley le Poer Trench, who has championed the importance of Tesla's contribution to mankind, has described his work as being 'on a colossal and cosmic scale'. I would agree. Tesla asserted that power could be drawn from the earth anywhere. However, this was never developed commercially, as were few of his magnificent inventions, and he died, aged 87, in 1943, and though a United States citizen for many years his records were sealed by the Custodian of Alien Property, and only government officials may inspect his papers. Though nothing so savage is involved, there are echoes here of the Wilhelm Reich witchhunt.

In simple terms electricity, or electromagnetic energy, generated by the Earth is what we call direct current because it flows in one direction only. We also know that a magnetic field builds up with the current. The current and field move together, but when a peak is reached the magnetic field 'collapses'. Tesla harnessed direct current by discovering how to keep the magnetic field from 'collapsing' at its peak. At the right moment the field must be given a boost. The way that this is done is to create various circuits and stagger their output, one behind the other, so that there is always a booster on schedule. This is alternating current, allowing uninterrupted flow.

As we seek to understand why prehistoric man placed stones upon leys, it is worth considering whether these in fact were instruments to boost the current. We know that they concentrate and store the power. Also it may be significant in this context that certain stones are placed at varying angles. The needles used in acupuncture are also placed at angles to produce the desired effect. In addition, early man esteemed jet and amber more precious than gold because of their electrical properties.

Tesla's work may not be purely scientific on a materialistic, capitalist level, for the New Age sect, Ruby Focus of Magnificent Consummation, based in Arizona, holds him in high regard.

The Ruby Focus is a 'new religion of the electromagnetic energy of the Great Central Sun'. Much New Age literature is almost impossible for any but the initiate to comprehend, but it can be stated that this group forms some type of battery for the changing of consciousness, and that 'this Earth is being transformed and will be catapulted into the fourth dimension as a mutation'.

The electromagnetism in leys is not felt by some people and has differing degrees of effect upon others, as I have found by demonstrations at a stone in Hart, County Durham. This suggests that there may be no true physical reality, but only a paraphysical, psychical or spiritual effect. The reader may decide this point for himself. That the basis is largely, or wholly, extra-dimensional is apparent to me, so let us look further into the wealth of spiritual interest in leys.

It may be, in fact, rather as Sir James Jeans wrote in *Physics and Philosophy* that:

> The physical theory of relativity has now shown that electrical and magnetic forces are not real at all; they are mere mental constructions of our own, resulting from our rather misguided efforts to understand the motions of the particles. It is the same with the Newtonian force of gravitation and with energy, momentum and other concepts which were introduced to help us understand the activities of the World.

21. Leys and Spirituality

'The great tragedy of megalithic civilisation occurred when men lost touch with the spirit.' – John Michell.[94]

When Dion Fortune commented, 'I don't think that it will be disputed that certain places exert a powerful influence on human beings,'[16] she was referring to sacred centres. She pointed out that every country has them, and, of course, leys join them and are sacred in themselves and also exert a powerful influence; the influence being upon man's spirit, soul, consciousness.

In our journey through the times from prehistory along the leys we will pass over spots where earlier worshippers have held their rites, where they gave to their god either their love or bloody sacrifices, where they begged for fertility or demanded it, where they met communally or clandestinely. Druids were here, witches too, Christians took over many sites, and now New Age groups such as the Aetherius Society have come. Other groups can be associated indirectly with leys, such as the Gnostics, or fairly directly, as with gypsies. The attitude of each to the pagan rites will be observed in the following pages, and assessments made of their relative interest in the sacred centres and their aims and reasons for choosing such sites.

As for the men who marked the system, it is now almost impossible to determine their spiritual relationship with the sites. It has been postulated that the stones and other antiquities on leys were used to control the energy in the ley. This would presuppose a technological people with scientific minds; but a scientific mind does not necessarily alienate spiritual belief within a person. It is compatible that science and spirituality can be the two sides of the coin that is man's being. Therefore if a man can be both scientific and spiritual there is no reason for leys not to be both at the same time and to be integrated as such.

Today we suppose that a clergyman will have little in common with a scientist, yet numerous clergymen could be quoted as furthering science, and there are scientists who have strengthened the precepts of religion. A technological society such as that which we associate with the megalith builder need not necessarily distinguish between what we regard as physical and spiritual manifestations. We all believe that invisible electricity exists, but can be largely sceptical of psychic phenomena. If we were not exposed in our schools to so much lesson time in physics, chemistry, biology, geography, history, mathematics and languages, and in most cases less than an hour a week on religion (rarely comparative religion, mostly Biblical history), then we would have a more balanced view of spiritual realities. It is suggested here that Megalithic Man and his children had a balanced teaching which gave them a full comprehension of the facts of living, which not only gave them a degree of control over their environment, but taught them how to become masters of their own personalities and spiritual welfare.

The history of ley hunting presented earlier in this book took the course of viewing its development on the level of periods of activity and advance, and fallow periods and those of stagnation. It could also have been categorized in three separate sections: a beginning in which trackways were the primary study and inspiration; a period in which theories of power currents and a UFO link fired investigators' imaginations; and latterly the view that there is a spiritual side to leys.

A supporter of the esoteric side to leys is the son of the late Alfred Watkins, Allen Watkins. In a covering letter sent to me with an article linking leys and ancient wisdom he wrote:

> Actually this particular link-up has been lying fallow in my mind for forty years. At that time I was interested in (theoretical) occultism and was reading all I could find on the subject.
> Indeed I spoke to my father on the connections I could see, and he was greatly interested and sympathetic as he always was, but he,

quite rightly, was first anxious to get on the record the solid physical
evidence for leys that could be pointed to on the existing landscape.

From the very start I have believed that leys have an esoteric
origin and meaning derived from some old culture . . . but have kept
quiet until now because I did not want to prejudice father's great
discovery by linking it with highly controversial matter.

I have stated my conviction in *The Ley Hunter* that the physical
fact of leys is beyond controversy, but when you get to esoteric
origins, very few folk are on that wave-length, and orthodox
scientists restrict all discussion to the earth-plane and so make it
difficult for their faithful followers to see any intelligent meaning in
anything.

These words may be suitably regarded as a statement
which could be validly applied to the leys mystery, for we
can assume that prehistoric man gained control of these
terrestrial currents through manipulation of solar power,
thereby producing a perfect environment. By doing so, our
ancestors utilized nature by scientific means, the construction of perfect monuments acting as instruments.

But man's nature is not wholly temporal; he has a spiritual
side. It would therefore be odd if his powers had not been
applied to furthering this facet of his nature, and this section
will deal with how leys themselves have a dual significance as
carrying energy which is both temporal and spiritual, either
as one power with two aspects, or two powers carried jointly.

In considering the various properties to be categorized, the
following words may help the reader to appreciate the
complexity of the problem and the multifarious nature of the
physical side of the power (as opposed to its spiritual nature).
Guy Murchie wrote: 'Nuclear physicists have long since
concluded that the nuclear binding force must be as distinct
from electromagnetic force as electromagnetic force is
distinct from gravitation. Although all three are undoubtedly
related and perhaps are just three aspects of the same
influence, each has its own properties.'[41] Here we meet the
notion that distinct properties can exist within a common
framework of influence. Scientists may be sceptical that such
is the case with ley power, and many will undoubtedly
blanch at the addition of mystical concepts. However, the
reader is not being asked to accept this idea if he judges it

fallacious. Perhaps only certain of the following inquiries into leys' properties will be acceptable.

It must be stressed that before the Iron Age Druids we have no record of a priesthood, so it is an open question as to whether one predated it or what its functions would be. It is my belief that any 'priesthood' of the Stone Age would have had the dual responsibility for teaching science and exploring spiritual matters under the single idea of spiritual physics. There would be no religion as such; no worship of a deity, deities or spirits. The Sun's relationship to the ley current, its constitution, its effect on fertility and warming welfare, and its astrological influence would be studied. If man felt any inner relationship with the golden orb it would not be one of superstitious awe and concern, but one of love, simple love, as for one's friends or the countryside.

The ancient Druids, by all accounts, were a scientific brotherhood with real knowledge, but in a debased form. Their secrecy is probably not to be applauded, for secrecy leads to the formation of an elite, and power, and power corrupts. Their behaviour seems not to have been without its bestial side. Human sacrifice can have no saving grace. It is my opinion that the ancient Druids were the inheritors of the ley network, already in decay, and that their comprehension was virtually nil. In fact, I would guess that they understood it much less than we do. Perhaps they were sorcerers and murderers whose spirituality was warped. But we must note that our information about the Druids was written by their enemies, the barbaric Romans, and therefore cannot be trusted implicitly, and could well be entirely false. Professor Stuart Piggott, writing in *Myth and Legend*, regarded human sacrifice as an important part of Druid ritual and claimed: 'This was more than the Romans, usually so tolerant in religious observances, could stand for, and the deliberate policy of stamping out Druidism within the empire is wholly understandable on this count alone.' Piggott was evidently forgetting the atrocities committed in the gladiatorial 'games'.

Alfred Watkins warned of two lines of research which he found 'dangerous to follow if one's chief aim is to convince others of the reality of the sighted track'.[60] One was place names; the other early religion. 'The gain to knowledge may be considerable,' he wrote, 'but most people do not want new knowledge in this, only confirmation of their existing idea or attitude, and are at once prejudiced.' This writer feels that the time is ripe for inquiries into the spiritual aspects of leys, and hopes that he has no prejudices on the subject; opinions, yes, but he has no intention of being dogmatic about these. He is not aiming to convince others of anything, but humbly provide evidence and speculations regarding leys.

So, in an open-minded spirit of adventure, the writer will lead the reader into the realms of a spiritual search for ley connections and truths by way of modern Druidic summer solstice rites, gypsy fairs, Abraxas, the etheric plane, astral travel, hermits, the Qabalah, numerology, elementals, witches' covens, Glastonbury Tor labyrinth and the Grail Quest.

Druidism

> 'By the middle of the Victorian era "reasonable people" came to regard Druidism as a topic to be avoided because of the militant attitude of those who so fiercely discussed its problems. It appeared to provide a platform upon which the retired Anglo-Indian officer, the village rector and the social bore, indeed every description of crank and eccentric, might rant and vapour to his heart's content.' — Lewis Spence.[48]

Ancient Druidism, like leys, is an embarrassment to modern archaeology which, far from adequately probing the problem, simply stresses that the Druids did not build Stonehenge, and leaves the matter there. No attempt is made here to explain or seek to prove anything at all about Druids. It can be left — the subject still being so thoroughly immersed in the melting pot — to the reader to decide for himself whether Druids were a beneficent tribal priesthood learned in ethics, morality, mathematics, natural sciences and philosophy, who provided a university of the arts and sciences, and who were associated with the oak, mistletoe and white bulls; or whether they were debased, frenzied, drug-crazed magicians who burned alive the innocent in huge wickerwork figures.

Any connection between ancient Druidism and the ley system must be tenuous, and it should be remembered that authorities associate them with oak groves rather than stone circles, though the former also have connections with the ley system. However, John Michell asserted a definite connection: 'Two things are certain: the stones were erected for magical purposes, and the Druids were themselves magicians, who as heirs to the occult system of the former race, would scarcely have ignored the ubiquitous instruments of their predecessors.'[40] If only we knew.

Today we have The Order of Bards, Ovates and Druids. No lesser authority than T.C. Lethbridge accepted that present Druid beliefs are perfectly genuine survivals, and this may well be so. So what does today's OBOD believe? Probably most important are the necessity for universal truth and love, and also the need to increase the awareness of seasons and localities, knowledge of which enriches lives. The Order seeks a reinterpretation of ancient monuments, which indicates the importance of their meaning, which in its view is as basic for us today as it was during the Neolithic period. The qualities of the Sun, Moon and stars, to which the monuments were commonly orientated, can be relearnt. An OBOD leaflet states: 'Mounds and stones form patterns that belong both to human and supernal truths.' Ley hunters and Druids today speak the same language. This ancestral interpretative wisdom is available to interested persons at the Order's public meetings, both lectures and ceremonies, whilst within the Order itself are further degrees of instruction. The Order transmits this knowledge to all by symbolic actions and words in public rituals at eight festivals: the solstices, the equinoxes, and the four Fire festivals, Candlemas, Beltane, Lammas, and All Hallows.

Witches and Gypsies

*'But what is witchcraft other than fallen and
debased occult methods of what were once great
spiritual accomplishments.' — John Foster
Forbes.*[14]

Two of the most maligned groups of people in Britain are
witches and gypsies. There are black witches and white
witches; there are good and bad gypsies. Both are guardians
of ancient wisdom and both play separate roles in our
society. Both have associations with leys and their energy.

Stone circles have always been associated with witches,
who do not bow down to idols, but instead worship living
forces by holding magical rites. Their work at prehistoric
sacred sites relates them to the power held by such places,
which they undoubtedly utilize for either good or evil
purposes. Four years ago rows of dead crows were found
upon the recumbent stone at Sun Honey stone circle,
Aberdeenshire, a most unpleasant place, and they had
indisputably been used in the working of black magic.

A gypsy told me that his people know the leys and use
them when travelling as they often afford some protection
from harassment. In Aberdeenshire I saw a lay-by where
mounds of earth had been dumped specifically to stop
gypsies using it as a traditional camping site. When I checked
my map I was not surprised to find that it was on a ley.

Gypsies are a knowledgeable and wise people who tend to
keep their secrets within their own people, but the reader
may be assured that their cultural level allows for more
sophisticated practices than roasting hedgehogs.

Christianity

*'I have had a lousy Xmas because I believe in Santa
Claus and someone's gone and crucified him.' —
Roger McGough.*

The Christians, as has been shown, utilized former pagan sites in Britain, and transformed pagan deities into saints. Not only that, but we find that the two fundamental dates in the Christian calendar, of the birth and rebirth of Christ, Christmas and the Easter resurrection, are marked by the time of the winter solstice and spring equinox. These Sun periods, when the days begin to lengthen, and when the days begin to be longer than the night, are significant and reveal how important the Sun's influence is in religion. Churchyards took the form of a circle with the church shaped like a cross at its centre – the circle and the cross.

With Christianity, men began to forget the old beliefs and misunderstood the meaning of the Sun's wedding to the Earth, the Male God joining with the Earth Mother, the fusion of solar rays with the terrestrial current. Yet the placing of churches upon leys not only at the introduction of Christianity into Britain, but continuing to the Reformation and in isolated cases even today, is evidence that some people knew the importance of positioning religious buildings on the sacred lines, and designing these places of worship to reveal to the initiate the nature and flow of power at such spots. Certain heretical sects retained great wisdom, such as the Gnostics, which are worthy of extended comment, and also we find the Holy Grail having great meaning beyond orthodox Christian traditional belief.

The Holy Grail

'Whom does the Grail serve?'

The Holy Grail presents one with a complex riddle and the decision as to what it stands for is only a start, for only then can the real quest begin. This vessel has an important place in The Matter of Britain and has been the scope of mystics rather than Christians. It is a key element in the Arthurian cycle, rather than the Christian creed.

It has appeared in various guises, and this in itself makes the task of understanding its import incredibly difficult. Suggestions as to its nature include:

1. It was a sacred vessel in pagan Celtic myth, the

Cauldron of Ceridwen or Dagda. Arthur and a knight went on a quest over water to seek it in Annwn, a Celtic otherworld.

2. It was the chalice of the Last Supper brought to Glastonbury by Joseph of Arimathea or his companions, containing drops of Christ's blood.

3. It is now in a castle surrounded by a wasteland, kept by the wounded immobile Fisher King. If the knight seeking it asked the correct question then the king would be healed and the wasteland be revived.

4. Wolfram von Eschenbach's *Parzival* describes it as an oracular stone.

5. It is a lance.

6. It is a sword.

7. It is a dish.

8. It is a scrying crystal.

9. It is a UFO.

10. It is the alchemist's crucible.

It can also be suggested that the romances on the theme are confused notions of an initiation rite, or psychological journey by meditation or drugs. The Grail legend, it seems, was Celtic in its inspiration with pagan elements Christianized, yet it must refer to the loss of the bountiful Neolithic society, and the Church has always been wary of the legend, and it has been associated with such heretical sects as the Catharists. From the Catharists came the idea that the Grail Castle was the centre of a mystery sect, and troubadours, who were usually believers in the heresies, spread the legend from castle to castle (by leys?).

It may be possible to understand the Grail legend more clearly by reference to leys. There is the hero knight with whom we may identify ourselves; he must come to the Hermit to learn the way to the Grail castle, and the Hermit is inextricably associated with Hermes and leys; at the castle lies the Fisher King, believed by some to be Arthur, wounded through the genitals (the thigh of most stories seems to be a euphemism) and consequently symbolizing a loss of fertility creating a wasteland. The hero's quest depends for its fulfilment upon his vital question, 'Whom does the Grail serve?', whether the culmination be renewed fertility or the hero's advancement to higher consciousness.

There are many intriguing points in the Grail tales, such as why, according to a Gnostic account, the original abode of the Grail was the star Alcoyne, one of the Pleiades.

But the basis is a quest; the content, symbolic archetypal images; the meaning, the alchemy of consciousness. The Grail, in its essentials, suggests a correspondence with the ley hunter's quest to comprehend his own nature and improve it; also the wasteland theme suggests the deterioration of the leys' fertilizing influence upon crops to nourish the body and the cosmic wisdom to feed the mind and advance the individual's spirituality.

The Fall

'There are no truths outside the Gates of Eden.' — Bob Dylan.

Approaching the problem posed by the Fall of Man it may be best to avoid the depths of Christian theology and, recalling the words of Frithjof Schuon, remember that 'it is not everywhere presented as a "shortcoming" but in certain myths takes the form of an event unconnected with human or angelic responsibility'.[45]

Schuon suggests that the Fall, or Falls, refer to states of manifestation or 'separation', or, to put it simply, dimensions of evolution from subtle to dense matter. Also the Fall may be accepted as none of man's doing by misdeeds, but a doctrine of evolution whereby man having become materially dense through the process of evolution may now take over the reins and retrace his way to the Light. The Fall crystallizes man's almost complete lack of access to the reality of divinity, infinity, God; and today's search for cosmic consciousness is a sign of a reawakening of this fact and the steps becoming found to achieve a return to the universal godhead.

In the Garden of Eden it was the serpent which brought knowledge to man, and that knowledge was his place in the evolutionary scale. The serpent could be regarded as ley power in all its manifestations as a life force and way-shower to higher realms. Schuon puts original sin in a nutshell; it is, he says 'indifference'. The indifference is to spiritual values, to a belief in God. The Fall is repeated by every action against universal harmony, and, as shown, Megalithic Man worked harder than anyone in history to achieve cosmic harmony. The lessons were almost entirely forgotten until now.

Abraxas and the Gnostics

'Gnosticism is currently fashionable. It is staging a come-back.' – A.D. Duncan. [11]

The serpent, emblem of leys, raises its forked-tongued head at the feet of Abraxas. Abraxas was itself an emblem of the Gnostics, a mystery cult which flourished in the few centuries immediately before and after the rise of Christianity, in the Middle East. Decoded, his name is 365, and his form is that of a human body dressed in Roman soldier's garb. He represented aspects of power whose sum was supreme intelligence.

The body was man himself.

The head, a cock with open beak, stood for intelligence and the hailing of light, which is the cock's habit at dawn.

The tunic represented the need for struggle.

The arms represented the protection and power given by the dedication to the Gnostics.

The shield, in his left hand, was wisdom.

The battleaxe (or whip) represented power.

The snakes were *nous* – insight; and *logos* – understanding.

Abraxas was the figure which taught that man can only reach full power by developing certain facets of his mind. We can all take a lesson from Abraxas and the Gnostics. We should also take special note that the Gnostic must strive hard for his supreme intelligence. This did not entail collecting facts or debating doctrines, but was arrived at through direct mystical experience, the initiate being guided in secrecy.

As well as being known as a mystery cult, Gnosticism has also been described as a Christian heresy. This seems particularly unfair as the Gnostics were not of any one religion, and Abraxas was not a god or idol.

The fact is that Gnostics teach that there is a supreme being or power which is invisible and without form. Nothing extraordinary in that; but they believed that this being/power could be contacted, and they helped their disciples to achieve this. It required exercise of mind and body. Ultimately man and power became identified, man becoming purified and enlightened. Whichever Gnostic society it was, its prime aim was to achieve this fulfilment.

They believed that the disciple should spend as much time and effort as possible to achieve identification with the infinite power – to become God; not everyone is capable of refining themselves – some have the divine spark and can be liberated from the material environment and some cannot; and that the mystical vision may come by any of a variety of methods – for some frenzy, for some meditation. They also put the individual before the community. In many ways their doctrine parallels the inner path of alchemy.

Gnostics believed that a man's place in the next world was determined by the knowledge that he acquired in this world, and that the knowledge was to be gained intuitively (note that advances in ley hunting and allied investigations have not come by reasoned deduction but by moments of intuition). They believed not only in the duality of mankind; but the duality of spirit, which is good, and matter, which is bad.

In studying giantlore the theory was propounded that we on the earth plane are at a low stage of evolution, devas being very high; but a percentage of people are attempting to raise themselves to a higher plane, which we once occupied. This is akin to Gnostic belief in that many of the cult's followers accept the notion that the divine Thought fell into defilement and resulted in the creation of the visible world; what one might term the earth plane which is mankind's. Simon Magus, the Gnostic, held that this primordial Thought gave birth to the lower orders which created the world. So the story tells, the lower powers captured the Thought and imprisoned her in a woman's body and through a series of incarnations she arrived in a prostitute's body. This woman was called Helena, whom Simon Magus found in a brothel, and she had once been Helen of Troy. Simon Magus regarded himself as God come to redeem her.

G.R.S. Mead believed that the Gnosticism associated with the name of Simon Magus 'is indicative of one of the main streams of the psychical heritage of early alchemy', with 'a highly developed doctrine of the divine fire and of the tree of life, and with psycho-physiological speculations which are entirely in keeping with the subtle body theory of psychical alchemy'.[37] Mead also wrote: 'Most of the Gnostics, at any rate, held that in spiritual rebirth something most real in all senses, some *substantial* as well as moral change, was wrought in them.'

Freemasonry and the Hidden Planners

'The structures of the Gothic cathedrals embodied the fusion of the Octahedron and the Cube, or, if we follow Platonic philosophy, of Air and Earth.'
— Julian Carlyon.[71]

The alchemist had his apparatus and did in fact work with metals and chemicals, although his real purpose was not the transmutation of base metals into precious ones. His materials, vessels and methods were not simply symbolic but did in fact achieve the desired results, physically in the metals, spiritually in the man.

Similarly the freemasons' architectural gems, such as the Gothic cathedrals, were not laboured upon to such heights of perfection for the sheer will to create grandeur, were not built to perpetuate a tradition of wonderful building stretching back through the centuries to Stonehenge and beyond; but the building process, from design to completion, was a process of spiritual regeneration, and the buildings were designed to perpetuate this upon generations of worshippers within the hallowed precincts.

Why is it that secrecy was involved in both the pursuits of

the alchemists and freemasons? The truth in the link between the two was not even guessed at until Fulcanelli made it plain. The builders of the Gothic cathedrals are still anonymous.

Research by John Michell, Keith Critchlow, Julian Carlyon and Guy Underwood has led to a new understanding of Christian places of worship, and examples of recently built parish churches, such as the one at Addlestone in Surrey, suggest that consciously or unconsciously position and design has been influenced by persons following sacred geometric principles handed down since prehistoric times.

Initiation

> '*On the plains on both sides of the Solway, mazes are also to be met with, and as in Wales herdsmen still cut labyrinthine figures upon the turf, which they call, for no reason except that their fathers used the same expression, the "Wall of Troy".*' — E.O. Gordon.[20]

Why is there an initiatory maze at Glastonbury, overlooking the zodiac? Why are turf mazes associated with the Trojans? Are leys initiatory paths? Did a Neolithic priesthood brainwash the populace by magical rites to give them the support and manpower to reshape the countryside, or were the secrets of the universe open to all?

Each of these questions raises interesting points about the prehistoric civilization, and may lead us to a greater understanding of leys themselves. Leys put man on to the right track to spiritual development and certain features upon them might not only mark, manipulate and control ley energy, but have a dual aspect in that they fitted into the scheme of the earth/fire/water/air elements. In fact, the whole question of initiation raises a serious doubt that mankind was held to comprise of equals during the Neolithic Age. The implications of the questions posed above are probably a complex intertwining of the heights to which man may rise and also the risks that man will allow his fellow to face; that to reach Heaven man may have first to experience Hell; that something sinister lurks along the path to enlightenment. Yet it is arguable that dangerous as it may have been, initiation may conceivably have been offered to all, and the individual had the choice whether to go ahead and at whatever pace suited him.

Glastonbury Tor maze, surrounding the steep summit, has yet to be verified by archaeologists, but reflecting on the fact that they cannot even accommodate leys and terrestrial zodiacs into their prehistoric universe we will not allow its non-authentication by them to unduly disturb us. Glastonbury's maze is perhaps unique, but just as the Glastonbury zodiac was once thought to be the sole representation of the heavens depicted upon the landscape, so there may be many other examples. Turf mazes also exist in Britain, often associated with churches; and mazes have been found depicted on Cretan coins and a rock carving at Tintagel, in Cornwall.

Geoffrey Russell has been a champion of Glastonbury Tor maze and linked it with the Grail Quest.[106] He also suggested that Glastonbury Tor is Caer Sidi, the 'Spiral Castle' and abode of the Celtic goddess Ceridwen, his contention being that candidates or pilgrims would have entered this three-dimensional maze and eventually arrived by seven circuits at the summit. Glastonbury would consequently have been an ancient mystery centre, and Joseph of Arimathea's delivery of Jesus Christ's blood in the Holy Grail — blood being equated with spirit — was probably not unexpected. Russell described the beginning of the journey as Hell and its culmination as Heaven.

John Michell has stated that other mazes exist on hillsides, but as for Glastonbury's he has suggested that it may have 'been enclosed with bushes, earth banks or hurdles so that nothing could be seen of the surrounding countryside until the top was reached'. He postulated that initiates encountered there some force, 'the full terror of which had to be experienced before those reaching the top were rewarded by the moment of enlightenment for which their years of training had prepared them'.[95] They met a manifestation of a force for which such hills were natural conductors.

Michell suggested that the vision could only be achieved by certain seekers and that some died of terror, and that in all probability candidates were in a drugged state – two hallucinatory plants being native to the Tor's lower slopes. In the ultimate vision, for those who survived, Michell suggested that the initiate understood the meaning of the experience and saw the lines of current stretch away below across the country, and that the initiate became attuned to a current of time which annihilated space.

Michell's view, right or wrong, raises the ugly questions of the value of hallucinatory experience (which many regard as never being truly mystical), and whether any teacher can morally justify allowing a pupil to face that which may lead to death. No criticism or justification is intended here upon the psychedelic drugs issue, but it is a fact that leys themselves must be equated with both physical and spiritual reality, outer and inner space, and our need to understand the boundlessness and topography of both. As to whether one should seek a vision which may never be achieved because its attainment may be curtailed by death, this leads us on the one hand to argue that nothing of value is or should be easily come by, and on the other hand there is the view that a vision such as that of Alfred Watkins should not be artificially induced but must come by way of intuition or inspiration.

My personal view is that Glastonbury Tor maze is not contemporary with the terrestrial zodiac below the Tor or the megaliths, but was created at a later stage. The society which erected the menhirs was in my view a peaceful and balanced one, which would have frowned upon drug-induced visionary techniques and any system which put anyone's life in peril. When mankind lost the ability to see beyond the veils of mystery with ease and man's senses became dulled, he went to great lengths to retrieve this state of vision. The heritage of a common link between the 'gods' and men had widened to the extent that the 'gods' became deified, mankind saw itself as vastly inferior, and physical and mental liberty was of little consequence; also any means by which the link with the 'gods' could be regained was permissible and morally acceptable.

During the Bronze Age some persons undertook trepanning, this being the removal of a circular piece of bone from the skull. Burial remains have provided skulls where new bone has grown around the edge of the cut. P.J. Helm suggested that the 'patient' was kept calm with the aid of drugs or hypnosis, and he regarded recovery as a 'startling fact'.[22] There is no questioning by him of the motive for the operation or credit for the obvious surgical skill involved. The flower power cult of 1967 brought new interest in, and keen volunteers for, trepanning, which it is claimed creates a permanent 'trip'. A relationship to the 'third eye' of mysticism is tantalising.

Small turf mazes, known commonly as Troy Towns, following the debatable belief in Trojan colonization of Albion, exist particularly in the Welsh uplands, where according to E.O. Gordon we find 'shepherds on the summit of every hillock making pictorial representations in the surface of the grass of the labyrinthine walls of ancient Troy'. He also stated the existence of mazes on both sides of the Solway; London's Blackheath, Southwark and Peckham Rye; Rochester; one near Dorchester; one at Leigh, between Yetminster and Yeovil; Wick Down at Downtown; Breame Down, near Salisbury; St Ann's, Sneinton, Nottinghamshire; near Ripon; Camberton, Cambridgeshire; Caerleon; Somerton, near Oxford; Saffron Walden; the Winton mound, St Catherine's Hill, Winchester; and Alkborough, Lincolnshire. Cretan coins, he claimed, show the designs of the three last-named mazes.

Before returning to consideration of the possibility that leys could be used to explain certain spiritual realities, the later developments of initiatory practices can be shown as indications of how man came to approach spiritual reality by degenerate means. A number of writers, including Arkon Daraul and the Revd A.D. Duncan, have drawn parallels between initiatory practices and depth psychology on the lines of Dr C.G. Jung.

The ancient mystery cults involved mind training, the

6. Arbor Low fails to visually captivate the imagination, but this Derbyshire stone circle seems to play a significant role in the scheme of siting of prehistoric monuments. (*Department of the Environment*)

7. Silbury Hill, seen from the air. The largest prehistoric man-made mound in the world, it has been the subject of much speculation as regards its purpose. (*Cambridge University Collection*: copyright reserved)

8. The Rollright Stones, Oxfordshire, are privately owned, and despite being subjected to ... are one of the best preserved stone circles in Britain. (*Depart-*

application of fear, tension, anxiety and conflict, producing a psychological state whereby the mind becomes pliant enough to allow various suggestions to be put to it which once accepted are almost impossible to remove. Certain religious and pseudo-religious organizations today use this method, either by creating anxiety that the Day of Judgement is at hand, or by carefully programmed psychotherapy. There are many such groups as these, and the writer, though not making any judgement upon them, suggests that caution should be exercised by those who approach such groups. Any kind of mindbending, whether by religious groups, total-itarian regimes, media controllers or psychiatrists, should be treated warily. Though dubious about the existence of free will, the writer has a high regard for the dignity of man, and any procedure by which one person seeks to influence another needs careful consideration before *carté blanche* is given for the application of a state whereby the patient, disciple or initiate gives control of his mind to a manipulator, who may implant whatever he chooses to be 'right' for another.

Arkon Daraul sums up one problem: 'The real mystery of the mysteries is how and when man first discovered the use of certain procedures to condition other men: and whether the discovery was instantaneous or gradual, or simultaneous or at different times and places. But one cannot date doctrines as one can archaeological finds, by radioactive carbon.'[10]

Whatever the reader's views upon the current rise in the use of drugs and the penalties, it is arguable whether the State has a right to legislate on what an individual can or cannot do with his consciousness so long as this does not affect anyone else's rights. Nevertheless it is clear that experiences gained without the use of chemical or herbal aids must be preferable, and would rule out any doubts as to their validity and reality. A reasoned argument on the value and history of hallucinogenic quests for knowledge has been given by Anthony Roberts.[103]

John Allegro caused a storm by stating that Christianity is based on a sacred mushroom cult, and at Scottish sites I have

visited fly agaric (*Amanita muscaria*) is not uncommon.
Whether drugs were taken at such sites in late prehistoric
times, when spirituality had waned, as an attempt to retrieve
the lost golden age, is debatable; but also it should be
considered whether 'trips' were a factor in the disintegration
of spirituality.

But according to Karana, drug-taking was prevalent during
the whole prehistoric period:

> By consciring [a special form of deep meditation] and by disciplined
> use of LSD, one may pass at will from one level of consciousness to
> another. One may have many strange and wonderful experiences
> during a trip, perhaps tap the very font of truth and knowledge, but
> there is no assurance that such experiences will be of benefit to the
> person or anyone else if he neglects to tune in with the conscious-
> ness *during* the trip and with his personal environment *afterwards.*
>
> The wise men of the Stone, Bronze and Iron Ages of Britain were
> masters in the art of consciring. Others took the trip after drinking
> from the Cauldron of Wisdom a potion brewed from *Amanita
> muscaria* and four herbs. It is clear from the bardic statements in the
> 'Book of Dwyfyddiaeth', 'Barddas' and 'The Spoils of Annwn' that
> the novice took his first trip with the assistance of a bard who
> monitored him in each level of consciousness. The novice was guided
> until he became aware of the racial consciousness, and here he
> remained for a long period before being allowed to pass to higher
> levels. Only when the novice became thoroughly tuned in to the
> consciousness of man, the 'dead' and the living, did he acquire the
> ability to recall and relive at will the knowledge and experiences
> obtained at other levels.
>
> With the power of recall men and women became exceedingly
> practical mystics. Living on the edge of a dream they sought to make
> it real. They built the Golden Age of Britain. Greek historians said
> they lived like gods, proud, free, fearing neither life nor death and,
> unlike other peoples, just and honest in commerce.
>
> Because they were able to retain and put their inner experiences
> into practice, life became a poem. The music of the spheres was a
> reality. For them the cosmic life was expressed joyously in wind and
> sailing clouds and in a glory which shone in all living things.[92]

Certain people have related that certain sacred sites can
produce within them states similar to those induced by drugs;
Chanctonbury Ring, for instance. Research would be profitable into how this happens, at what times or in what state of

mind the person must be, and whether anything is revealed.

Magic seeks to know, to know knowledge; mysticism seeks to give, to give to the Creator. Science also seeks knowledge. I believe that the megalith builders did not differentiate between science, magic and mysticism, and I believe that we should not either. In gaining knowledge of leys and allied subjects, we should approach our task hoping to achieve both physical, scientific proof together with esoteric magical knowledge; and remember that to give is as important as to receive. Our receipt of knowledge must be balanced by our giving back what we have learned to others, to the land, to our heritage. Some occultists, however, aim to gain power as opposed to knowledge, and ley hunting and kindred interests are not free of such persons, so take care.

Much of the leys' fascination stems from their magical quality. This is hard to define if we confine ourselves primarily to leys as geometrical patterns or lines of a physical current, but as is being attempted within these pages, we must also consider them on a spiritual level. The question of spirituality cannot be divorced from realms of higher consciousness. So we turn to Dion Fortune's definition of magic, that it is 'the science and art of causing changes in consciousness to occur in conformity with will'. The writer is fascinated by the concept of changing consciousness, but being wary has approached the subject of occultism by purely theoretical means and has not taken part in any ritual practices. It is left to the reader to decide whether a step into practical occultism is wise.

As for prehistoric initiation, Allen Watkins has suggested that candidates wishing to be initiated into the pagan mysteries 'were indoctrinated by ritual, drama and actual ordeals, rather than by oral instruction. The body of occult truths they absorbed is called by the convenience names of The Ancient Wisdom, which included a morality teaching expressed in terms of the four elements'.[112]

Allen Watkins warned that the notion that the four elements constituted man's crude attempt at physical science is wrong and that 'they were the technical terms used in a very deep system of psychology and morality which claimed, and still claims, universal validity in all ages', such a teaching being that the elements existed within man and also on the face of nature.

He gives the classifications as being:

Earth — the physical side of man.
Water — the emotional side.
Air — the intellectual side.
Fire or aether — the divine side.

He also quotes St Paul as classifying the four 'bodies' in his First Epistle to the Corinthians as:

Earth — the fleshy body.
Water — the 'natural body'.
Air — the 'spiritual body'.
Fire or aether — the 'heavenly body'.

He relates that The Ancient Wisdom saw man as the complement of seven bodies, of which the lower four were successively discarded at death. These were the four main bodies quoted above, with three intermediate bodies.

He continues his thesis:

> Between Earth and Water there is Mire, which is a mixture of the physical and the sensual elements in Man. Between Water and Air there is Mist, which nicely describes the confused thought consequent on mixing emotion (Water) and reason (Air). The last intermediate is the Halo or Rainbow, which is the fiery barrier between reason (Air) and final intuition or revelation (Aether). By these seven symbolical terms we can express the whole range of post-mortem experience of the human soul, as well as the whole range of subjective experience during life.
>
> The central Wisdom teaching was that Man had fallen from the highest plane (Aether or Fire) to the lowest plane (Earth), and that if he wished to recover his lost estate he must retrace his path upwards through all the elements.
>
> The ritual initiations of the pagan Mysteries expressed through the actual experiences of the candidate the difficult stages in Man's ascent through the elements. There were three initiations. The first was from Earth to Water, the second from Water to Air, and the third from Air to Fire or Aether.
>
> Again we find these initiations repeated in early Christian custom, but under the form of Baptism. St John the Baptist expressly mentions all three in the Third Chapter of St Luke's Gospel. There

he contrasts his own lower baptism by Water with Jesus's higher
baptism with the Holy Ghost and with Fire. 'Holy Ghost' is the
translation in the Authorised Version of the Greek word 'pneuma',
which means Breath or Air. The correspondence is exact.

Allen Watkins then draws attention to the identity of the
teachings with a walk along a ley. The physical features
encountered correspond at every point:

> He starts from a high initial point and descends from high estate to
> EARTH. He goes along a stoned causeway through a muddy pond:
> MIRE. The old track leads straight through a ford: WATER.
> Visibility is bad: MIST. He climbs upward into a clearer atmosphere:
> AIR. The blazing beacon on the summit is reflected in a circular
> moat: HALO. He arrives at the terminal beacon point: FIRE.
>
> After two millenniums we still continue to use exactly the same
> ley-metaphors to express the permanent realities of Man's inner life.
> They are born in us as part of our heritage from the past. We
> describe a man whose mind and conversation is purely material as
> 'down-to-earth'. We refer to a sensualist as 'wallowing in the mire'.
> We say a passionate man is overcome by a ·flood of emotion'
> (Water). We speak of a brave man as having received his 'baptism of
> Fire'. We speak of a strikingly true thought as a 'flash of intuition'
> (Fiery Light). An honest man is said to 'go straight', identifying the
> Path with right conduct and morality.

Links between the pagan initiations, the philosophy of the
elements and leys are to be found in classical, mediaeval and
modern literature, Allen Watkins states, and he gives as
examples the Old Testament, New Testament, Vergil,
Apuleius, Dante, Shakespeare, Bunyan and Belloc. He
believes that it can be deduced from reading such literature
that leys were involved in pagan initiations and are identical
with the philosophy of the elements. He suggests that ancient
man would have seen that leys had a magical as well as a
secular side, and that the two sides grew up together, and
early man would have regarded leys as sacred, useful, and
bringing success and luck. In posing the question of leys ever
having been used for initiation, he answers that their being so
'perfectly fitted for such use, that it is hard to believe
otherwise. Where else could ancient man look for a medium
to hand that expressed his philosophy so exactly'.

Allen Watkins ended his article by noting that Major F.C.

Tyler had also come to the conclusion that prehistoric occultism was bound inextricably to the ley system. What Tyler said was: 'There must be that ancient worship (we call it "Sun Worship", but know so little about it) behind it all,' and 'What the purpose of this arrangement was is a problem for the future; but it seems to me that it was connected with the practice of the Ancient Wisdom, which we know so little about, but which was bound up with what we call "Religious Worship".'[54]

I find Allen Watkins's line of reasoning sound and in keeping with the speculations of leys being particularly sacred and also lines of inspiration. Also leys do not engender the sinister implications of the labyrinthine maze concept of Glastonbury Tor. It may be that such an initiatory use of leys as paths of theoretical occultism was superseded by the ominous presence of a Glastonbury maze.

Yesod

> 'The Qabalah is a development of the creation myth about which Judaism has speculated to a much greater extent than most Christians believe.'
> – A.D. Duncan.[11]

More complex than the speculations that leys may be associated with the four elements is the possibility that they can be similarly linked to the Qabalah. A.D. Duncan refers to the Qabalah as a ' "map" of manifestation', a symbolic diagram of the stages from the unmanifest to the successive stages of manifestation represented by the Sephiroth, or Tree of Life. The Christian understands 'manifestation' by the term 'creation', though the two terms are not absolutely interchangeable. In a work such as this there is not room to even adequately explain the Qabalah, and this writer has not the qualifications to do so. What is to be attempted in this brief discourse on the Qabalah is to suggest that our study and that of the Qabalah can be shown to cover certain common ground.

Stated simply, the Tree of Life charts how the soul may

progress from dense to higher levels (reincarnation or by learning of these levels during this life); and is a mind system of symbols and archetypes, a guide to the structure of both the macrocosmic collective unconscious and the microcosmic individual conscious.

Duncan's commentary on the Tree of Life is my major source and has been chosen as it takes an objective view of the subject. The following is, however, a subjective selection of information on the Tree of Life as it may have correspondences with leys. It must be stressed, however, that though I believe certain links are strong, others are tenuous, and my purpose in presenting these speculations is to spur occultists to seek from their point of view whether such correspondences exist, in preference to ley hunters, uninitiated in occult matters, jumping in head first.

Duncan follows the Tree from top to bottom in his book. My choice is the reverse. We should imagine that in our search for greater knowledge of leys and ourselves we begin our initiation into the Mysteries from the low, dense level and go towards the higher levels, physically and mentally. So, sephirah by sephirah, we will seek correspondences.

Malkuth: This is the level of the four elements – earth/water/air/fire. It is also the end result of creation. Spirituality made physically manifest.

Yesod: Here we enter the dimension of esoteric ley hunting, for the purpose and practicalities for which the marking and manipulation of leys was made exists on this level. If we are to assume that leys, as energy currents, have existed since the beginning of creation, and believe that they form the framework of the Earth, we can take a few cautious steps forward, making assumptions which nevertheless seem rational in our context of thought.

This is not to say that etheric energy is in the leys and nowhere else. I understand the truth to be that ether is, as occultism states, existing everywhere, and that leys somehow hold concentrations of such – perhaps generating it for the Earth. Perhaps also a greater amount of this may have been produced in prehistoric times, and the Fall of Man resulted from a disintegration of knowledge of leys and subsequent withdrawal of much of this power, resulting in man's fall to a denser level.

Man has a physical body and an etheric body, according to esoteric science. It is the etheric body which 'feels'; is one with the nervous system. This ether is the framework of matter.

According to Gareth Knight the ether is 'the vehicle of the life forces' and 'can be manipulated within the limits of its nature, which are by no means inconsiderable. All miraculous and supernatural happenings, therefore, are brought about by the manipulation of the natural qualities of the aether, and if we understood the nature of the aether, we should understand the rationale of their production'.[26] This is the agency of psychic phenomena and spiritual healing. Here is the sphere for magic.

Therefore, if we were to assume that leys are concentrations of ether, then it would explain why ley centres were used for magic, the cases of 'getting high', why healing is associated with them, why ghosts are associated with them, their association with life forces and fertility. People like to walk the leys, and the symbols for Yesod are perfumes and sandals; the latter seemingly significant, which the occultist regards as helping him 'walk with ease' on psychic levels, but we may determine as having physical reality during Neolithic times, worn by those who trod the old straight tracks. Perfumes (incense and joss sticks), being an aid to changes in consciousness, may then as now have been used for that purpose.

The magical image for Yesod is a beautiful, strong, naked man. What other than this is the Cerne Abbas giant? His nakedness is fully apparent, and the club he wields signifies his strength. Yesod's correspondence in microcosm is the fertilizing, reproductive organs, so handsomely displayed at Cerne Abbas.

The spiritual experience associated with Yesod is vision of the machinery of the universe, and there is no doubt that Megalithic Man comprehended this.

This level is undoubtedly the most significant for our study, and many generalizations touched upon here are worthy of greater explanation, and can be returned to in later passages, particularly that regarding the ether.

Hod: This sphere is also important in our study, for here we encounter Mercury and St Michael, important factors to be dealt with later and at length. Hod is the sphere of ceremonial magic, the sphere where the magician actually works. Michael is Hod's archangel and his is the element of fire. Christianity venerated St Michael as protector and guardian. Here also are Hermes, Mercury and Thoth. Here are the ley guardians.

Netzach, Tiphareth, Geburah, Chesed, Daath, Binah, Chokmah and Kether: These spheres are higher than Yesod and Hod, our particular areas of interest. To discuss them and any particular correspondences with our study would probably be confusing and do more harm than good at the present. A full understanding of Yesod and a consideration of Hod should be our aim at this stage, and not until these are fully comprehended should we move on. We must crawl before we can walk. This is not to say that little of interest lies beyond. Temptations to seek correspondences between physical features in the landscape and these spheres or levels of the mind are many: Daath with its kundalini, inklings of links with Druid Beltane bonfires, its misty peaks, pyramids, supreme wisdom and the masters one may contact telepathically; or Duncan's 'hilltop mass-hysteria shrines' of the Celts, which may be 'traced on the map, in triangles and pentangles, by those interested in such matters' in Tiphareth's sphere.

Duncan states that man, the microcosm, must progress from the physical world to the Light. There are thirty-two paths to trace in the Qabalistic system if the occultist is to perform the Great Work completely. This writer, being wary, if not downright cowardly, has contented himself with theoretical occultism, and has in this work drawn attention to points where he believes the occultist and ley hunter share common ground, and is convinced that leys and the Tree of Life have correspondences.

As for the thirty-two paths, the last (or for the occultist working his way from the physical upwards, the first) is from Malkuth to Yesod, and Duncan relates this to one's probing

the unconscious mind, it being the mythological level of the
Celtic Underworld and the way of psychoanalysis (Jung's
process being to follow the images until they become
symbols). A description is quoted in Duncan's book, from a
work by Israel Regardie, which describes the 'visions' seen on
the thirty-second path. Its resemblance to the imagery and
symbolism of Bob Dylan's songs is striking, and I suspect that
many songs by Dylan, Leonard Cohen and others are
similarly depictions of these paths and manifestations of the
unconscious. Gareth Knight believes Lewis Carroll to
similarly be 'a writer who wrote of the deeps of the
unconscious mind'. On the thirty-second path one meets
representations of the four classic elements already referred
to. This world, Duncan states, is also referred to the ether,
called by him the fifth element – 'quintessentializing the
lower elements'. The temple in the 'vision', whose four doors
represent the elements, is the ether.

To stress once more, ether is all-important in our understanding of leys. Also the Celtic Underworld is not an exact,
physical country as most works state (researchers seek these
locations on maps), but has only an inner reality. It is also
feasible that the location of Atlantis is, and has only been, in
the mind – but at a different level to that of the Celtic
Underworld.

It may be that ley points were used in yet another way.
Today's psychoanalyst asks his patient to visualize certain
symbols, and from the descriptions given he judges the
patient's general psychological health. Perhaps an initiate was
asked a number of questions on ley power, his description of
an initial peak and his tactics to reach it being indicative of
his level of aspiration, a barrow giving his attitude towards
death. Or maybe he was instructed to meditate at various ley
points and then describe his experiences to his teacher.
Similarly he could be sent to various segments of a terrestrial
zodiac to learn their differences, and so comprehend differences within himself and between himself and other individuals.

A.D. Duncan makes little differentiation between the
occult and certain Christian practices, both being associated

with the mind. He is not particularly interested in the study of 'power lines', whereas we are. It is therefore not surprising that he is somewhat off the mark, his interest and conclusions being totally on the side of inner reality. He gives no indication for a belief in the exoteric existence of a King Arthur or Merlin, knights or a round table. This writer does not suggest a physical reality for men named in the Arthurian legends, but he does suggest that what the occultist seeks inwardly can also be found outwardly. By this I mean that leys and terrestrial zodiacs (round tables) are outward signs of inner realities and cosmic truths, prehistoric man having helped mark and design this land to correspond to these, to provide maps for the soul, for man's journey through the levels of creation, the ladder to higher consciousness.

Though the inner meanings of leys must be found by attunement with the mind, the ley hunter must not lose sight of the basic fact that leys have an outward reality as lines of peace, harmony, and inspiration, and are a remarkable expression of our ancestors' interest in the truths of spirituality and bond with nature. One's feelings towards leys need never reach a high/deep level, and can remain on the level of admiration for the effort put into marking or manipulating the current by ancient man, and they can be enjoyed as expressions of his need to create harmony within his surroundings.

However, the full content of the argument for a spiritual reality for leys is far from having been fully presented, and the crux of the matter will be tackled in later pages. This is the etheric angle to the study, already met several times. But before coming to this matter we may extend our study of the Qabalah by its relation to mental wellbeing and the general welfare of one's health, and also consider the validity of numerology.

Numerology

'Twenty-two, two little ducks.' — Bingo caller.

Application of numerology to aspects of ancient wisdom can

be enlightening; it can be annoying. Sometimes it works; sometimes it does not. In a work such as this space does not permit a deep and extensive examination of this system of discovering truths, and those who find this chapter interesting are urged to read the section on the subject in Richard Cavendish's *The Black Arts*.[7]

I have chosen the 'Hebrew' system, based on the Hebrew alphabet with additions from the Greek, which neither uses the figure 9 nor lists the alphabet in normal order.

1	2	3	4	5	6	7	8
A	B	C	D	E	U	O	F
I	K	G	M	H	V	Z	P
Q	R	L	T	N	W		
J		S			X		
Y							

For persons or places the numbers are added. If they come to a number greater than 9, then the number is reduced to its digital root. For instance, 'Paul Screeton' adds up to 52, i.e. 5+2 = 7. Exceptions are 11 and 22, numbers to be handled with caution.

The numbers which we shall consider are 1, 9 and 11, all odd numbers, which are male numbers, and 22, an even, female number.

No. 1   Stands for positive, pioneering, independence, creativity, domineering, one-track-mindedness. It is the number of God. And Albion, the wisdom teaching name of Britain. Also it is Glastonbury's number.

No. 9   The number of high mental and spiritual achievement. Of visionaries and idealists. Impulsiveness, charm, urge to help. People often considered by their duller contemporaries as wild, unorthodox and impractical. It is the number of completeness.

Alfred Watkins was a 9. Ley is a 9, and so are most of the 'ley deities'. Cole, king of the leys, is a 9; so is Elen, his daughter; Saint Michael, Christianized guardian angel of leys; Hermes Trismegistus; Dunwal Molmutius, the prehistoric law-giving road-maker, and according to Hollinshed, Britain's first king; Jesus; Christ; Jesus Christ.

However, Thoth is a 7, and Mercury a 5. But in the Tarot, the Hermit has card 9. Silbury is 9.

No. 11 Revelation is the keynote of 11. It represents a higher, supernatural plane of knowledge and achievement. It is interpreted as God (1) added to the world (10). People whose number is 11 have a special message to give to the world. Cavendish regards them as 9 on a higher plane. I would draw attention here not to people but places. Stonehenge is 11; so is Woodhenge.

Even more interesting is the fact that the three confirmed centres of terrestrial zodiacs known to me are 11: Butleigh (Glastonbury zodiac); The Middles (Stanley); and Fleet Shot Hill. Also King Arthur disappeared in 542 A.D. – an 11.

No. 22 This is the number of the master. For persons it is the number of an exceptional man. He may be great spiritually, or a great criminal, tycoon or master black magician. 22 has creation as its keynote and enshrines all the secrets of the universe.

Stanley, with its zodiac, is 22, as is the nearby cathedral city of Durham. Dragon is 22. There are 22 major trumps in the Tarot pack.

There are many objections to numerology – too numerous to mention – and it is suspect. But the reader may judge for himself, and if he then regards it as dubious, he may dismiss it.

The theory that anything's essential nature is revealed in its name, and that names can be expressed in numbers, is not specially complex; no more so than astrology. The theory and structure of it is basically Greek in origin, and seemingly quite sound in practice. That universe is constructed to a mathematical pattern and that this involves opposites and their reconciliation should be self-evident.

Gematria is another numerical system, whereby the letters of a word are converted into their number equivalent and

then added before substituting another word which adds up
to the same total.

Psychotherapy and Spiritual Healing

> 'Diagnosis and treatment at a distance are both
> inevitably related to thought, in fact I contend that
> without the directive power of thought no cure
> would be effected.' – David V. Tansley.[110]

As has already been noted, the Qabalistic system is insepar-
able from the current techniques of psychotherapy, based on
the findings of C.G. Jung. Depth psychology has revealed the
unconscious to be a vast area whose inner space limits are as
boundless as those of the astronomer's outer space. The
importance of this discovery is on a par with the Renais-
sance's maritime and astronomical discoveries, for it has
opened up unsuspected vistas. It gives us a clue to the
scientific reality of so much psychical phenomena and myths,
symbols and images. It provides a basis for occultism's
credibility as an exact system, while removing some of its
awesomeness.

Psychotherapy and hypnotherapy attempt to reach the
unconscious and find the deep-rooted fears and causes of
mental disturbance, and help the patient overcome his
failings and lead him back to normality. Hypnotherapy will
place in the unconscious, by suggestion, a revulsion for
something, such as cigarettes, to cure a person of smoking, or
will similarly find the seat of some trouble and release the
offending blockage. As mentioned, there are in Britain
certain groups which use therapy to condition members.
Readers are warned to be wary of any group which seeks to
process his mind.

Psychotherapy is a direct system by which the mind's ills
are treated; but what of treatment for other ills of the body?
Psychic or spiritual healing has produced an immense number
of verified cures, often with people orthodox medicine has
classified incurable. They are not infallible, of course, and
negative results bring them into disrepute and lead to a

rejection of psychic therapy. But to this writer's satisfaction, spiritual healing will work and is worthy of being taken as seriously as the treatment given under the National Health Service.

There is a school of thought which believes that some, if not all, human ills have their origin in the mind. The hypothesis is gaining ground because of an increase in well-attested cases being brought to the notice of medical circles. Ulcers are now generally accepted as being caused by worry. Cancer is likely to follow in acceptance. Worry is a process of the mind, and it is worry which would seem to be capable of producing chemical changes in the organs of the human body.

It follows then that the mind causes illnesses, so why should not, under reversed circumstances, the mind be led to not only cure illnesses but improve the physical constitution of the body and produce physical and mental supermen of great bodily strength and intellect? If the mind is responsible for the ulcer, then an 'outside' reaction on the body could cause changes in the body which would directly affect and change the mind.

If the reader is a little confused as to what this has to do with leys and sacred centres, then one of Iris Campbell's psychometric readings will make it clearer.

Mayboro, south of Penrith, is a henge monument with one huge monolith within. She describes it as 'an experimental area for the trying out of the sun's rays at certain angles and conditions . . . where the magnetism was induced from the four points of the compass . . . it subsequently received too much power . . .'. And 'the teachings and Ministry of this place . . . would be directed towards . . . the lymphatic glandular system . . . These glands are the storehouses of energy on the etheric plane'. She adds: 'You have here a house which was ordained for the purpose of co-ordinating light for the benefit of the glandular construction in Man . . . it was as if it were built over with a dome of glass.' John Foster Forbes adds that many speculative writers on megalithic sites had hinted at the constructions being covered over, not with glass as we know it, but he asks the reader to envisage 'a specially induced volatile substance transparent in nature, bordering on the atmospheric, yet spiritually substantial, having powers of absorption, transmutation and refraction; something too that at the same time veils and reveals. Can one say jasper?' (In 'The Revelation of St John the Divine' the first foundation of the New Jerusalem was jasper.)

Iris Campbell states that the monolith's position, not quite at the centre, accorded with the solar rays being 'induced at a certain angle in order to bring about the accurate influx that the body could take of solar force without being overwhelmed by too much power; this was essentially a healing and upbuilding centre'. She states that the 'soul is the influxatory of man through which are drawn Cosmic Rays', and that at Mayboro the combined magnetic content of Sun and Earth united treated man not on the physical but on the soul plane. She also comments, maybe very significantly, that the distribution of the colours of the Sun was different then, for there was less of the violet and more of the blue in the rays (blue being the colour of the etheric).[15]

This is extremely important for just as leys and sacred centres have their outward and inner realities, their material and spiritual levels of existence, we find here evidence for the heightening of consciousness by way of an outside source, solar energy, through the lymphatic glands, benefiting the spirituality of man. Again we have met the etheric. This provides a reason why the Sun was accorded such importance, and the value to early man of the etheric and the need for raising his consciousness.

From the prehistoric period a return to the present day is necessary to state with regard to modern spiritualist and psychoanalytic workings that it seems that just as forces of the mind can create organic diseases, the same forces can be used to eradicate them. It will now be worthwhile to look at certain other unorthodox healing methods, and we will not be far at all times from leys, the etheric and the ancient wisdom.

In associating leys and sacred centres with health, it will be seen that there is a viable connection between them and

9. Avebury stone circle. Many of the stones have been destroyed, but this view presents a fine selection of the remaining stones. (*Department of the Environment*)

10. A village within the environs of the huge Avebury stone circle. (*Department of the Environment*)

orgone energy, the practice of radiesthesia, and also that the centres themselves provide effects.

As for the centres themselves, we will content ourselves here with a brief consideration of the physical, as opposed to the spiritual, effects.

Rickets and Rheumatism

Geoffrey of Monmouth, writing about 1136, stated that Stonehenge's stones had healing virtues. Merlin tells Aurelius: 'Laugh not so lightly, King . . . For in these stones is a mystery and a healing virtue against many ailments.'

An eight foot high monolith at Minchinhampton, Gloucestershire, has a hole through it, and in past centuries mothers would pass babies through it if they had rickets, as this bone disease was apparently cured in this way.

An example of a stone which I know to have cured friends of mine is at Hart, in County Durham. One woman's rheumatism was so bad that she could not put her hands behind her head, but after sitting on the stone she found she was capable of doing this. Another man had injured an arm in a road accident, and several minutes after sitting on the stone the pain was 90 per cent gone.

Guy Underwood claimed that his water lines appear to be harmful (causing rheumatism) and that aquastats are beneficial (curing rheumatism).

One reference to healing from a prehistoric site which struck me as significant is from an eighteenth-century manuscript, in which it is stated that a rock basin on Ben Newe, Strathdon, is 'renowned among the vulgar for marvellous cures; there is said to be a worm abiding in it, which, if alive when the patient comes, he or she will live; if dead they are condemned to die'. Could this not be a garbled understanding that if the ley power is at the time active then healing occurs; if dormant then the patient receives no benefit and consequently dies?

Orgone Energy

Dr Wilhelm Reich is best known for his orgone energy

accumulator, for a book on the orgasm, and for an apparatus which seemingly withdrew cosmic energy from 'space machines'. The work of this physician and scientist requires further study, as his findings were revolutionary and startling – and upsetting. Reich died in a United States federal penitentiary. He was imprisoned for resisting an injunction regarding his experiments. The sad end to the life of this great man has many bizarre ramifications. It was a twentieth-century witchhunt.

In a book by Brad Steiger and Joan Whritenour, there is a chapter entitled 'The Silencing of Wilhelm Reich'. The authors state that Jerome Eden, a student of Reich's work, is 'convinced that there was a conspiracy to stop Reich's research and destroy him because of what his discoveries threatened'.[49] Herschel Sales, in *Flying Saucers*, No. 48, wrote that he believed Reich's death to be the culmination of ten years of 'harassment and persecution at the hands of carefully concealed conspirators, who used the U.S. Federal agencies and courts to defraud the people and prevent them from knowing and utilizing crucial discoveries in physics, medicine, and sociology'. These are harsh accusations indeed. Even if the motives of the nameless conspirators are unclear, there are certainly sinister overtones. Reich's findings had been published and reputable scientists verified his results. The orgone energy accumulator had been acclaimed by the late Dr Theodore P. Wolfe as 'the greatest single discovery in the history of medicine'. In his later years, Reich turned his attention to UFOs and deduced that they are motivated by primordial, mass free, cosmic orgone energy.

John Michell wrote: 'There can be no doubt that the dragon current refers to some natural flow of force, related to the earth's magnetic field and only rediscovered in modern times by the late Wilhelm Reich who called it orgone energy';[40] the dragon current being ley power. He added that orgone energy is present in every part of the universe, is mass free and consequently hard to isolate, and provides the medium through which magnetic and gravitational forces manifest their influence. However, it can be accumulated in a chamber lined with some inorganic material, covered outside with alternate layers of organic and inorganic matter. A person in an orgone accumulator will become charged with this vital energy.

Michell believes that the chambers below the great megalithic edifices were utilized by prehistoric man in this way — and that they were layered according to the principles rediscovered by Reich. Long barrows and fogous are examples, and he notes the trouble taken to select materials of clay and stone, and the great distances over which these were brought.

Comparisons between etheric energy and orgone energy show such great similarities that it would be surprising if they were not identical. Both are everywhere, both can be accumulated. As to whether Reich ever found lines of orgone energy I have no knowledge, but according to Steiger and Whritenour he demonstrated orgone energy's presence with a geiger counter — perhaps along a ley. Incidentally, his Orgone Institute was on an estate at aptly named Rangeley, Maine.

Reich's association of orgone energy with UFOs is also interesting, and also that as a psychoanalyst who studied under Sigmund Freud, he believed in an outer, physical reality for UFOs.

Radiesthesia

The quotation of David V. Tansley's which introduced this section might not find acceptance with your friendly family GP, but readers who have considered the achievements in the medical field by Edgar Cayce will find it believable enough. Such diagnosis and treatment is effected via the etheric and the thought regarding the illness reaches the patient as energy with curative power. But without explanation of the etheric plane it would be pointless here to follow this argument fully and this will be dealt with later in this work.

As for the acupuncturist, who sticks needles in his patients as a curative measure, he is often regarded with suspicion, derision or hostility. Yet he deals with the body's vital energy, just as the ley hunter deals with the raw energy of the Earth. This energy, called by the Chinese 'Ch'i', permeates man, has twelve main meridians and it flows from one to another in set sequence, making a complete cycle in twenty-four hours, and is controlled by the Sun. There are also seasonal and lunar cycles. In addition there are eight extra 'mei' meridians which act as regulators, and it cannot be coincidental that leys in China were called 'lung mei'. These lines are also believed to be involved in psychic development.

John Wheaton, the Devon acupuncturist, wrote: 'If one builds up Ch'i or psychic energy to the extent that it starts to raise one to a higher level mentally/psychically, then the surplus energy flows through the extra meridians in the same way as Ch'i normally flows through the "Ching lo" or ordinary meridians.'[117]

The network is made more complex by linking meridians, and the energy is bi-polar. Wheaton believes that leys and acupuncture meridians are both circulatory systems with centres for the tapping or control of this energy.

Thus we note that the acupuncturist deals with the life force and its circulatory passage in the human body, just as the ley hunter deals with the same force and network on the Earth. The theory is that the life force must be in the right place at the right time, in correct amount and polarity. In a patient, if this was imbalanced then disease occurred, and the cure is by transferring life force within the body. Sometimes the treatment is accompanied by an electrical tingling.

The acupuncturist in China was believed not only to be curing anything from manic depression to piles, but the therapy was meant to provide a means by which imprisoned evil spirits might be expelled.

Another oriental therapy is moxibustion – the burning of mugwort upon the skin, even far from the particular ache itself. May there be a connection here with the beacon fires of prehistory?

Death

'Given the greater number of dead than living on this earth, a revolt of the dead against the living

who had buried them would certainly end in defeat
for the latter.' — Ornella Volta.[56]

To everything there is a positive and a negative side. Leys can
be seen to be important for a better life, either with regard to
fertility or the higher aspirations of man's inner life. Leys,
however, may also be connected with death.

Archaeologists, because it is simple, perhaps rational,
suppose that prehistoric man had a superstitious dread of
death. They would have us believe that early man was afraid
of the dead. But what if he attempted to comprehend the
stages and paths taken by the soul upon death, while he was
alive?

But as with every accepted statement by archaeologists
there is another view worthy of consideration, and one which
fits our framework more easily. This involves funerary urns.
The readily acceptable explanation is that bodies were put so,
foetus-like, to stop the dead coming back to harm the living.
To stop it getting out. What if the opposite is true? What if
such a position — a return to the womb symbolic of
rebirth — was the motive, and placing corpses upon leys was
to allow the etheric body to move on in its natural
environment, the etheric?

Many occultists believe that after death the body releases
the etheric body and this still has a faint spark of life,
desiring to live again and can be attracted back to life,
absorbing life energy from living creatures to continue
indefinite life, and that Spiritualist seances are not contacting
'spirits' but astral corpses. Is there an echo here of a reality in
the belief that Arthur can be summoned back to life?

There are traditions of the dead being carried along leys
and the bearers pausing at crosses and stones, where they
rested or prayed and placed the coffin for a while.

Fertility

> *'The plant sucks up the juices of the stars and*
> *makes these juices available in a recipe we can*
> *swallow.' — Richard Grossinger (Io, No. 5).*

The gently murmuring Dee was low when my wife and I waded over the slippery stones to a large slab of rock in the river's midstream. We crawled through the large hole in it. Tradition associates this stone at Pannanich with conferring fertility.

Throughout Britain there are stones of Neolithic origin believed to possess the ability to promote fertility in barren women. J.M. McPherson quotes the above example in *Primitive Beliefs in the North-East of Scotland*, and also a granite mass in Braemar and a recumbent stone in King's Park, Edinburgh. Newlyweds embraced the menhir of Plouargel in Brittany and Stone of Chantecoq, Eure-de-Loire, in the hope that they would have offspring. Around a Carnac standing stone childless couples ran naked.

The phallic imagery involved may be the reason for the association of the stones with fertility, but there is also the possibility that somehow these stones produce an effect which removes impediments which make certain women barren.

Health has been shown to be an area in which leys play a part, and the sub-division of fertility is an important one. In addition to the legends of standing stones being instrumental in procuring fertility, there is the wasteland in the Matter of Britain cycle, which details a country's fertility devastated and awaiting renewal by the hero whose quest is dependent upon a critical question.

It is possible that in early prehistoric times the land may have been more fertile, and perhaps several crops a year were grown without consequent reduction of fertility, through manipulation of leys and help from the elementals.

Evidence will be provided to show that leys play a part in plant growth, but further than this, speculation alone exists.

Guy Underwood stated that geodetic lines caused no difference in colour or rate of growth in plants, but that they affected germination and shape. For instance, mistletoe, the Druidic, aphrodisiac parasite, was found to grow only above blind springs or nodes; the same being the case with the yew, the longest-lived British tree, yet one associated with death, prehistoric earthworks and Christian churchyards. Isolated hawthorns – the meeting places of elementals – such as Glastonbury's holy thorn, are mostly located upon blind springs. At Risbury Camp I watched Andrew Kerr dowsing apple trees and finding them corresponding to geodetic lines.

Jimmy Goddard has found that ley power has caused several species of trees, such as the copper beech and Scots pine, to grow with double trunks. Ley power can also cause spiral growth in tree trunks. It may be deduced that the form of energy flow is thus made manifest to our sight, in the third dimension, and that the spiral is suggestive of the snakes upon Mercury's caduceus. He theorizes that the double trunk became the sign of benediction (the forerunner of a sign now indicating abuse), and the spiral symbolized the serpent power.[91] A correspondent in Midlothian, Mrs L.F. How, planted green beans along a ley and was astounded by the enormous quantity of double beans which sprang up.

H.J. Massingham said of pine trees: 'The accidence of pines upon so many barrows and earthworks is too frequent to be ascribed to natural grouping.'[35] Perhaps they made such ley points easy to find, but the pine also has many traditional properties, being good for the teeth, stomach, bowels, and apparently stirring up lust and increasing sperm.

On 21 October, 1968, the *Daily Mirror* published a report on a tree which local people refused to have cut down at Ballymagroartyscotch, in Ireland, and so a ring road was to be routed around it. Not many trees are held in such high esteem, but this enchanted whitethorn had survived Hurricane Debbie, which raged at 120 m.p.h., and uprooted 500 trees on a nearby estate.

The Cerne Abbas hill figure is associated with fertility. 'The fecundity of the local herds and fields were believed to depend upon the preservation of the hill figure', wrote Guy Underwood, adding that it is said that if a girl sleeps on the giant she will bear many children.

As referred to earlier, certain wells were believed to endow fertility when the water was drunk, often sweetened with sugar. King James II and his second queen visited St Winefrid's Well, at Holywell, Flintshire, on 29 August, 1686, with the hope of procuring a son.

Stone circles, as opposed to single standing stones, are not generally associated with fertility, but there is a legend that into one of the Stapeley Hill stone circles, near Shrewsbury, a cow made a daily appearance. This was during a famine and a fairy provided the cow. The legend tells how a wicked witch milked the beast with a bottomless pail in order to stop the villagers getting any milk, but a sudden flash of lightning revealed to the cow what mischief was afoot. The cow kicked the hag and vanished. The witch remained rooted to the spot and is now the single upright stone of the circle. (Lightning, incidentally, is attracted to oak trees and by percentage strikes them far more often than any other species.)

E.M. Nelson, however, stated that men and women ran naked nine times around stone circles, perhaps as a fertility rite, but I know of no other reference, though the number nine is significant.[42]

References to orgiastic rites, mostly in very modern times, associated with prehistoric or early Christian sites, are common. This raises the question of whether the sex was simply the natural culmination of magical practice or was enhanced upon a supraphysical level by power peculiar to the site. Readers may have experienced the electrical tingling of the body or even the blue inner flash of love associated with sex. Is there a link here with leys, sacred centres, the blue etheric, Wilhelm Reich? Guy Underwood claimed that animals chose blind springs as places to bear their young. But did they ever consciously choose to become impregnated at such spots?

The Etheric

> 'No one knows what simple, natural forces of which we know nothing but which are within our grasp could be made use of by a man endowed with an "awakened" consciousness.' – Louis Pauwels and Jacques Bergier.[44]

I argued earlier in this work the possibility that the current passing between ley points has an electromagnetic base and carries with it concentrated matter on the etheric level, this energy being a concentration of a force existent throughout the universe, present in every atom and of great importance in the human body. Just as we disabuse our physical bodies by eating animals' flesh, smoking tobacco which affects the lungs, drinking coffee which harms the chromosomes, drinking alcohol which harms the liver, so we similarly disabuse the etheric double by failing to raise our consciousnesses by turning our intellects and emotions towards the spiritual source of creation. That an etheric framework, in the form of leys, holds our planet together is a strong possibility, and that prehistoric man knew that he and his environment each had their different vibratory levels, and the notion that both could interact beneficially was his belief, and so strove to find a correct balance between them. He found the centres where the etheric current was drawn from the land by the heavenly bodies and co-ordinated the power centres to function harmoniously. It is a possibility that ley power from such a fountainhead would be dissipated into the atmosphere before man's discovery of it, or flow between the centres via electro-magnetic lines in a weak form. His efforts were directed to accumulate such energy at mounds, a stone or stone circle, and later churches and cathedrals, both for his owns spiritual benefit, and also by placing stones between centres he created or increased the energy's flow.

Before examining the evidence, an explanation is required as to the use of the term 'etheric'. Firstly, the ether under consideration here is not the anaesthetic discovered by Paracelsus, which aptly, however, carries the same name and also causes a change in consciousness.

It was first used to explain ley points by Frank Lockwood, who writes under the pen name Circumlibra.

The universe has seven distinct vibratory rates of conscious being. Contemporary names for the first three of these may be expressed as: 1, Physical; 2, Etheric; 3, Astral. The divisions are somewhat arbitrary and merge. Some speak of twelve rates. If we choose to regard leys as lines at a higher frequency than our normal conscious state, we will readily understand why etheric is an apt name. Man's aim should be to raise his consciousness to just such a level of perception, and the more we probe the leys' realities the nearer we come to identifying with them and their level of existence.

Frank Lockwood's own words explain his reason for using the term etheric:

> We are told there are several levels of matter in addition to our own dense, physical matter. I would place the substance the Earth breathes both in and out mainly on the etheric level, which is considered to be matter next to our own in density. This being so I may speak of the centres as 'etheric centres', but as they are also centres of energy then it would seem in order to call them 'energy centres'. Certain of these centres have been so worked upon, usually in the remote past, as to become definite 'power centres'. . . . As the Sun passes over the breathing centres its energy impinges on the more benign energy of the centres and forces it forward, creating a major surge at certain times, especially at noon. Other bodies also create tides which do not necessarily coincide with those of the Sun.
>
> It is most difficult to use terms to describe the centres, and the energy which floats is pushed and pulls almost at one and the same time without borrowing and/or violating the generally accepted meaning of various words which have been created or claimed in other directions. The most important thing is to convey a fact in a manner that can be understood by all.[76]

One of those who has speculated as to man's not merely concentrating ley power but extending its scope of activity is Ross Nichols, Chief of the Order of Bards, Ovates and Druids. He wrote:

> It seems clear that the leys usually exist first and that men recognise it by placing monuments such as their temples, stones and other aids to identification at significant points of emphasis . . . There are also cases where men seem to have created or completed a line of power, using natural features, by some instinct, presumably for the UFOs to use. A clear example is at Selworthy, a hill in North Devon where for some time UFO observers used to congregate, although no reason was at the time adduced for the appearances there. Surveying this after the gatherings had ceased to be so common however, a reason appeared. The line between two summits of the hills, together with the position of a small Neolithic pillar at the base of one of them, formed a sharp isosceles triangle whose acute point was directed precisely to the North-East – the traditional point of power at midsummer. Man therefore by erecting this pillar – quite without

other purpose — at this particular spot, had created the triangle that made what witches call a cone of power.[99]

Did early man concentrate the energy and merely manipulate it within the framework of the grid, or could he direct it as he chose? Let us look farther into the nature of the energy. Ideas about power currents are relatively new and no tradition has yet been created to provide support for them, as is the case with the idea that man's physical body is an exteriorization of an invisible subtle embodiment of the life of the mind.

Such a belief has persisted through many centuries and countless generations of mankind around the world.

'It is, however,' wrote G.R.S. Mead, in his work on the subtle body,

> the prevailing habit of the sceptical rationalism of the present day to dismiss summarily all such beliefs of antiquity as the baseless dreams of a pre-scientific age, and to dump them all indiscriminately into the midden of exploded superstitions. But this particular superstition I venture to think cannot be disposed of in so contemptuous a fashion.[37]

Mead, who wrote these words in 1919, hazarded a guess that psychology would add weight to his argument, and this has proved to be so.

The subtle body is of the material order, though of a more dynamic nature than man's physically sensible body; is normally invisible and not a diaphanous double, being fundamentally constituted of the nature of a dynamic system of energy. Mead stated, and I agree with him, that man arrived at such conclusions by analysing 'the whole of living experience without prejudice, by ·speculating on the phenomena of dreams and visions as well as on the facts of purely objective sense-data, by reasoning on what happened to them without any arbitrary exclusion of everything not given in physical perception'. Mead surmised that this speculation was determined mainly by biological and psychological considerations, and stated significantly: 'The subtle body notion may be said without exaggeration to have been what might be called the very soul of astrology and alchemy' — two subjects already discussed.

We will follow Mead's reasoning further, for it is in harmony with a particularly vital line of ley hunting thought. He claims that there was an astral or sidereal religion of antiquity which regarded man as the microcosm and the universe as the macrocosm, and that this 'philosophic astral theory set up a ladder of ascent from the Earth to the light-world'. This was the 'path of ascent'. Hand in hand with it went astrology and alchemy, the one straightforward and the other perversely camouflaged in its true purpose.

Ley hunting is a modern speculative process, far from being fully worked out, and in this book an attempt is made to be as straightforward as possible, though the author recognizes that it may well be that the great truths will be so profound as to lead in the future to a creation of an 'underground' system of contact between initiates. The end purpose is the same as that of astrology and alchemy, to come to a full understanding of one's relationship with the cosmos, and it is the subtler regions which require exploration.

This section deals with the etheric, and the problems with regard to definition have been stressed. For simplicity's sake let it be stated here that a link is being drawn between the Earth's leys as lines of etheric or spiritual/psychical energy and man's subtle body or soul – his psychical embodiment. There is so much in the ley hunter's universe pertaining to realms of the psyche, inwardly and outwardly, that to neglect this would be the creation of spectacular imbalance.

Mead attempts to make distinctions among the miasma of old and modern terms relating to the subtle body, but to avoid confusion we will work in terms of a gross physical body: a spiritual etheric body pervading the whole gross body and surrounding it; and an astral body or augoeides or radiant body, centred like a light-spark in the head, the only part of its contact with the physical body.

It is suggested here that physical, etheric and astral bodies all have a special relationship with leys. The physical body is attracted by them as pleasant routes for rambles and a challenge to make them believable as far as archaeology is concerned; the etheric body is attracted by their latent spiritual content, which is its natural environment; the astral, seemingly, also finds them an easier natural environment for release.

W.E. Butler, in *The Magician, his Training and Work*, discussing ceremonial magic, writes: 'During the many magical operations undertaken through the years, the robes become "charged" with a certain etheric energy.'

Also, while on the subject of religious rites, it seems that the gross physical body is cleansed with water, while the etheric body is cleansed or nourished with such vapours as incense.

Elementals – denizens of the etheric plane – are the subject of a separate section, but it is worth just mentioning here that there is no reason for not holding it possible that extra-terrestrial beings live on the etheric plane of certain planets of our galaxy, vibrating at their different rate and invisible to us, our astronomers and space probes, also that their vehicles exist in this dimension and that certain sightings are privileged only because someone tunes in his inner vision to them, quite probably while on a ley, and even that the dragons seen in the sky had such a real existence as manipulations of the intelligence which now chooses the more 'scientific' UFO forms.

The entry of ley hunting into the etheric domain has brought researchers into contact not only with occult and spiritual bodies and individuals, but also the dowsing fraternity. The writer has spent much time drawing attention to the link between ley hunting and widely divergent religious thought, and treated dowsing in a relatively simple manner. It is now worth re-examining the nature of dowsing and the branches of radiesthetic practice.

Northrop and Burr, in 1935, put forward an electrodynamic theory of life, which led to the idea of man as an energy field. Subtler than this electrodynamic field is the psi-field, posited for the formation of theories regarding precognition and extra-sensory perception, the psi-field being etheric.

It is through the psi-field that the dowser perceives by feedback the object sought for, and radiesthetic diagnosis is performed similarly. The practitioner utilizes a geometric arrangement to find the required answer and the psi-field has a functional geometric pattern. This pattern also exists in DNA (deoxyribonucleic acid), the genetic information store-house

According to David Tansley, the atoms of a man's physical body are derived from the physical plane, and his psi or etheric force field is derived from the planet's etheric field. Therefore the physical cell should reflect the archetypal pattern of the etheric web, which in turn should reflect the energy field pattern in which he is immersed. We are back to 'as above, as below', and into molecular biology.

As long ago in modern, as opposed to prehistoric, times as 1661, Joseph Glanville concluded that thoughts may be transmitted through the ether as sounds through air. Tansley's following comment can be read just as well, I believe, with regard to ley power: 'Anyone dealing with psi phenomena, and theorizing about the transmission and reception of information over distances, as occurs in dowsing, is going to have to seek beyond the known electromagnetic fields in order to find answers to the problems this phenomenon poses.' This echoes the ley hunter's need to seek an answer to ley power beyond electromagnetic fields.

I have been told by an entity, through a psychometrist, that leys are partly a communications network, though not in such specific detail as Iris Campbell received from a psycho-metric reading at Long Meg and her Daughters stone circle in Cumberland. She wrote:

> This was the central wireless receiving station where they, so to speak, 'tuned in' to all other stations throughout the land. They picked up the Earth vibrations on these stones and they transmitted their messages on the stones by tapping . . . The contact was made by any ordinary psychometric means; it seems that in this case, and in order to pick up the currents, they would use the palms of the hands and transmit to the pineal by the nervous system, i.e., transmitted to the mental receptive consciousness and then to the spiritual body.

All the stones are tuned to the principal pillar outside the circle, this being of local Cumberland stone unlike the granite stones forming the main ring of the circle. The large pillar was of a 'lower vibration', which tuned in to the Earth's vibrations at the site, the other stones being valueless for picking up 'terrestrial vibrations'. However, Long Meg converted the vibrations to a 'higher vibration' which the granite was able to take up.

Miss Campbell also referred to the site as the 'control room' or 'engine room', and 'in conclusion I would say that this was an *absolute* wireless station, in fact a telepathic junction for healing centres as well'. She added that the magnetism is withdrawn by fairies and conveyed to the 'flower and vegetable kingdom' they tend.

The Revd A.D. Duncan has also commented on the telegraph system which leys form as one of their functions:

> The magical-cum-religious system of the Celts established lines of psychic communication, traceable on the map as a system of triangles and pentangles. It has been the experience of not a few psychic people to find themselves, when on a 'line', either knowingly or unknowingly, suddenly and inexplicably aware of what is going on at the other end of the line. The points of intersection and the apices of the triangles are normally the sites on which the cult was practised and they are frequently places where a considerable disturbance can be made, psychically, by unwise 'dabbling'.[11]

There are other ramifications to a theory of an all-pervading ether which allows thoughts to be carried over great distances. This could account for persons unknown to one another in different parts of the world making the same discovery simultaneously and the requirement that patents give not only the day but hour of registration. It could also explain how the same symbols occur around the world, and identical edifices exist in different continents, the ideas which created these being transmitted via the ether, and therefore, conceivably, making the diffusionist theory unnecessary, as too the belief in a single worldwide civilization. Such psychic transmissions would produce from a common origin architecture and myths styled to suit a race and its environment but broadly similar. This leads to the possibility that an Atlantean culture was not carried around the world by survivors and colonists from a physical Atlantis, but that separate civilizations drew from a knowledge storehouse which existed, and may still exist, on the etheric plane. Another possibility to account for similarities of design and expression around planet Earth is that astral travellers returned to their homes after seeing structures in other parts of the world and repeated them in their own lands.

It is also possible that leys act as transmitters for emotions, rather than messages. There is a theory that a strong emotion or feeling carries a charge of force which can affect the person at whom it is directed, and the rites of Christians, occultists, witches and members of such New Age groups as the Aetherius Society seemingly point in this direction.

A ley point at which a rite of this kind is performed could well be a focal point from which emotions, good or evil, would radiate with the ley energy. I understand that the Aetherius Society, in 'charging' its hills, believes that the resultant energy released remains at the focal point and continues to radiate from there, whether by leys or not I do not know, but this seems probable. It also would seem that witches' activities at ley points may also act similarly, though there is no indication that witches are generally aware of ley power. Neither is there any reason to suppose that Christians' worship does not similarly radiate from churches on leys.

The effect upon the ley should be relative to the strength of the transmission from the transmitter(s), but the effect upon the receiver may not be simply relative to his own sensitivity, for he may have no awareness if it was beneficial or unpleasant psychic attack.

If this sounds far-fetched, consider those people you know. Can you sometimes 'sense' a person's kindness without even knowing them, or feel evil radiate from someone, or sensuality? Do some people invigorate you simply by their presence, while others depress you and make you feel drained? You register instinctively some people's inner nature by a kind of receiving mechanism, while you can feel others drawing vitality from you. Some may arouse erotic feelings, or hostility, or others make you feel warm and nearer mankind, while others cause feelings of uncleanliness and suspicion.

Witches, it seems, develop emotional capacity and project to deities in the sky; Aetherius Society members by a reverse process will power down from the sky; Christians send emotional power out to their universal God; and the magician will project it at an enemy; Spiritualists in faith healing project to those who are ill.

The argument for leys as transmitters of thought has been stated, and it can be developed to include encouragement of fertility of plants. Cleve Backster, director of Backster Research Foundation, New York, employed a polygraph — used to test emotional stimulation of human beings — on plants, and found that they registered pleasure, apprehension, fear and relief, and that such responses not only covered threats to their well being but even to persons with whom they were closely associated. Even more remarkable, he found that the responses were registered when the plants were threatened by him from considerable distances away.

It is not, I think, idle speculation to suggest that what we call fertility rites with mumbo-jumbo incantations to 'the gods' were in fact reasoned appeals and encouragements to the plants to grow to the best of their abilities. The rites were aimed at the crops and not at deities. Such rites, performed at ley points, would have concentrated etheric energy to radiate their thoughts and hopes across the country.

The implications in this are enormous, presuming that the notion is viable. By willing plants to grow by appeals or threats, much famine in the world could be alleviated.

It is here important that we consider again geometry in the context of medicine and leys.

Our model for the medical basis of the argument is the psionic chart, used by radiesthesists to diagnose and treat patients. It is composed of three basic geometric symbols of specific dimensions. Symbolically the square represents personality, or the four combined energies of the physical, etheric, emotional and mental force fields. At the centre is a circle, the symbol of centres of power within the etheric field. It is within a downward pointing triangle, representing material and involutionary activity.

David Tansley describes the psionic chart as 'a graphic

example of combined, symbolic geometric forms that key themselves to the patterns emerging from the etheric formative forces'.[110]

Throughout the chart energies can manifest and reveal 'the subtlest imprints of disease upon the human life field', the combination of geometric symbols providing the basis for exploring 'energy relationships in health and disease'. The hypothesis is that patient and practitioner are geometrically linked during the diagnosis.

Tansley develops his argument by drawing two triangles with a common base, forming a diamond with emanative energy at the apex of each and the points at each end of the base being receptive. The points are:

Emanative – at apex of upward pointing triangle; patient who gives off energies into psi-field.

Evocative – left end of the base line; represented on physical level by any one of the Turenne witnesses.

Magnetic – right end of the base line; represented by patient's blood spot.

Distributive – at apex of the other triangle; a positive centre of force within the psi-field of the practitioner.

There may be much here to coax ley hunters and dowsers into seeking correspondences with the ley system and ancient wisdom. Could such triangles of ley points provide clues as to the direction of ley energy flow? Does the blood spot have any correspondence with debased human sacrifice practices which various authorities have claimed to sometimes be utilized for divinatory purposes?

I am struck also by the words of Alice Bailey, in *Esoteric Astrology*: 'This diamond shaped formation of the interrelated energies is the prototypal pattern which lies behind the etheric network and is its final conditioning influence as far as our earth is concerned.' I have noted a diamond pattern on the recumbent stone of the Aberdeenshire stone circle at Midmar.

Tansley adds:

The symbol is a single unit of the psi-field. By taking its pattern and extending it into a multi-dimensional network, it forms a vast geometrically structured force field. Each line is potentially positive and negative, and each confluence of lines contains the potential of emanative, evocative, magnetic and distributive qualities.

This should interest researchers as it is accepted that the ley system is a vast geometrical layout, is multi-dimensional, and to most researchers is a network of forces.

David Tansley refers to Buckminster Fuller's geodesic domes having the psi-field pattern utilized for practical purposes. He also mentions Fuller's comments upon the geometric patterning and states, 'high energy charges refuse to take the long way round to their opposite pole'. Fuller says that triangular systems represent the shortest, most economical network of energy.

Tansley also refers to G.D. Wasserman's assumption that though psi-field energy interacts with ordinary matter fields, it is almost absent or extremely small, so psi-fields can be propagated over long distances without absorption. This is really about E.S.P., but it suggests that ley power may in fact during flow not lose any strength — which may be considered in opposition to the idea that stones were placed as 'boosters' into the system, rather than 'markers'.

Yet it is these stones which mark the way for seekers to not only comprehend the etheric, and gain the inner vision necessary to see its lifeforms, but return to a time when beings on this earth had less dense bodies which were better attuned to natural sources of power. The Fall of Man could consequently describe the process which led to man's loss of sensitivity and degeneration into a denser state. The Aquarian Age may be bringing the influences which, if tapped, will raise us to a higher frequency. Atlantis, as has been suggested, may be an etheric area and civilization of beings on such a level, and perhaps Atlantean influences played a part in the harnessing of ley power by Megalithic Man.

Many individuals and spiritual New Age groups are pursuing an interest in the etheric and seeking to raise their vibrations. Roger McGuinn, of the Byrds, a folk-rock group, told *Record Mirror* (19 June, 1971), referring to the group's version of Bob Dylan's song, 'Mr Tambourine Man':

To me the 'Tambourine Man' was Allah. The eternal life force — it was almost an Islamic concept. '5D' was very intellectual — a metaphysical trip based on the ethereal mesh of the universe. I was aware of the ambiguity which some people might read into it about drugs but that was not my intention, nor was it my intention with '5D' or 'Mr. Spaceman'.

This recognition of the ether's power and value has been felt by many sensitives, who understand the nature and importance of the etheric double. Geoffrey Hodson has described the etheric double as 'the connecting link between the inner and outer man and the container of the vital energy or *prana* received physically from the sun and superphysically from the spiritual sun'.[24]

It is an occult truth that planets have their devas and a spritual nature, and it is this which astrologers are aware of and make their calculations from. John Foster Forbes has written of the spiritual sun:

I know that it is common knowledge to look upon the sun merely as a physical mass of burning substance; to think of the sun otherwise as a live world, the home of many glorious inhabitants, conveys with it to the material mind nothing more than ridicule; one's powers of appreciation of Celestial things are not centred in material concept; you must have had at some time long before these incarnations something of the element within your being that makes for solar consciousness, otherwise the very mentioning of such things is as anathema.

How greatly the peoples of this world have lost this consciousness! Even those who once had it are slow to regain it. Such a consciousness brings back to one the memory and understanding of all true spiritual science. Physicists of today will never recover the knowledge and wisdom of the cosmos. Such things are not recoverable on the mental, intellectual plane; their apprehension, comprehension and final realisation are dependent on a re-correlation of all the powers of one's being; a gradual but most purposeful return along the true Masonic path of reinitiation until stage by stage the ancient wisdom and knowledges are reached again in a sense that 'become' within ourselves as part of ourselves; not as mere beliefs which are handed out to you, but as integral elements of our own selves. This is the Bread of Heaven, the Celestial manna for weary souls retracing their steps from out of this world's wilderness. .

The emphasis is most strong therefore where the Sun or Solar Myth is concerned. For nine-tenths of the great myths are linked up with the Sun. Why should this be? Simply because in most ancient times the dwellers upon this earth knew what the Sun was. To them it was a most glorious world, for they had power (in higher vision and under circumstances of high transcension) to draw into their very being elements of solar content which gave to them an entirely different conception of life to the debased material concept that now obtains here; they experienced thereby a joyance and, as it were, a kind of ecstasy which is far beyond any appreciation of what we can formulate in these days; it was an ecstasy so sublime that it was there very all in all and all sufficiency; nothing in those days was hurtful; there was no pain, no want, no loss of separation; no injustice, no jealousy; for true conscience and consciousness brought open vision in all things and absolute understanding. These are the conditions that all celestial worlds live under; yes that even this world lived under and will live under again when the veils are parted and we shall see as we are seen.[14]

The megalith builders, I assume, understood this and sought not to draw extra warmth from the Sun, but spiritual energy. Their lives were spent in applying spiritual physics to get maximum benefit by their stone machines from the Sun.

The physical effects from the Sun, not the spiritual ones, are the harmful ones. Varying effects from too much sunlight include sunstroke, kidney failure, sunburn (a first degree burn), scarring, cancer (malignant melanoma), heat exhaustion, blind spots in the retina, and much more.

Jimmy Goddard has taken a particular interest in harmful aspects of solar radiation as he is particularly susceptible. He claims that seasons and the Sun's position in the sky can affect health.[87]

So treat the Sun with the respect it deserves.

Pneuma

'It is clear then that, while men believed in the pneuma as agent in nature and in man's mental operation, and called the manipulation of that pneuma by the name alchemy, this word could be applied to several different processes: first, to operations with distilled and sublimed substances in the laboratory, to something that we could call a

material chemistry of volatile bodies; secondly, to a mental process in which a magician attempted to draw on the pneuma outside him and to project that pneuma into a vessel and fix it so that it could be handled as a material substance; thirdly, to manipulations of the pneuma or spirit of man, which could in fact amount to a truly mystic process. Let alchemy be called "a chemistry of the spirit", and it will be possible to understand its many aspects and the conflicting views of those who have not grasped its essential features.' — F. Sherwood Taylor (The Alchemists).

Ley hunting can be archaeological alchemy, a process by which the spiritual nature of our prehistoric heritage can be known and the researcher achieve the same quality of spirituality.

The alchemy accredited, perhaps dubiously, to Hermes Trismegistus has as its key a doctrine of pneuma. In Latin the term *spiritus*, and in Indian *prana*, have the same significance, but the term has no correspondence in the English language. This writer will attempt to show it to have a correspondence in some degree with the doctrine of the ether. The Ancients regarded pneuma as the agent which linked the universality of all matter and was the agent in effecting all changes in nature. It was a life force which caused not only growth, as in living things, in physical or spiritual stature, but was instrumental in change, physically as in transmutation of metals or human spirituality. Also the alchemists identified pneuma with the substance mercury. Pneuma linked Heaven and Earth, contained all the power of the cosmos.

The Philosopher's stone was to be solidified pneuma.

The concept of pneuma is now discredited. As chemistry sprouted from alchemy, the notion of subtle matters of the seventeenth and eighteen centuries such as ether, which was a descendant of pneuma, were no longer regarded as having life or being akin to mind. Ether was the last to be withdrawn from respectability by science, and went underground into the realms of the occult.

A new lease of life for the pneuma concept was brought about at the point in history when strict scientific disciplines were gaining ground. Science found the religious account of the world and that of science incompatible, but the idea of a middle pneuma to resolve the old with the new materialistic view was welcomed by the seventeenth-century public, under the name of hermetic philosophy.

Hermetic philosophy not only has a number of writings given Hermes's name within its framework, but was culled from several sources. The philosophy sought to defend such sciences as alchemy, astrology and natural magic. Like ley hunting it was a science in which spirituality had a rational place. It was, of course, mysterious, but then nuclear physics seems like a secret doctrine to the uninitiated.

At its core the philosophy had a chain of descent from God to matter, which was compatible with Christian theology, and as has been shown is essential to the esoteric view of leys and their special place in this scheme.

As now, this philosophy was inspiring, but only to a minority. As science could not weigh or measure such substances as pneuma, and influences such as those of the stars were incalculable to their satisfaction, the philosophy was discarded. Refuted, discredited, but not dead; like God, hermetic truths are subtle but can be reached by patience and understanding.

The Greek Stoics who developed the theory of pneuma postulated several kinds of pneuma coexisting in a body; uniting it, giving it animation and giving the power of rational thought. As with the ether it was the fifth element, the quintessence. It also introduced the theory that several substances could share the same volume at the same time, which is a great truth and a much disputed one. Those who have seen elementals know its reality. Aristotle explained heredity within the framework of pneuma, and we now see that the comparable ether has the pattern of DNA.

In religious conjecture some Stoics identified pneuma with God, which was a reasonable supposition considering its infinite interpenetrative nature, the monotheistic view it upheld in a predominantly polytheistic world, and its linking man and the cosmos in a marvellous unity.

A writer who signed his article, 'Beyond the Material Plane', in the March 1972 issue of *Cosmic Paper*, Georges O., gives a list of names attributed to this linkage between man and the universe —

> Ancient Chinese — vital energy; Ancient Hindu — prana; Polynesian Huna —· mana; Paracelsus — Munis (alchemy); Van Helmont — Magnale Magnum [i.e. Holy Grail]; Mesmer — animal magnetism; Reichenbach — odic force; Keely — motor force; Blondot — N-rays; Radiesthesists — etheric force; L.E. Eeman — 'X' force; Current Western medicine — psychosomatic field [?]; Soviet scientists — bioplasmic energy; Czech scientists — psychotronic energy.

Elementals

> *'It was found that someone's aunt had one day been sitting in a train when she looked up and saw what was obviously a little gnome, sitting on the railway embankment, pulling a flower to pieces. He looked up, gave her a wry disinterested glance and returned to his flower.' — Betty Wood.*[118]

The road into Carlisle from the massive marshalling yard at Kingmoor is narrow, and while walking down it towards the overgrown tump by an old empty mansion house, I had to step on to the verge as a car approached. Continuing walking through the grass that sunny afternoon I stepped on to a stone. I halted, looked down, and it glistened. It was quartz: it had been worked into a convex shape and was deeply embedded. I touched it for about half a minute and then walked a couple of paces. Then I saw something move a yard or so in front of me. The thing leapt like a frog and was frog-shaped, but about three feet high. It was brown but its form was hazy, difficult to describe, but the effect was not dissimilar to a television screen when the lines go crazy. I had the impression that what I had seen was an elemental and that I perceived it at the edge of my consciousness.

It was an earth gnome, described by Geoffrey Hodson as lanky, sometimes solitary, and disproportionate to our senses. He regarded them as relics of Lemurian days and possibly representations of such times. In England they are always black or, as I saw, peat brown, but he, unlike me, found their atmosphere decidedly unpleasant.[23]

I never expected to see an elemental, though I was perfectly willing to believe in their existence.

Two aspects of my experience are worthy of consideration, that is if my testimony is to be believed and that I did not have an hallucination. One is the fact that the experience took place on a ley; the second is the possibility that the quartz itself was instrumental somehow in bringing about the sighting, i.e. raising my consciousness while I touched it.

In dealing with the phenomenon of elementals, a belief in a different rate or rates of vibration is essential, and also the reality of persons with clairvoyant vision, capable of tuning in to a subtle world around us inhabited by life forms of a different nature to ours. Certain people, by discipline, open up correct channels for seeing and communicating with entities on this other dimension. A person on a drug trip, someone at a crisis during an illness, or when drunk, may open the door to perception of elementals for transitory periods, whereas others achieve self-conscious control of inner vision. It is suggested by the author that on touching the quartz boulder near Carlisle he momentarily raised his vibrations to the level at which elementals exist, and that this would indicate the etheric and extra-dimensionality of ley power. It suggests that a person on a ley is more likely to see an elemental, and also that ley power is their environment.

But the quality of the sighting of an elemental may vary considerably, and also the object seen. Betty Wood recalled the case of the police station where the staff were baffled by the fact that all the drunks they took in saw the same pink crocodile in the same corner of the same cell. However, it is not pink crocodiles which interest us, but nature spirits. As to the quality of the sighting, E.L. Gardner, in a preface to Geoffrey Hodson's book *Fairies at Work and Play*, writes: 'Their motion or vibration is so comparatively rapid, their laws of activity so subtle, compared with the physical world that words fail to describe what is seen, and the vision often fails to record all that one might wish to know of any given fact.'

Frank Lockwood, however, related to me an occasion when he came face to face with an elemental, who was almost completely green but of basically human form. The elemental told him that he was human and then after some conversation walked away and vanished. His disappearance was by a prehistoric mound which had been truncated by farming. Here again we find a prehistoric monument taking a critical place in an encounter.

If we refer again to Gardner's preface, another point of similarity, though more hypothetical, emerges.

> And what is it he [Hodson] has observed? A vast variety of etheric and astral forms, large and small, working together in organised co-operation on what we must call the *life* side of Nature, stimulating growth, bringing colour to the flowers, brooding over beautiful spots, plunging in waves and waterfalls, dancing in the wind and the sunlight – in fact, another order of evolution running parallel to and blended with our own.

A study of prehistory along the lines laid out in this book brings the researcher to the obvious conclusion that prehistoric man lived not only in harmony with nature, but sought to retain the ecological balance and enjoy nature's splendour. He lived to the same fundamentals as the elementals.

Before delving further into the world of elementals it is necessary to dismiss the theory that fairyfolk are a memory of a race of tiny humans who existed in prehistoric times, as some authorities have suggested. Elementals are ultra-terrestrials. Where they fit into the whole spectrum of ultra-terrestrial life is not easy to answer. Are fairies at one vibratory level and ghosts, poltergeists, giants, etc., each at another level? Who knows? Let us just consider first what we may call elementals – the fairies, goblins and other nature spirits.

Elementals need not be seen as lower forms of life than man – or higher. Their tasks are generally associated with plants, and it should be remembered that for prehistoric man growth was all-important and therefore was presumably carried out in harmony with nature, in partnership with the activities of elementals.

Geoffrey Hodson has written of 'small sub-microscopic etheric creatures' energizing plants, and this led him to some revolutionary insights into the nature of growth. Those who would laugh at Hodson's revelations of tiny 'builders' making flower stems and petals, watching over blooms for a while even after being cut, to the point of following them into a house, should consider whether it is the elementals who work exceptionally hard when a grower threatens to destroy a plant if it will not bloom.

As for the forms of the larger elementals, Gardner's opinions are most interesting. He states that such beings have no fixed body, but if they materialize they will usually use the thought-form created by the observer and appear in traditional gnome guise as in children's picture books. 'The elemental life rejoices to jump into a ready-made thought-form as much as an active child delights in dressing up,' writes Gardner. But the elemental I saw was an exception, as it differed completely from what my notion of an elemental would be. And what of the beings regarded as ufonauts? They seem to fit whatever guise is expected — black 'diving' suit with helmet, angelic hermaphroditic features, slant-eyed and pixie-eared, etc., to suit the investigator's personal expectations. Thus we may connect two wholly separate branches of ultra-terrestrial life.

If we examine another passage we may discover other links between leys and elementals.

> They may live as the ensouling life of a tree or group of trees, the magnetism of their bodies stimulating the far slower activities of the tree, the circulation of sap, etc.; or they may be engaged in raying out strong influences over certain spots, termed 'magnetic centres' which have been put under their charge . . .[23]

Hodson's words suggest a number of speculative ideas: they could explain why certain trees are regarded as sacred; that a co-operative agriculture in which man and elemental worked together could produce better crops, perhaps three a year; that by agreement there was concentration of effort in only certain areas which would result in a totally different landscape to that hypothesized by those archaeologists who build up a Neolithic scenery based upon only geological and meteorological considerations; and that the psychic atmosphere of certain sites is maybe partially dependent upon the elemental incumbents' nature.

I am told that a Scottish New Age group is working in partnership with elementals and having extraordinary agricultural results. If so, this bears out Gardner's comment:

> As we cease to ignore the activities of the devas and nature-spirits, and recognise their partial dependence on human mentality and the amazing response forthcoming when recognition is given, we shall find many of our difficulties and problems solved for us and the world far more wonderful than anything we have yet conceived.

Those who seek the ageless wisdom are attracted to the sacred spots, the places where elementals also find greatest joy. Our love for such places can only help make extra-dimensionals work harder.

The speculation that there is a ley intelligence and that Albion is a living god or goddess is viewed favourably by many researchers, and notes such as these indicate lines along which such ideas may be extended and verified. The giants are ultra-terrestrials much involved with the ley system and I find it a feasible hypothesis that each area of Albion will have its own chief deity and that these in turn are bigger and more evolved than many stages of evolving consciousness on other levels.

Hodson deals with manmade entities formed by black magicians and this would tie in with the fact that sensitives have determined that certain sites have been defiled psychically. Do unpleasant entities of this nature still lurk at certain sites? Certainly some sites should be approached with great caution.

Perhaps a comment by Hodson gives us the clearest indication by a sensitive as to the relationship between elementals and leys, when he notes that these beings operate instinctually, 'largely by playing along the lines of force — stimulating to them — which form the geometrical patterns set up in the all-pervasive ether by the emitted and vibrating THOUGHT — WORD — FORCE'.[24]

It is as James Stephens comments in his work of fiction, *The Crock of Gold*: 'A leprechaun is of more value to the Earth than is a prime minister or stockbroker, because a leprechaun dances and makes merry, while a prime minister knows nothing of these natural virtues.'

One winter night with three friends I was out for a walk in Hartlepool. We were aged about ten years old and were passing a mansion house, then closed and boarded up, but now a Roman Catholic school. The grounds were overgrown and it had an eerie atmosphere. We were contemplating whether to explore, when two of us saw a smoky, white phantom shape, man-sized and of a vaguely human shape. Two of my friends could not see it, but after it disappeared we climbed the wall and threw stones in the direction of its dematerialization, until a woman from the house next door came out and yelled at us. We were more afraid of her than the ghost . . . and fled.

Years later a schoolfriend to whom I was relating this tale said that he had been outside the same house and seen a hand hanging out of a window. Tramps, apparently, were then in the habit of dossing down in the building, but my schoolmate ventured inside . . . and found no one.

The house is not on a confirmed ley, but is on high ground not far from some ancient sites and places where prehistoric artifacts have been found.

That ghosts exist, I am, of course, convinced, having seen one, but the fact that two out of four people present saw it suggests that psychic faculties are involved.

Whether we accept that all ghosts are, in fact, dead persons who have not completely 'passed over' is debatable. Are they 'live' ultra-terrestrials like elementals? Whatever they are, they are elusive, may be demonic, mischievous, friendly, confused, ancient or modern, inhabiting castles or council houses.

When it comes to an attempt to link leys and ghosts, the evidence is so far as tenuous as the ghost's attachment to this plane which we commonly inhabit. Philip Heselton, a former editor of *The Ley Hunter*, tried to discover from the Society for Psychical Research locations of ghost sightings in order to plot them, but the society was unable to furnish this information. Ghost sightings are publicized less than UFOs and though on the earth rather than in the sky, it is not easy to determine exact locations. Hartlepool cases known to me fit no special pattern, connected with leys or otherwise. There is a famous grey lady who occasionally walks the wards of St Hilda's Hospital to the consternation of patients and staff; the hospital is close to a pre-Reformation church. But other cases in the town are seemingly unconnected with leys.

A subdivision of ghost phenomena is the headless horseman. Ian Rodger researched these and found that they had particular haunts, 'beacon hills, sunken roads and groves, cross-roads, and, rather naturally, churchyards and cemeteries'. He also found many associated with the building of a church, in which the non-Christians – the Devil, witches – were involved in attempts to stop the construction work. Rodger stated that occasionally not only is the building stopped, but the church is built elsewhere, and quoted the legend of a headless horseman commuting between the Devil's site, Rodmarton long barrow, Gloucestershire, and the church.

Less spectacular, but equally interesting, are the black dog legends. These may be not unconnected with leys and further investigation is required. Two cases which interested me involve a church and a road. There was a black dog the size of a calf which haunted Bungay, Suffolk. It allegedly ran amok in St Mary's Church on 4 August, 1577, and killed many worshippers. Scratches on the doors are attributed to it. It was still around in 1940, when a coastguard fired a bullet at a point-blank range through it. Of a different character is a friendly black dog in Essex which escorts women on a lonely country road. A woman who was rather frightened of this companionable phantom prodded her umbrella right through it to no effect.

Ley Deities

'The pyramid belongs above all to Mercury or Hermes, called by the Egyptians Thoth, the quick-

*silver deity that hovers over the straight tracks and
standing stone.' – John Michell.*[40]

Mercurial leys, quicksilver lines, elusive currents, serpent
power under the dominion of Thoth, Hermes, Mercury, Elen
and others; straight alignments between the haunts of St
Michael. There are gods and saints whom the seeker after ley
wisdom must pay homage to.

Thoth, the Egyptian precursor of Hermes and Mercury,
was also, according to John Michell, called Theutates by the
Druids, and is remembered in Albion's Tot and Toot hills.

Hermes, born in a cavern on Mount Kylene, guides
wayfarers on unknown paths, was god of tradesfolk, patron
of skilled athletes, wears wings on his hat and shoes to
indicate swiftness, was a messenger of the gods, guided souls
to the netherworld, was science or rationalization, ruled
Cancer, was patron of thieves, and had a magical wishing-rod.
Hermes Trismegistus is supposed to have written:

> It is true, without falsehood, certain and very real,
> That that which is on high is that which is below,
> And that which is below is that which is on high,
> In order that the miracle of Unity may be perpetual.

A man of many parts he is closely linked with Mercury.

Mercury, even more so than Hermes, is joined indisputably
with leys. Mercury the god, Mercury the metal and Mercury
the planet.

Mercury, the Roman deity, was the messenger of the gods
and himself the god of intelligence, eloquence and mer-
chandise. He is a middleman between the other gods and
humanity, connecting the celestial and terrestrial, just as leys
are charged by cosmic forces emanating from the heavens
uniting with forces from the Earth's interior. According to
Henry Cornelius Agrippa, the spirits of Mercury are attributed to come as a king riding on a bear (this suggests an
Arthur and Great Bear correspondence), a beautiful youth, a
woman holding a distaff, a dog, she-bear, a magpie, or a rod
(caduceus?). He has also been regarded as a guide of souls,
bearer of life and change.

Mercury the planet, though not necessarily affecting leys,

is well befitted to be called the leys' star. It is, like ley power, elusive. It dances close to the sun, generally heralding daybreak, and is devoured by its light. It rules the mind. Its gender is neuter and convertible, taking the gender of the planet in closest aspect. Mercury above all is a transmitter, whether of traffic, speech, or dissemination of knowledge.

Those born under Mercury have ley-like temperaments of being active, electromagnetic, lymphatic-nervous and herm-aphroditic; their destinies show restlessness and much travel. Success may be expected in literature, among other things. The sense with which it is associated is eyesight. It is the messenger by which we communicate between our spiritual god-self and our physical entity. Its sign is the crescent (moon symbol, representing personality), surmounting the circle (sun symbol, representing individuality), over a cross (of matter). It represents mortal mind. Mercury rules Virgo.

The sign's serpent connections are of great interest. Iris Vorel stated:

> Virgo is also represented by a serpent and so is Scorpio. Because these two symbols are frequently confused on account of their similarity, I will take them up together and explain their difference. Virgo is represented by the garter snake, that harmless and useful little destroyer of rodents and vermin. Hence it is used in the caduceus of the medical corps. In the symbol of Virgo you will easily recognise a coiling serpent with the 'staff of Hermes' drawn across its tail.
>
> Scorpio, however, is represented by the venomous reptile, a poisonous serpent, whose bite is fatal. Therefore you might find the 'sting of Scorpio' suggested in the dart at the end of its symbol.[67]

Iris Vorel also remarks that the glyphes for other zodiacal signs are related to serpents: Leo, a spermatazoa — infinitesimal serpent; Capricorn, uncoiling serpent; Aquarius, two serpents gliding in opposite directions, or a serpent gliding over the waters of truth followed by its shadow.

The caduceus was also a symbol for Aesculapius, the Roman god of medicine, and Asklepios, the Greek god of healing.

Mercury, the metal, was distilled from cinnabar by the alchemists. It is a mysterious metal which is a liquid and which can enter a mysterious amalgam with other metals and yet be distilled away from them. Ley power is a part of our earth and atmosphere, a part of and yet separate, having motion and being mysterious. Alchemists symbolized mercury in a number of ways, one of which was, significantly, as a dragon or winged serpent. This revealed the opposites of solidity (snake, earth) and mobility (wings, air). Its changeable nature made it easy to pair with the rapid movements of the little planet Mercury.

Elen, reputedly the daughter of King Cole, is Albion's equivalent of Thoth, Hermès and Mercury. She, according to *The Mabinogion*, built a system of roads 'from one castle to another throughout the Isle of Britain'. This suggests the construction of trackways following the placing of stones, mounds, etc., to mark leys. Elen, or Helen, or the Christianized form St Helen, has given rise to such names on leys as Heel, Hele, Heol and Ellie stones, Elen's roads and Elen's Causeway. Being the daughter of King Cole, or Coel, she links with the cole, coel, cold and coldharbour names common to leys. Even ley and lane are names similar to Elen.

Dan Butcher has written at length on Helen and her Middle Eastern counterpart, Semiramis, on their road-building works, connection with astral travel, UFOs, fire, and shape-shifting – particularly in the form of a dove.[66],[67] The dove connection interested this writer, and Dan Butcher's comments provided a clue as to why a dove is shaped in the landscape at Dove Cote, on the perimeter of Fleet Shot Hill zodiac, County Durham, by the Virgo sector.

Dan Butcher wrote to me:

The dove, of course, features in the Glastonbury Zodiac ... and in that representation it seems to be escaping from the head of the rider on the horse and flying straight towards the 'wheatsheaf' held in the Virgin's outstretched hand. We might see in this a representation of astral projection, the rider on the horse being the astral projector – the horse being a common symbol of the astral vehicle. The dove represents the realeased, mobile centre of consciousness. The Virgin stands for Helen or Semiramis ...

It may all sound rather far-fetched, but ...

The Fleet Shot Hill zodiac dove lies between Elwick (El – Elen) and Dalton Piercy.

There is also the Greek goddess Helen, sister of Castor and Pollux, who is associated with the pine, or as John Allegro suggests, fly agaric. Allegro also claims that Hermes, in Sumerian, means 'erect penis' and refers Castor and Pollux to the mushroom cult.

The letters EL suggest correspondences with leys: the letters form two-thirds of the word ley; the *ell* is 45 inches, 4+5 = 9, a ley number, as is *el*even; *El*ohim, gods; *el*emental, *el*f; *el*ectric; *el*an, French for vital, living force; *el*der, leader; *el*evate, levitate; *el*ect, raise to higher state; *el*astic, lengthen; *el*ope, a journey; *el*ation; etc.

From Hermes we seem to have gained the true meaning of hermits, for such people were not solely solitary mystics, but people with a duty to help direct wayfarers along unfamiliar tracks or across fords or ferries. Alfred Watkins gave several examples, to which I might add Friar Tuck.

Tuck, formerly Michael Tuck, left Fountains Abbey to become Hermit of Copmanhurst, where he tended a ferry. He fought Robin Hood and joined his band of 'merry' (a ley word) men. A fascinating account of the symbolism in the Robin Hood legends, by Gareth Knight, appeared in *Quest*, No.5. But as for Friar Tuck, it seems more than coincidence that his name was Michael. John Michell noted correspondences between St Michael and Hermes. Both were connected with high places and 'their common attribute as guides on the pathway between life and death identifies these two with the same archetype, for both Hermes with his serpent entwined wand and St Michael, impaling the dragon on his sword, represent the principle known to geomancers as the dragon current'.[40]

St Michael churches and chapels, usually perched on high places, occur particularly in the West of England and Wales. St Michael is an archangel who is captain of the heavenly host. He was regarded by early Christianity as the one who was instrumental in casting the Devil, in the form of a dragon, out of Heaven and 'into the earth'. This is stated in the Book of Revelation, which Peter Ratazzi stated in *Quest*, No. 3, is 'a rare minglement of Christian teaching, number wisdom and Hebraic clairvoyance . . . It is the most enigmatic part of the New Testament'. Does the dragon refer to a UFO or UFO dispatched from another planet as a punishment and which came to Earth? Or do we look for a reference to the impregnation of ley power, which in certain of its manifestations does seem somewhat hostile to man's well-being? The tors, as Guy Underwood claimed, have been partially altered by man and several St Michael churches stand upon these ley centres, such as those on the summits of Rough Tor and Rame Head in Cornwall, and Devon's Brent Tor. St Michael can be recognized in churches by his sword, wings, feathered legs and arms, with the devil/dragon under his feet, or by scales he holds in one hand. There is much to learn and investigate here.

St. George is the knight in armour depicted with cross on banner stepping on a dragon and thrusting a spear into the beast. He is perhaps an odd choice as England's patron saint, for it is unlikely that he ever even set foot on these shores. He was a Roman soldier, reputedly martyred for his Christian faith at Lydda, a place now in Israel, on 23 April, A.D. 303. Crusaders brought back the legend of his dragon-slaying exploits from the Middle East, and this is why he is portrayed so often as a mediaeval knight. Nevertheless it seems odd that if a dragon saint had to be chosen as patron saint, why it should not be Michael.

St Catherine of Alexandria's churches and chapels are also frequently on hill tops. Her body was supposedly transported to the top of Mount Sinai and discovered in the ninth century. She had been beaten and beheaded after having been bound on a wheel (Catherine wheel) by order of the Emperor Maxentius. A virgin, martyr and learned princess, she was the saint of young girls, nuns, scholars and wheelwrights.

St Margaret, of Antioch, was another virgin and martyr. She was swallowed by a dragon, so the legend goes, made a sign of the cross, and this caused the dragon to swell and split. This led to her being invoked by women in childbirth.

St Andrew was another dragon saint.

These saints took the place of deities in the Christian religion, which appeared following the distintegration of much of the knowledge of the ley system.

Quartz

> 'Scientists say that some of man's most difficult
> problems may be solved by crystals.' – G. Hunt
> Williamson.[62]

One of the most extraordinary aspects of the ley hunter's
researches is the somewhat baffling question of the properties
of quartz, of which no one has so far given a full appraisal.
The fact is that quartz is present in a great number of
megalithic structures, and I have seen large crystals of it at
Aberdeenshire sites, and a quartz stone led me to see an
elemental. Admittedly quartz is the commonest of minerals,
found in every class of rock, and forming under all sorts of
conditions. Flint, so greatly used by early man, is a black
compact variety of quartz, valued for the sparks given when
struck.

On the physical level, quartz possesses piezo-electric
properties; that is flawless crystals of clear quartz expand and
contract slightly when subjected to an electric field. These
are used for quartz resonators and oscillators in radio and
telecommunications. Brinsley le Poer Trench has postulated
that a piezo-electric effect is utilized in UFO propulsion. The
communications value of quartz is important for the control-
ling of radio frequencies and this aspect may be related to the
etheric vibratory level too.

If we accept that an experience of the inner light indicates
spiritual rebirth, and noting that the mystic light plays a part
in certain initiation ceremonies, we are approaching the
quartz question from a spiritual angle. Mircea Eliade records
a ceremony of Australian medicinemen in which young
aspirants are sprinkled at the initiation with 'a sacred and
powerful water', which is liquefied quartz. The aspirant is
considered to be filled with crystals and given many
supernatural abilities. 'Quartz', says Eliade, 'owes its extraordinary prestige to its celestial origin.'[13] Baiame, the master
of initiation, dropped to the Earth fragments from his quartz

throne. 'In other words,' states Eliade, 'the crystals are supposed to have fallen from the vault of heaven; they are in a sense "solidified light".' Eliade gives examples of special powers conferred upon medicinemen by quartz crystals, including seeing souls, seeing into the distance, ascent to Heaven and seeing spirit beings.

An excitingly enigmatic reference to quartz appears in a work of fiction by J.G. Ballard: 'Ignoring Quinton, he took a piece of quartz from his flying jacket and laid it on the surf. From it poured the code-music of quasars.'[4]

George Hunt Williamson has also commented on crystals and believes that they had great significance in past civilizations. He quotes Thoth as having written in his Emerald Tablets: 'In the apex of the (Great) Pyramid set I the crystal, sending the ray into "Time-Space", drawing the force out of the ether.'[63] The crystal was a capstone of crystalline copper. (Not all agree that the capstone was such, including John Michell.) Williamson also wrote: 'Copper is a stratified attention crystallized consciousness ... Copper can be the bridge between time and timelessness.'[62] All other metals have their effects in a three-dimensional world, but not copper. He also suggests that crystals may be able to 'think'. Quartz standing stones therefore might have intelligence 'within them' rather than 'behind them', though it could have something to do with elementals of the mineral kingdom which hold the intelligence. Or it may be nonsense.

It may be significant that a brief copper age followed the Neolithic, before the Bronze Age.

But to return to the communications aspect of crystals. Lapis lingua (a corrosive state of copper in its natural state) crystals cause a definite increase in telepathic powers when taped over four gland centres – pituitary, pineal, thyroids and thymus – and it seemingly stimulates their vibratory rate to allow the development of psychic forces. Edgar Cayce has described it as an aid to meditation, influential in making decisions in dealing with mental attributes and making the body more sensitive to the higher vibrations. Lapis lazuli was also recommended by Cayce.

Williamson also referred to quartz in another book, where

he wrote of granite sculptured figures around the world which at times hum, and he claims that such humming is growing louder year by year. He suggests their use to be as batteries and refers to the quartz displaying a piezo-electric effect due to tremendous pressure on the crystallized substances. Williamson first noted this at Marchahuasi, Peru.

Quartz is referred to by E.O. Gordon in his description of the Cornish circle of Boscawen-un: 'Near the centre of the nineteen standing stones is a monolith, 8ft. out of the ground, which inclines to the north-east; one of the stones is a block of quartz 4ft. high. It was "obviously placed in a post of honour", reasons Lockyer.'[20] Druids' Circle, Penmaenmawr, had its central area originally paved with quartz.

UFOs have also been linked with the crystals on leys. A correspondent to *The Ley Hunter* wrote:

> Suitable crystals, built into a ley, would provide the anode of an electric circuit, with the cathode in the UFO overhead; together they would provide something similar to a photo-electric beam — anyone stepping on to the ley would break the circuit and trigger off the reaction — in this case, the embodiment of the UFO. In the laboratory, such a circuit produces coloured images similar to an Adamski saucer. Such a circuit, probably low voltage and VHF, would explain other effects. I feel that this is one UFO theory that is open to scientific proof, and could be tested.

'Fogging' on photographs has been allied to the quartz composition of many standing stones or to the current transmitted by them. The first to report this was John G. Williams, who noticed a 'fog' patch on a contemporary photograph, and subsequently on prints taken years earlier which he had not then noticed or attributed to faulty technique. There is a strong suspicion that this is not caused by the refraction of light through the crystals, but is the result of ley power.

Others have since found 'fogging' on prints. Desmond Leslie has written of visiting Stonehenge in 1954, and on all of the photographs he took 'a column of light, like a searchlight beam, can be seen rising into the cloudswept February sky from the very centre of the Trilithon'. He suggests that archaeologists should dig deep to seek mysterious crystalline stones beneath prehistoric monuments.[28]

Referring to photographs of the Glastonbury zodiac, Muz Murray wrote: 'We tend to assume that a photograph is something without life, yet recent radiaetheric research has shown that the negative emulsion absorbs something of the psychic energy of whatever is photographed.'

I have heard one explanation that photographs taken at certain quarries and on beaches may show 'fogging' due to refraction of ultra-violet light, but it would be interesting to find cases of where a stone is particularly active or inactive and photograph it at both times and compare results.

Quartz, in its smallest unit, consists of three molecules of silicon dioxide arranged in a spiral or screw form, which can be right- or left-handed. It has the power of rotating the plane of polarization of light in either direction. The spiral and light are great symbols, and suggest the great value of quartz. In fact a book on the symbolic nature of the spiral would be greatly appreciated by researchers in several fields.

Also quartz does not have the same velocity of light through it in all directions. So when a light beam enters, it will generally be split into two rays internally, and they become polarized and vibrate according to certain lattices in the crystal as they have different refractive indices. To make a lens in the crystal you will end up with two different focuses depending on which ray you're looking at.

Quartz is the subject of some interesting folklore, which is worthy of study. Albertus Magnus said that if quartz is placed in direct sunlight, and if cold, it throws out fire; it decreases thirst if placed under the tongue; and if powdered and mixed with honey and taken by women, it fills the breasts with milk.

The Aquarian Age

'Signs of an imminent revelation of inconceivable scope are now so abundant and clear that only the wilfully blind can be unaware of the change in the psychic atmosphere that 1967 has brought.' – John Michell.

'Even in the year that has passed [1967] in production of this book the keynote of violence has become predominant in the international sub-culture, invigorating tired and sentimental forms of popular music and overshadowing the pseudo-mysticism of the John Michell/Glastonbury/Flying Saucer cult.' — Jeff Nuttal (*Bomb Culture*).

The decaying Christian tradition of the present day, with crumbling country churches, locked except on Sundays, with death-watch beetles and leaking roofs; the congregations who attend out of habit or for social esteem; the incumbent who is more a welfare worker than a go-between for God and the parish; a religion which has failed to meet the questioning attitudes of the old on after-life, who flock to Spiritualism; the young, with a spiritual sense which probes beyond hymns and sermons, who have looked towards drugs, meditation and the prehistoric heritage; and the middle-aged who send their children to Sunday school while they sleep off the effects of roast beef and Yorkshire pudding.

Yet there are those today, with an Aquarian Age being born and a coming millennium to support their view, believing that a new era of cosmic consciousness, a returned paradise on Earth, a blessed eternity, is dawning. The rediscovery of leys, a comprehensible and true vision of prehistory, widespread use of drugs, the coming of UFOs in abundance, are factors which have been promulgated as indicators that a new consciousness is imminent. Should we accept this? There is a cosmic renewal doctrine. Will there be a physical or psychical Second Coming? Has it already come? Has Atlantis risen in our consciousnesses? Is the Wasteland to be revived? Who is the Grail Knight? Is Arthur walking the old straight track at this very minute? Fanciful ideas?

I believe in reality, and as I look around me and read the papers, it is obvious to me that such an idealistic view can only disappoint. Yet magic is afoot. A generation is grasping truths which are surfacing in their consciousnesses, which can be made manifest and lead to a richer life individually and socially. Others are becoming activated by the persons who first comprehended the vision of past, present and future.

The impetus increased significantly in 1967, and deplorable though the view of Jeff Nuttal's quoted above is, it was inevitable that flowerpower would wither, for the original purity of it was debased by materialistic, capitalistic intervention.

I have always been dubious about old and new religions, and prefer to regard spiritual values as one's own, and that their development can only be personal, and not collective. Alchemists of old worked alone, and so must today's. It is extremely romantic to have a belief in the Great Year with its regeneration of the cosmos by a destruction of all existing forms, a return to chaos, and then a new creation. It has about it an attractiveness in that it is not associated with any dogmatic religion, no particular dates for it are computed and its fulfilment gives one something not only to look forward to, but presents a reason for living. Many people in the New Age groups and ufology preach a gospel of coming chaos followed by a Golden Age. I cannot help but feel that this is wishful thinking, while being not a little perplexed by the vitality of young people's unswervable belief and longing for a New Age. I admit to a degree of cynicism here which may sound at odds with everything in this book. The true meaning of the incredible realizations and discoveries during the past fifty years in the subject of speculative archaeology is not yet fully understood. We are far from the end of the old straight track. But it has given me new insights into many subjects and into deeper consciousness, yet it has not yet reached the politicians, the armaments manufacturers, the military, the racial extremists, all those who act to reduce civil liberty, the Church's hierarchy, the judiciary, the town planners, the chemical plant owners, and all who have the power of life and death and disharmony over the populace and the environment. Our slight realization in scope and numbers may penetrate a 'collective consciousness', but it has to compete with the forces of evil, greed and *laissez-faire.* We are but nightingales singing in a midnight thunderstorm.

I know that many people in New Age Groups have become interested in leys and sought to include them within their philosophical framework, and that their spirit guides have given approval to the network linking power centres. Many such groups warn of chaos and/or preach of a coming glorious age. But are we on the threshold of either? Changes will come, but they will be slow and of little immediate consequence spiritually. Individuals will benefit spiritually from this subject, but it need not necessarily follow that any noticeable change will come to humankind, or that this spirituality will be recognized by orthodox religions. Mind cults, spiritual societies, New Age communes may win converts, but their numbers are small compared with the apathetic, grey, nine-to-five zombies which make up the greater part of society.

There have always been those who have chosen a spiritual path outside orthodox religion, and I number myself among these. But such have always been in a minority and the lure of idiotic, messianic cults has always been present. I would only warn that one must not be gullible, but carefully assess, rationally, anything spiritual, and not be drawn simply by the cries of salvation from an apocalypse.

The subject matter of this book promises no chaos or Golden Age; no certainty of spiritual fulfilment; no set pattern of consciousness expansion. The subject can be seen, in one form, as antiquarian alchemy, but the ley system is only a guide and fabric to this and not a means to an end, for the individual must be receptive to its influence and use it how he sees fit, how it best suits his aims. Not everyone in a Christian church expects to find God there, and nor should an inquirer into prehistoric truth expect to find anything which is not within his heart and his mind.

The ley hunter need not approach his subject with the slightest wish for spiritual enlightenment, just as many visitors to old parish churches go there to admire the architecture and not seek God.

For those who do wish to learn spiritual truths, leys offer an alternative to the staid traditionalism and dogma of the Church, and provide what only promises to be a possibility. Of course, they need not be necessary in this context, for the ability to become spiritual, in whatever sense one determines this, is in the final analysis within oneself.

The paradisal syndrome is rather pathetic. It means a

plenitude of food, yet there is no foreseeable end to famine; absolute liberty, when dictators of every kind from parents to teachers, to shop stewards, to bosses, to religious leaders, to politicians in general make this laughable; to the abolition of work, when all we find are growing dole queues of men who want to work; to immortality, while paradoxically heart surgeons prolong lives in a world of population explosion; peace, when each nation seeks more lethal weaponry.

Most spiritually oriented people believe we are now in the Age of Aquarius. It has been predicted as starting as long ago as the time of Elizabeth I; the Baha'i faith dates it from 1844; perhaps magical flowerpower 1967 was the start; Arthur Shuttlewood gave the beginning as 16 May, 1968; and others give dates in the future up to 2062. I favour 1967.

Three New Age groups which look forward to a better future are The Atlanteans, White Eagle Lodge and The Aetherius Society, each aware of and interested in leys.

The Aetherius Society, founded in November 1960 by Dr George H. King, believes that the UFOs' mission and that of their crews is a spiritual one, and the group has 'energized' various peaks in Britain, especially around Warminster, such as Glastonbury Tor, Silbury Hill, Stonehenge, Cadbury Castle and Hill, Cradle Hill, Battlesbury, Teffont Magna, Chew Magna, Cley Hill, Heaven's Gate and also points on the outskirts of Bristol and Marlborough.[46]

Whether we look upon these societies with cynicism or not, the notion that leys and centres may be reactivated or superactivated is a strong one. I have seen the result of human intervention between the Sun and the terrestrial current, and been astonished. This book is a spur to research into this, and the means whereby we can make our dreams come true. Megalithic Man had a dream and he was 'awakened'. We have little but nightmares and slight control over them. Many have their daydreams of an Edenic future. The gates of Eden are on the leys and in our heads. Few have the strength to open them.

22. Further Aspects of Leys

Research into leys has bred an extraordinarily broad amount of speculations into a diversity of aspects of life, and some of these not investigated earlier in this work can be summarized for investigators to probe.

Crimes of violence. It has been suggested that these, and perhaps also suicides, occur more frequently by percentage on leys, because of the electromagnetic field disturbing the brain.

Road accidents. These also have been related to leys and the possibility of an electromagnetic field affecting the driver's brain or the vehicle's mechanism. I tend to take this seriously, having been the victim of a bad smash by a pond, where within one month at least three other cars left the road within a hundred-yard stretch.

Illness. The late Guy Underwood found that certain geodetic lines had effects upon the body, causing rheumatism, etc., and leys have also been seen to engender healing powers. However, as Arthur Lawton found, the energy can cause disease, and I have heard that the Black Death travelled not from person to person, but was transmitted along leys.

Good and evil. The dualities in ley influence lead one to surmise that one may apportion good and bad influences occurring. It is said that the Chinese dragon has 117 scales imbued with powers of good and 36 with powers of evil. $1+1+7 = 9$; $3+6 = 9$; and the total 153 is $1+5+3 = 9$ — the ley number. Also, in the Bible, 153 is mentioned by St John with reference to fish scales.

Serial time. Perhaps a person on a ley may see into the past or future. Any reports of such happenings could be checked to see if there is strong psychic energy at the spot, as an associate of Arthur Shuttlewood has stated that the mechanism for Dunne's serial time is largely governed by terrestrial magnetism.

Disappearances. I have been told by a reliable person that an officer working in the field of aircraft safety has discovered two places where aircraft vanish as if through 'a hole in the sky'. One is off Malta, the other is the Bristol Channel. If the latter exists then certain other perplexing facts may be linked. In *The Illuminer* magazine for September/October 1970, Gerald Lovell quotes a couple who saw a UFO descend into the sea off Minehead, Somerset. He then postulates a subterranean passage through Somerset and even Wiltshire; refers to fresh water reputedly appearing in the middle of salt water between Brean Down and Steep Holm Island, and states that this fresh water patch is on a suspected orthoteny.

There is perhaps a slim chance that people could disappear while on leys, as there is the possibility that they are connected to other dimensions and another time-space sequence.

Misfortunes. Those who cause damage to prehistoric sites may become the victims of 'coincidental misfortune'. An Irish correspondent, Tim O'Sullivan, wrote to me of a farmer who had a rath destroyed in one of his fields. Within a year he and his cattle had died of rare diseases; a horse was strangled in the field; one of his children was frightened by something indescribable and in panic broke a hip; the bulldozer driver was injured immediately afterwards when the vehicle capsized on him, then his house burned down, he moved away and his next residence burned down.

People who have attempted to move the 'dragon's tombstone' at Sockburn had also had misfortunes, and there are many other such tales. Also the remains of an old oak standing in Carmarthen has been the cause of alterations to two road schemes, for Merlin is said to have prophesied:

When this oak shall tumble down,
So will fall Carmarthen town.

Ley sound. Tones are created, according to one sensitive, when the Sun creates a 'high tide' of ley energy. Among the tones are a 'burr' and 'whinny', on an ultra-dimensional level. If ley power is generated, then it must produce a sound as friction will be in action.[76]

Ley colour. The same sensitive has referred to elusive energy colours visible on an ultra-dimensional level.

Astral travel. Dan Butcher has suggested that astral projection may be aided for a projector if he finds himself on a ley. This could mean that structures of great similarity around the world could be the result of projectors returning and imposing foreign structures with local refinements. Man may also have gone to other planets by this means.

Iris Campbell, in a psychometric reading, states: 'It seems that all these sites were probably interconnected – it seems too that the astral bodies could travel and remember in the morning where they had been.'[15]

Leys in space. The late Professor Percy Wilkins, at one time regarded as the leading lunar astronomer, told Desmond Leslie that in the crater Gassendi, on the Moon, were parallel lines, triangles and geometric shapes. Where these intersect are pits or dome-like structures. If these patterns were natural cracks, they are unique to the Moon. Some parallel lines run up to the crater wall where there are what look like entrances to tunnels, and regular rows of dots then march over the wall to rejoin the parallel line on the far side from where they continue for many miles. From these tunnels bright lights had been observed emerging. Leslie reports that another astronomer, as long ago as 1871, had recorded geometric patterns in the crater Plato.[28]

Jimmy Goddard has also suggested that Mariner space-probe photographs indicate the presence of alignments on Mars.

Conclusion

'It means something — that we're in light, that we live in light now . . . but in our minds we are not in light.' — Marianne Faithfull.

Obviously one man's lifetime is not long enough to spend researching fully any one of the topics dealt with in this book. Work need not, and must not, be done by individuals in complete isolation. Neither should anyone tackle any single facet of the study, for they interlock and interweave. Nor should a researcher feel that he is alone or that his speculations are so way-out that to publicize them would bring complete ridicule. I hope that I have an open mind and that the reader will have too. Increasingly, people are turning to off-beat subjects, having been appalled by the narrow-mindedness of academics, and are becoming experts themselves, by not worrying about what others will think of them. We must assemble facts and find relationships between facts, especially those which official science regards as heresy, ignores or dismisses.

Revelations, now that many of us are walking the leys, are coming with greater ease and being seen to be of greater significance than anything which has gone before. Cross-pollination between exact science, calculated guesswork and psychic intuition has brought prehistory almost into true perspective, and we must focus our attention on this until all is clear.

Bookends

'Archaeologists are fierce and will tear to pieces one of their number who makes an insecure generalisation. An outsider can afford to take more risks.' — P.J. Helm.[22]

'There are so many aspects of this study that it can
never die. Almost everything is energised by this
power, not only in the physical world we know but
in the lesser known spheres of activity. The basic
truths are few, the implications manifold and so it
may be necessary to seek through many implications before the basic truth is revealed.' —
Circumlibra.[74]

'The fact is I'm turning to gold,
turning to gold.
It's a long process, they say
It happens in stages
This is to inform you that
        I've already
        turned to clay.'
              — Leonard Cohen.

"Would you tell me, please, which way I ought to
.go from here?"
"That depends a good deal on where you want to
get to," said the cat.' — Lewis Carroll.

References and Bibliography

This bibliography is not simply a compilation of works referred to in the text, but lists books and articles of interest to those following the subject matter of this book. Some are easily obtainable, others are long out of print; some are of only specialist interest; some have not been consulted by the writer, owing to their great rarity. However, though incomplete, this collection represents a fairly comprehensive index of works bearing upon the problems dealt with in this book. Because many of the books deal with a wide range of subjects, it has been impracticable to put them into sections.

BOOKS

1   Allcroft, Revd. Hadrian *Earthwork of England*, 1908, Macmillan (examples of alignments; theory undeveloped).

Allcroft, Revd. Hadrian *The Circle and the Cross*, 1930, Macmillan.

Allegro, John M. *The Sacred Mushroom and the Cross*, 1970, Hodder & Stoughton.

Anderson, R.M.C. *The Roads of England* 1932.

2   Andrew, F.W. *Memorials of Old Derbyshire*, 1907.

Anonymous *A Defence of Sacred Measures*, 1972, Radical-Traditionalist Papers.

Anonymous *The New Jerusalem at Glastonbury*, 1972, Zodiac House.

Atkinson, R.J.C. *Stonehenge*, 1956, Hamish Hamilton.

3   Ashe, Geoffrey *The Quest for Arthur's Britain*, 1968, Pall Mall.

4   Ballard, J.G. *The Atrocity Exhibition*, 1970, Cape.

5   Barondes, R. de Rohan *China*, 1959, Peter Owen (dragonlore).

Belloc, Hilaire *The Old Road*, 1911.

Belloc, Hilaire *The Stane Street*.

Berlitz, Charles *Mysteries from Forgotten Worlds*, 1972, Souvenir Press.

Blake, William *Jerusalem*, 1964, Allen & Unwin.

Bord, Janet and Colin *Mysterious Britain*, 1972, Garnstone Press.

Browne, Rt. Revd. G.F. *On Some Antiquities in the Neighbourhood of Dunecht House, Aberdeenshire*, 1921, Cambridge University Press.

Bunyan, John *Pilgrim's Progress*, 1687.

6   Burland, C.A. *The Arts of the Alchemists*, 1967, Weidenfeld & Nicholson.

Burland, C.A. *Echoes of Magic* 1972, Peter Davies (old customs).

Cathie, Bruce *Harmonic 33*, 1968, Reid, New Zealand (UFOs).

7   Cavendish, Richard *The Black Arts*, 1967, Routledge & Kegan Paul.

8   Clark, Grahame *Prehistoric England*, 1962, Batsford.
     Cooke, Grace and Ivan *The Light in Britain*, 1971, White Eagle.
     Cox, R. Hippisley *The Green Roads of England*, 1914, Methuen;
          1973, Garnstone Press.
9   Crawford, O.G.S. *Archaeology in the Field*, 1953, Phoenix
          House.
     Danaher, Kevin *Folktales of the Irish Countryside*, Mercier (fairy
          paths).
10   Daraul, Arkon *Secret Societies*, 1961, Muller.
     Dinnie, R. *A History of Birse*, 1864 (extract reprinted *The Ley
          Hunter*, No. 28, 1972).
11   Duncan, Revd. A.D. *The Christ, Psychotherapy and Magic* 1971,
          Allen & Unwin.
     Dutt, W.A. *Standing Stones of East Anglia*, 1921.
     Dutt, W.A. *Ancient Mark Stones of East Anglia*, 1926, Flood.
     Eitel, E.J. *Feng-shui*, 1873, Trubner.
12   Elgee, Frank and Harriet Wragg *The Archaeology of Yorkshire*,
          1933, Methuen.
     Elgee, Frank *Early Man in North-East Yorkshire*, 1933.
13   Eliade, Mircea *The Two and the One*, 1962, Gallimard, Paris;
          1965, Harvill.
     Eliade, Mircea *Patterns of Comparative Religion*.
     Elliot Smith, Sir G. *The Evolution of the Dragon*, 1919,
          Manchester University Press.
     Evans-Wentz, J.D. *The Fairy Faith in Celtic Countries*, 1911,
          Henry Frowde.
     Falconer, Alan *The Cleveland Way*, 1972, H.M.S.O.
     Farrar, Stewart *What Witches Do*, 1972, Peter Davies.
     Forbes, John Foster *The Unchronicled Past*, 1938, Simpkin &
          Marshall.
     Forbes, John Foster *Ages Not So Dark*, 1939.
     Forbes, John Foster *Living Stones of Britain*, Parts I and II.
14   Forbes, John Foster *Britain: The Land of Lost Magic*.
15   Forbes, John Foster *Giants of Britain*, 1945, Thomas's Publica-
          tions.
     Forbes, John Foster *The Castle and Place of Rothiemay*, 1948,
          Aird & Coghill (extract reprinted *The Ley Hunter* No. 27,
          1972).
16   Fortune, Dion *Aspects of Occultism*, 1962 reprinted, Aquarian
          Press.
     Garner, Alan *The Moon of Gomrath*, 1963, Collins.

17 Gauquelin, Michel *Astrology and Science*, 1970, Peter Davies.
    Geoffrey of Monmouth *Histories of the Kings of Britain c.*1139 (old roads).
18 Gleadow, Rupert *The Origin of the Zodiac*, 1968, Cape.
19 Goddard, Jimmy *Handbook of Leys and Orthoteny*, 1966, private (extract reprinted *The Ley Hunter*, No. 1, 1969).
20 Gordon, E.O. *Prehistoric London*, 1914; reprinted 1946, Covenant Publishing Co.
21 Grigson, Geoffrey *The Shell Country Book*, 1962, Phoenix House.
    Haining, Peter *The Anatomy of Witchcraft*, 1972, Souvenir Press.
    Harris, Rendel *A New Stonehenge*, 1929, W. Heffer & Sons.
    Hartley, Christine *The Western Mystery Tradition*, 1968, Aquarian Press.
    Hawkins, G.S. *Stonehenge Decoded*, 1966, Souvenir Press.
    Hearn, Lafcadio *Some Chinese Ghosts*, 1948, The World Press (geomancy).
22 Helm, P.J. *Exploring Prehistoric England*, 1971, Robert Hale.
23 Hodson, Geoffrey *Fairies at Work and Play*, 1925, Theosophical Publishing House, London.
24 Hodson, Geoffrey *The Kingdom of the Gods*, 1970, Theosophical Publishing Co., India.
    Holder, Richard *Songs of Mu and Atlantis*, 1972, Zodiac House.
    Insole, Alan V. *Immortal Britain*, 1952, Aquarian Press.
    Jackson, G. Gibbard *From Track to Highway*, 1935, Ivor Nicholson and Watson.
    Johnson, Walter *Byways in British Archaeology*, 1917, Cambridge University Press.
25 Keel, John A. *Operation Trojan Horse*, 1971, Souvenir Press; 1973 Abacus (UFOs).
    Kendrick, Sir T.D. *The Druids*, 1927, Methuen.
    King, Francis *Sexuality, Magic and Perversion*, 1971, Spearman.
    Kirk, Revd. R. *The Secret Commonwealth*, 1933, Eneas Mackay (fairies).
26 Knight, Gareth *A Practical Guide to Quabalistic Symbolism*, Vols. I and II, 1965, Helios.
    Kolosimo, Peter *Not of this World*, 1970, Souvenir Press (UFOs and the past).
    Larsen, Egon *Strange Sects and Cults*, 1971, Arthur Barker.
27 Lawton, Arthur *Mysteries of Ancient Man*, 1939, private; reprinted 1971 privately.
    Layne, Meade *The Ether Ship Mystery and its Solution*, private.

28   Leslie, Desmond, and Adamski, George *Flying Saucers Have Landed*, 1970 edition, Neville Spearman.

29   Lethbridge, T.C. *Gogmagog: The Buried Gods*, 1957, Routledge & Kegan Paul.

      Lethbridge, T.C. *The Legend of the Sons of God*, 1972, Routledge & Kegan Paul.

30   Lockyer, Sir Norman *Stonehenge*, 1909 edition, Macmillan.

      Long, Max Freedom *Recovering the Ancient Magic* 1970, Cedric Chivers.

31   Maltwood, Katherine *A Guide to Glastonbury's Temple of the Stars*, 1924; reprinted 1964, James Clarke & Co.; Air View Supplement, 1937.

32   Maltwood, Katherine *The Enchantment of Britain* 1946, Victoria, Canada.

33   Maltwood, Katherine *King Arthur's Round Table of the Zodiac*.

34   Maltwood, Katherine *Itinerary of The Somerset Giants*, 1946, Victoria.

      Mann, Ludovic MacLellan *The Scots 'Druid' Temple*, 1939, private.

      Mann, Ludovic MacLellan *Moles of Men: Druid Temple near Clydebank*, 1945, private.

35   Massingham, H.J. *Downland Man*, 1926, Cape.

36   Massingham, H.J. *Fe, Fi, Fo, Fum – The Giants of England*, 1926, Kegan Paul.

37   Mead, G.R.S. *The Subtle Body*, 1967, Stuart & Watkins.

38   Michel, Aimé *Flying Saucers and the Straight Line Mystery*, 1958, Criterion, New York.

39   Michell, John *The Flying Saucer Vision*, 1967, Sidgwick & Jackson.

40   Michell, John *The View Over Atlantis*, 1969, Sago Press; 1972, Garnstone Press; 1973, Abacus.

      Michell, John *City of Revelation*, 1972, Garnstone Press.

      Miller, S.H., and Skertchly, S.B.J. *The Fenland, Past and Present*, 1878 (old roads).

      Morton, H.V. *In Search of England*, 1927 (old roads).

41   Murchie, Guy *Music of the Spheres*, 1961, Dover.

42   Nelson, E.M. *The Cult of the Circle-Builders*, 1909, Robert Atkinson (extracts reprinted *The Ley Hunter*, Nos. 26, 27, 1971).

43   Ogston, Sir Alexander *The Prehistoric Antiquities of the Howe of Cromar*, 1931 (extract reprinted *The Ley Hunter* No. 25, 1971).

44 Pauwels, Louis, and Bergier, Jacques *The Dawn of Magic*, 1963,
      A. Gibbs & Phillips; 1964, Panther.

Pauwels, Louis, and Bergier, Jacques *The Eternal Man*, 1972,
      Souvenir Press.

Pennick, Nigel *The Nuthampstead Zodiac*, 1972, Endsville Press.

Petrie, Sir W.M.F. *The Hill Figures of England*, 1926.

Pixley, Olive *The Trail*, 1934, G.W. Daniel.

Reich, Maria *Mystery on the Desert*, 1970, Sago Press (Nazca).

Reich, Wilhelm *The Discovery of the Orgone*, 1942, Orgone
      Institute.

Reichenbach, Baron C. von *Letters on Od and Magnetism*, 1926,
      Hutchinson.

Roberts, Anthony *Atlantean Traditions in Ancient Britain* 1971,
      parts I and II; 1972, part III; Zodiac House.

Sale, J.L. *The Secret of Stonehenge*, 1965, private.

Sangharakshita, Sthavira *On Glastonbury Tor*, 1970, private.

'Sarana' *Ley-Line Linkage of Radio-Activity and the Containers*,
      1972, private.

45 Schuon, Frithjof *Light on the Ancient Worlds*, 1965, Perennial
      Books.

Scott-Giles, C.W. *The Road Goes On*, 1946, Epworth Press.

Sharpe, Sir M. *Earthworks in Middlesex and Hertfordshire.*

Sherlock, Helen Travers *The Wryley Stones*, 1929, W. Heffer &
      Sons.

Shuttlewood, Arthur *The Warminster Mystery*, 1967, Neville
      Spearman (includes notes on leys by J. Goddard).

46 Shuttlewood, Arthur *Warnings From Flying Friends*, 1968,
      Portway Press.

47 Sitwell, William *Stones of Northumberland*, 1930, Reid & Co.

48 Spence, Lewis *The Magic Arts in Celtic Britain*, 1970, Aquarian
      Press.

Spence, Lewis *The History and Origins of Druidism*, 1971,
      Aquarian Press.

49 Steiger, Brad, and Whritenour, Joan *New UFO Breakthrough*,
      1968, Tandem.

Sykes, Egerton *Meteor Strikes and the Hoerbiger Theory*, 1971,
      Markham House Press (gravitic anomalies, etc.).

Tansley, David V. *Radionics and the Subtle Anatomy of Man*,
      1972, Health Science Press.

Taylor, F. Sherwood *The Alchemists* 1951, Heinemann.

50 Thom, Alexander *Megalithic Sites in Britain* 1967, Oxford
      University Press.

51 Thom, Alexander *Megalithic Lunar Observatories*, 1971, O.U.P.
Thomas, Edward *The Icknield Way*, 1929.
52 Toulmin, Stephen, and Goodfield, June *The Fabric of the Heavens*, 1961, Heinemann.
Trench, Brinsley le Poer *The Sky People*, 1960, Neville Spearman; 1971, Tandem.
53 Trech, Brinsley le Poer *Men Among Mankind*, 1962, Neville Spearman.
Trench, Brinsley le Poer *The Flying Saucer Story*, 1966, Neville Spearman.
Trench, Brinsley le Poer *Operation Earth*, 1969, Neville Spearman.
Trench, Brinsley le Poer *The Eternal Subject*, 1973, Souvenir Press.
54 Tyler, Major F.C. *The Geometrical Arrangement of Ancient Sites*, 1939, Simpkin Marshall.
55 Underwood, Guy *The Pattern of the Past*, 1969, Museum Press; 1970, Pitman; 1972, Abacus.
Underwood, Peter *Into the Occult* 1972, Harrap.
56 Volta, Ornella *The Vampire*, 1965, Tandem.
57 Vorel, Iris *Be Your Own Astrologer*, 1942, Quality Press.
Watkins, Alfred *Must We Trade in Tenths?*, 1919, Watkins Meter Co.
Watkins, Alfred *Ancient Standing Crosses of Herefordshire*.
58 Watkins, Alfred *Early British Trackways*, 1922, Simpkin Marshall.
Watkins, Alfred *The Watkins Manual of Photography*, 10th edn. 1924, Simpkin Marshall.
59 Watkins, Alfred *The Old Straight Track*, 1925, Methuen; 1971, Garnstone Press (with notes by Allen Watkins and John Michell).
Watkins, Alfred *Photography, its Principles and Applications*, 3rd edn. 1927, Constable.
60 Watkins, Alfred *The Ley Hunter's Manual*, 1927, Simpkin Marshall.
61 Watkins, Alfred *Archaic Tracks Around Cambridge*, 1932, Simpkin Marshall.
Watkins, Allen *Alfred Watkins of Hereford*, 1972, Garnstone Press.
Wedd, Tony *Skyways and Landmarks* 1961, private; reprinted 1972 privately (leys and orthoteny).
Wheaton, John *Acupuncture*, private.
Wildman, S.G. *The Black Horsemen*, 1971, Garnstone Press.

61   Williamson, George Hunt *Other Tongues – Other Flesh*, 1953, Amhurst, U.S.A.
63   Williamson, George Hunt *Secret Places of the Lion*, 1958, Neville Spearman.
     Williamson, George Hunt *Road in the Sky*, 1959, Neville Spearman.
     Zinner, Ernst *The Stars Above Us* 1957, Allen & Unwin (extract reprinted *The Ley Hunter*, No. 36, 1972).

ARTICLES

64   Allen, J. Robin, 'The Straight Track Business Again', *Cheshire Life*, June 1940.

65   Atkinson, R.J.C., 'Barbarian Brains', *The Listener*, No. 2, 122, 1969 (review of book 50).

Anonymous, 'His Influence Lives On', *The Hereford Times*, 26 March 1971 (Alfred Watkins).

Anonymous, 'The Old Straight Track', *The Hereford Times*, 2 July 1971 (Hereford picnic).

Anonymous, 'Stanton Drew Stone Circles', *TLH**, No. 6, 1970.

'Atun', 'Gypsy Lore, Zodiacs and Albion', *TLH*, No. 19, 1971.

Bateman, Michael, 'Straight Talking', *The Sunday Times*, 7 March 1971 (John Michell interviewed).

Beebee, Marjorie, 'The Old Straight Track', *Headway*, February 1972.

Benham, Patrick, 'The City Revealed', *Torc*, No. 4, 1972 (The Canon).

Benham, Patrick, 'The Canon of Being', *TLH*, No. 34, 1972.

Benham, Tina, 'Glaston and the Phoenix', *Torc*, No. 2, 1971.

Bird, Alfred J., 'Geometric Principles and Patterns Associated With Two Megalithic Circles in Wales', *Britain* (RILKO book of articles), 1971.

'Boots, Jiving K.', 'The Weekly Adventures of a Loser Musician', *Melody Maker*, 19 June 1971 (leys and fayre spoof).

Bord, Colin, 'The Aetherius Society', *Gandalf's Garden*, No. 4, 1969.

Bord, Colin, 'The Cosmic Continent', *Gandalf's Garden*, No. 6, 1969 (Mu).

Bord, Colin, 'The Sacred Science of Antiquity', *Torc*, No. 3, 1972 (review of book 40).

* *TLH* denotes *The Ley Hunter* throughout this section.

Bord, Colin, 'Thoughts, Crystals and Cosmic Energies: Shape Power and the Aetherius Society', *TLH*, No. 32, 1972.

Borst, Lyle B., 'English Henge Cathedrals', *Nature*, 25 October 1969.

Borst, Lyle B., 'The Megalithic Plan Under the Houses of Parliament', *TLH*, No. 11, 1970.

Bosanquet, Henry, 'Glyn Daniel: Patron of the Arts', *Braingrader*, February 1971.

Bradley, John, 'Salt Hill, the Montem and Stabmonks', *TLH*, No. 35, 1972.

Brooke, John, 'Saint George', *Pendragon*, Vol. 4, No. 3, 1970.

Butcher, Dan, 'A Mysterious Alignment in the Western Desert of Egypt', *TLH*, No. 12, 1970.

66   Butcher, Dan, 'Astral Projection, UFOs and Leys', *TLH*, No. 15, 1970.

Butcher, Dan, 'Some Notes on the Names of UFO Entities', *Cosmos*, Summer 1971 (Elen and leys).

Butcher, Dan, 'The Wandering Turf: or The Psychography of Leys', *TLH*, No. 16, 1971.

67   Butcher, Dan, 'Helen and Semiramis — Builders of Roads', *TLH*, No. 20, 1971; reprinted *The Atlantean*, No. 139, 1971.

68   Caine, Mary, 'The Glastonbury Giants', *Prediction*, series beginning December 1968.

69   Caine, Mary, 'The Glastonbury Zodiac', *Gandalf's Garden*, No. 4, 1969.

Caine, Mary, 'Is There a Kingston Zodiac?', *Prediction*, series beginning June 1971.

Campbell, Iris, 'The Straight Lines or Leys', *TLH*, No. 10, 1970.

Campbell, Iris, 'Magnetism in Relation to Prehistoric Sites (and Others)', and 'Some Memories of John Foster Forbes', *TLH*, No. 12, 1970.

Campbell, Iris, 'The Origins of Glastonbury Tor', *Torc*, No. 4, 1972.

Campbell, Iris, 'Solstice Thoughts', *Torc*, No. 5, 1972.

70   Carey, Mollie, 'The Real Stonehenge', *Enigmas of the Plain* (booklet produced by J. Goddard).

Carey, Mollie, 'The Secrets of the Megaliths', *TLH*, No. 19, 1971.

Carey, Mollie, 'The Sacred Hills', *TLH*, No. 26, 1971.

Carey, Mollie, 'Yarnbury Castle Hillfort', *TLH*, No. 28, 1972.

Carey, Mollie, 'Alvediston — shades of Avalon', *TLH*, No. 30, 1972.

Carey, Mollie, 'Some "Impressions" at Stonehenge', *TLH*, No. 31, 1972.

Carey, Mollie, 'The Stone Alignments at Uffington', *TLH*, No. 33, 1972.

Carey, Mollie, 'Ancient Fields', *TLH*, No. 34, 1972.

Carey, Mollie, 'Ancient Dorchester', *TLH*, No. 37, 1972.

71 Carlyon, Julian, 'A Theory Towards the Further Understanding of Gothic Architecture', *Britain* (RILKO booklet), 1971.

Carr-Gomm, M.C., 'They Knew Where They Were Going in the Bronze Age', *Atlantis*, Vol. 11, No. 6, 1958.

72 Chaundy, Douglas, 'The Salisbury Star Map and the White Horse Triangle', *Enigmas of the Plain* (booklet).

73 Cleary-Baker, John, 'A criticism of leys', *BUFORA Bulletin* Vol. 2, No. 2, 1967.

'Circumlibra' (Frank Lockwood), 'Mistress Luna About to Retire', *The Atlantean*, April 1960 (Moon).

'Circumlibra' 'The Tides of the Sun', *Fate*, December 1963.

'Circumlibra' 'Progress or Progression – which?', *The Atlantean*, Sept./Oct. 1967 (elementals).

'Circumlibra' 'A Forgotten Science', *The Atlantean*, Jan./Feb. 1968 (ley power and carvings).

'Circumlibra' 'Did Atlantis Exist?', *The Atlantean*, Mar./Apr. 1968.

'Circumlibra' 'The Face of Sunny Jim', *The Atlantean*, Sept./Oct. 1968 (carvings and 'charging').

74 'Circumlibra' 'Robin Hood and his Stride', *The Seeker*, Vol. 1, No. 2 (ley power).

'Circumlibra' 'Carl's Wark and Carl's Wain', *The Seeker*, Vol. 1, No. 3 (ley power).

75 'Circumlibra' 'Etheric Centres', *TLH*, No. 2, 1969; reprinted *Times For The Times To Come Together* (booklet produced by P. Screeton), 1970.

'Circumlibra' 'The Ley on which I Live', *TLH*, No. 5, 1970; reprinted *Time For The Times To Come Together*, 1970.

'Circumlibra' 'Leys and Tides of the Day', *TLH*, No. 6, 1970.

76 'Circumlibra' 'The Earth Breathes', *TLH*, No. 7, 1970.

'Circumlibra' 'A Thousand Miles Apart', *TLH*, No. 9, 1970.

77 'Circumlibra' 'An Elemental and its Effigy in Stone', *TLH*, No. 13, 1970.

'Circumlibra' 'What is the Influence of the Leys?', *TLH*, No. 15, 1971.

'Circumlibra' 'Only a Gatepost', *TLH*, No. 18, 1971.

'Circumlibra' 'A Couple of Leys – Plus', *TLH*, No. 29, 1972.

'Circumlibra' 'Black and Bright', *TLH*, No. 35, 1972.

'Circumlibra' 'Pieces for the Jigsaw Puzzle', *TLH*, No. 38, 1972.
'Circumlibra' 'The Little Green Man', *TLH*, No. 40, 1973 (elemental).
Clasen, Charles, 'Glastonbury Lives', *Time Out*, 28 April 1972 (review of *City of Revelation*).
Cochrane, C., 'Looking for Lost Roads', *Ago*, No. 4, 1970.
Cohen, Alan, 'Sacred Stones', *TLH*, No. 16, 1971.
Cohen, Alan, 'Britain, Albion and the New Jerusalem', *TLH*, No. 24, 1971.
Cohen, Alan, 'Some Remarks Upon *City of Revelation*', *TLH*, No. 33, 1972.
Cohen, Alan, 'Australian Aborigines' Sacred Paths', *TLH*, No. 34, 1972.
Cohen, Alan, 'The Other Kind of Dream', *TLH*, No. 39, 1973.
78   Cole, Tom, 'One of the Durham Zodiacs', *TLH*, No. 14, 1970 (Stanley zodiac).
Collier, Mary, 'Mysteries of the Fosse Way', *The Atlantean*, No. 144, 1972.
79   Craddock, Marjorie, 'Pioneer Watkins', *Hereford Times*, 7 Oct. 1966.
Craddock, Marjorie, 'Unravelling the Great Stone Mysteries', *Hereford Times*, 4 Nov. 1966.
80   Critchlow, Keith, 'Notes on the Geometry of Stonehenge with Comments on the Ming Tang', *Britain* (RILKO booklet).
Croft, G.D., 'Linking Leys and UFOs', *TLH*, No. 21, 1971.
Croft, G.D. 'The Church of Holy Sepulchre of the Knights Templar', *Arcana*, June 1972.
81   Crump, Barbara, 'A Lost Network of Ancient Ways', *TLH*, No. 5, 1970; reprinted *Time For The Times To Come Together*, 1970 (Fosse Way).
Crump, Barbara, 'The Ley Line Through Monk's Ford', *TLH*, No. 22, 1971.
Crump, Barbara, 'A View of the South-West', *TLH*, No. 22, 1971.
Crump, Barbara, 'Ley Lines between Wales and the West Country', *TLH*, No. 34, 1972.
82   Davidson, Andrew, 'Silbury Hill', *Britain* (RILKO booklet).
Davidson, Michael, 'Two Fenland Leys', *TLH*, Vol. 2, No. 1, 1965; part reprinted *TLH*, No. 17, 1971.
Davidson, Michael, 'Fenland Past and Present', *TLH*, Vol. 2, No. 3, 1966.
Davidson, Michael, 'Idle Thoughts on Pubs', *TLH*, Vol. 2, No. 4, 1966.

Davies, Roy, '666', *Azoth*, No. 5, 1972.

Davison, R.C., 'In Britain as in China', *The Atlantean*, No. 143, 1972 (dragon paths).

83 Edwards, Lewis, 'The Welsh Temple of the Zodiac', *Research*, Vol. 1, Nos. 2, 3, 4, 1948; reprinted *TLH*, Nos. 15, 16, 17, 1971.

Farren, Joy, 'The Matter of Britain', Parts 1-3, *I.T.*, Nos. 98-100, 1971.

Farren, Joy, 'Scapegoat', *I.T.*, No. 121, 1972 (William Rufus).

Farren, Joy, 'Twang', *I.T.*, No. 124, 1972 (Robin Hood legends).

Farren, Joy, 'The Vampire Walks Among Us', *I.T.*, No. 125, 1972.

Forbes, John Foster, and Campbell, Iris, 'What Glastonbury Revealed', *Torc*, No. 1, 1971 (from a 1946 issue of *Avalon*).

Ford, Nancy, 'Glastonbury Vision', *TLH*, No. 23, 1971.

Forrester, Geoffrey, and Odell, Nick, 'A Sussex Ley Hunt', *TLH*, Vol. 2, No. 3, 1966.

Forrester, Sylvan, 'The Gog Magog Hill Figures', *Arcana*, June 1972.

84 Furness, Peter, 'Are Leys Due to Chance?', *TLH*, Vol. 2, No. 1, 1965.

Glob, P.V., 'The Old Track'. *Politzen*, 26 July 1971; reprinted *TLH*, No. 25, 1971 (review of book 59).

Goddard, Jimmy, 'A New Meaning to Leys', *TLH*, Vol. 1, No. 3, 1965 (orthoteny).

85 Goddard, Jimmy, 'The Great Isoceles Triangle of England', *UFO Magazine*, Summer, 1966; reprinted *Saucer Album*, 1967.

86 Goddard, Jimmy, 'The Porlock Ley', *TLH*, Vol. 2, No. 4, 1966.

Goddard, Jimmy, 'The Warminster Centre', *Enigmas of the Plain* booklet; reprinted in A. Shuttlewood's *The Warminster Mystery*.

Goddard, Jimmy, 'The Great Ley', *Enigmas of the Plain*.

Goddard, Jimmy, 'A Somerset Ley Hunt', *Awareness*, Aug. 1969; reprinted *TLH*, No. 3, 1970.

87 Goddard, Jimmy, 'Harmful Aspects of Solar Radiation', *Awareness* March 1970.

Goddard, Jimmy, 'UFOs and the Scientific Approach', *Awareness* Dec. 1970 (leys and ridicule).

Goddard, Jimmy, 'Detecting the Power in Leys', *TLH*, No. 7, 1970.

88 Goddard, Jimmy, 'Stone Circles and Patterns of Power', *TLH*, No. 12, 1970.

89 Goddard, Jimmy, 'Some Leys Around Addlestone', *TLH*, No. 16, 1971.
Goddard, Jimmy, 'The Somerset Zodiac', *TLH*, No. 18, 1971.
90 Goddard, Jimmy, 'An Unexpected Virgin', *TLH*, No. 20, 1971 ' (zodiacal figure).
Goddard, Jimmy, 'Orthoteny – Dead or Alive?', *TLH*, No. 21, 1971.
91 Goddard, Jimmy, 'Unusual Trees – Symbols of Ley Power?', *TLH*, No. 23, 1971.
Goddard, Jimmy, 'Britain – the Haunted Island', *TLH*, No. 36, 1972.
Jimmy Goddard has also written on leys and orthoteny in the following:
Flying Saucer Review, Mar./Apr. 1964; *Hermes*, Jan. 1966; *Orbit*, Feb. 1966; *Spacelink*, Spring 1966; *In Perspective*, Summer/ Autumn 1966; *Flying Saucers* Aug. 1966; *Spacelink*, Winter 1966; *In Perspective*, Feb./Mar. 1967; *In Perspective*, Apr. 1967; *S.I.G.A.P. Bulletin* Nov. 1968.
Griffin, John, 'Programming the Unconscious', *Journal of the British Society of Dowsers*, No. 154, 1971 (geodetic lines).
G.T., 'Scientists Coming into Line', *The National Message*, Aug. 1971 (leys and speculative archaeology).
Haddingham, Evan, 'The Sky-Watchers of Stonehenge Britain', *Arcana*, Feb. 1972.
Hall, Simon, 'Place Names and Leys of Southern Cambridgeshire', *Arcana*, Feb. 1972.
Hatton, Joan, 'Notes on Coldharbour Names', *TLH*, Vol. 2, No. 2, 1965.
'Hawkeye', 'The View from the Tor', *Torc*, No. 6, 1972.
Heinsch, Dr, 'The Principles of Prehistoric Cult Geography', *Proceedings of the International Geographical Congress*, Amsterdam, 1938 (in German).
Heselton, Philip, 'Alignments on the North Yorkshire Moors', A Bulletin From the Ley Hunter's Club, Oct. 1964.
Heselton, Philip, 'Alignments on Salisbury Plain', *TLH*, Vol. 1, No. 1, 1965.
Heselton, Philip, 'Strike the Trail', *TLH*, Vol. 1, No. 3, 1965 (introduction to ley hunting).
Heselton, Philip, 'Isle of Man Primary Ley System', *TLH*, Vol. 2, No. 1, 1965; reprinted *TLH*, No. 33, 1972.
Heselton, Philip, 'Leys in Britain', *TLH*, Vol. 2, No. 2, 1965 (ley patterns).

Heselton, Philip, 'Fifty Years of Ley Hunting', *TLH*, No. 5, 1970; reprinted *Time For The Times To Come Together* booklet.

Heselton, Philip, 'Major F.C. Tyler Reviewed', *TLH*, No. 11, 1970.

Heselton, Philip, 'The Holderness Zodiac', *TLH*, No. 25, 1971.

Heselton, Philip, 'Tending – an Awakening Realisation of an Old Responsibility', *TLH*, No. 36, 1972.

Hollingworth, Roy, 'Hey Ho, Come to the Fair!', *Melody Maker*, 19 June 1971 (leys and Glastonbury Fayre).

Howard, H. Theodore, 'New Light on the I Ching', *The Monolith*, March 1969.

'Jino', 'L'Apocalisse', *Torc*, No. 7, 1973 (Glastonbury).

Jones, Alan S., 'Whatever Happened to Lancelot Quail?', *Torc*, No. 7, 1973.

Jones, Dedwydd, 'The Eternal City', *Arcana*, June 1972 (review of *City of Revelation*).

92   'Karana', 'The Code of the Sacred Islands', *I.T.*, No. 35, 1968.

Kellaway, G.A., 'Glaciation and the Stones of Stonehenge', *Nature*, 3 Sept. 1971.

Knight, Gareth, 'The Robin Hood Legend', *Quest*, No. 5, 1971.

Knight, Kenneth, 'The Window Remains Shut', *TLH*, No. 7, 1970 (review of book 40).

Knight, Kenneth, 'The Northern Entrance to the "Kingdom of Logos" Identified?', *TLH*, No. 14, 1970; reprinted *Pendragon*, Vol. 5, No. 2, 1971.

Knight, Kenneth, 'The Gematria of the Hebrew Cabbala: A System for Interpreting Ley Lines?', *TLH*, No. 24, 1971.

Koop, Kenneth H., 'The Earliest Survey of Britain', pamphlet, Cairo, 1946; reprinted *Research*, Vol. 1, No. 1, 1948 (leys).

Koop, Kenneth H., 'Coldharbour Investigations', *Atlantis Research*, Vol. 3, No. 3, 1950.

Koop, Kenneth H., 'Coldharbour Alignments', *Atlantis*, Vol. 4, No. 4, 1951.

93   Koop, Kenneth H., 'The Earliest Survey', *Atlantis*, Vol. 11, No. 5, 1958.

Krysiak, Stanley, 'Earth's Harmful Radiation', *Journal of the British Society of Dowsers*, March 1969.

Larsen, Kenneth Lloyd, 'Quartz Crystal, UFO Reports and Mathematical Measurements', *Cosmos*, No. 11, Sept. 1970.

Leader, Elizabeth, 'The Somerset Zodiac', *Glastonbury* (RILKO booklet), 1969.

Legon, John, 'Lines of the Element Air', *TLH*, No. 36, 1972.

Legon, John, 'The Descent of the Canon', *TLH*, No. 38, 1972.

Leroux, V.L., 'Energy Chart', *Journal of the British Society of Dowsers*, No. 148, 1970 (henges as giant energy charts).

Lovegrove, Chris, 'In the Land of the Giants', *Pendragon*, Vol. 5, No. 3, 1971 (Cornish ley hunting).

Mackinnon, Kenneth, 'North-South Alignments Around Newbury and Reading', *TLH*, No. 31, 1972.

Marr, Leslie, 'Wilhelm Reich', *TLH*, No. 40, 1973.

Maughling, Rollo, 'A Defence of Sacred Measures', *Torc*, No. 4, 1972 (summary of book of same name).

Maughling, Rollo, 'Awakening the Enchantments of Britain', *Torc*, No. 6, 1972.

Maughling, Rollo, 'The New Jerusalem', *Central Somerset Gazette*, 1972; reprinted privately in booklet.

Merlin, R.H.A., 'Monoliths and Stone Circles', *TLH*, Vol. 1, No. 2, 1965.

Michell, John, 'Centres and Lines of the Latent Power in Britain', *I.T.*, No. 19, 1967.

94   Michell, John, '1850 B.C.', *I.T.*, No. 23, 1968.

95   Michell, John, 'UFOs and the Message from the Past', *Albion*, No. 1, 1968 (lecture to Contact U.K., 24 Feb. 1968).

96   Michell, John, 'Lung Mei and the Dragon Paths of England', *Image*, June 1968.

Michell, John, 'Flying Saucers', *The Listener*, No. 2,048, 1968.

Michell, John, 'The Word is *Unidentified*', *Vogue*, 15 Sept. 1968.

Michell, John, 'Agreement is Illusion, Harmony is Reality', *Moving Into the New Age* (Findhorn Trust booklet), 1969.

Michell, John, 'Glastonbury Abbey: A solar instrument of former science', *Glastonbury* (RILKO booklet).

Michell, John, '1850 Revisited', *I.T.*, No. 61, 1969.

97   Michell, John, 'Cornish Alignments', *TLH*, No. 10, 1970.

Michell, John, 'John Michell's Dream', *TLH*, No. 13, 1970.

Michell, John, 'A Ridiculous Episode', *TLH*, No. 14, 1970.

Michell, John, 'The Sacred Origins of British Metrology', *Britain* (RILKO booklet).

Michell, John, 'Professor Thom and the Ley Hunters', *TLH*, No. 21, 1971.

Michell, John, 'Iamblichus', *TLH*, No. 29, 1972.

Michell, John, 'The Canon Within Us', *TLH*, No. 34, 1972.

Michelle, J., 'The Spiritual Science of Antiquity', *Journal of the British Society of Dowsers*, March 1972.

Miller, Karl, 'Midsummer Night's Dream', *The Listener*, No.

2,048, 1968 (John Michell interviewed).

98 Moorhouse, Geoffrey, 'Temple of the Stars', *The Guardian*, 25 Jan. 1966 (interview with Mary and Osmund Caine).

Munro, Andrew, 'The Gog-Magog Hill Figures', *Cambridge Voïce*, Series 2, No. 4.

Neal, John F., 'Notes Towards an Understanding of the "Key of the Cosmos" ', *TLH*, No. 10, 1970.

Newham, C.A., 'Stonehenge – A Neolithic Observatory', *Nature*, Vol. 211, No. 5,048, 1966.

99 Nichols, Ross, 'Man's Monuments and the Leys', *TLH*, No. 11, 1970.

Nichols, Ross, 'Notes on some Orientations in the Brown Willy Complex', *TLH*, No. 18, 1971.

Nichols, Ross, 'Cones and Triangles of Power in Man's Development', *TLH*, No. 23, 1971.

Nichols, Ross, 'God-Names and Sighting Lines on Exmoor', *TLH*, No. 23, 1972.

Nichols, Ross, 'Ivinghoe Beacon and the Diagonal Ley Across Southern England', *TLH*, No. 35, 1972.

100 Northwood, Tony, 'Leys and Mathematical Probability', *TLH*, No. 8, 1970.

Oliver, Norman, 'Mystery Hill', *Cosmos*, No. 12, 1970 (UFO over ley centre).

O'Neill, Bob, 'An Introduction to Leys', *S.W.U.A.P.I.G. Bulletin*, Jan./Feb. 1970.

'Patrick', 'Why and Wherefore', *Torc*, No. 1, 1971 (leys and New Age).

101 Pennick, Nigel, 'The Nuthampstead Zodiac' (A), *Cambridge Voice*, Series 2, No. 3, 1970.

Pennick, Nigel, 'Geomancy' (A), *Cambridge Voice*, Series 2, No. 4, 1970; reprinted *TLH*, No. 13, 1970.

102 Pennick, Nigel, 'The Nuthampstead Zodiac' (B), *TLH*, No. 11, 1970.

Pennick, Nigel, 'Geomancy' (B), *Walrus*, No. 8, 1971.

Pennick, Nigel, 'Holy Commons?' and 'Ex Cathedra', *Arcana*, Feb. 1972.

Pennick, Nigel, 'The Knights of Christ', *The Oracle of Albion*, No. 1, 1972 (Templars).

Pennick, Nigel, 'Cambridgeshire Dikes and Earthworks', *Arcana*, June 1972.

Pennick, Nigel, 'The Church of St Nicholas and Our Lady in Cambridge 1446-1968' and 'The Pudding Stone Track',

Arcana, No. 3, 1972.

Perrett, R.D.Y., 'The South-North Alignment in the City of Sheffield', *TLH*, Vol. 2, No. 1, 1965.

Perrett, R.D.Y., 'An Alignment 5½° South of West Through Stones at Fulwood, Sheffield', *TLH*, No. 8, 1970.

Peters, Pauline, 'Take Me To Your Saucer', *The Sunday Times*, 1968 (John Michell interviewed).

P.H.S., 'Mystics' Picnic', *The Times*, 3 July 1971 (Hereford picnic).

Ratazzi, Peter, 'Island of Revelation', *Quest*, No. 3, 1970 (Patmos and numerology).

Richardson, John, 'Hawkins in Perspective', *TLH*, No. 37, 1972.

103 Roberts, Anthony, 'The Search for the Mystic Vision from Atlantis to the Age of Aquarius', *I.T.*, No. 101, 1971 (drugs).

Roberts, Anthony, 'Magic and Christian Symbolism', *TLH*, No. 19, 1971.

Roberts, Anthony, 'The Monk's Ford Ley', *TLH*, No. 20, 1971.

Roberts, Anthony, 'Glastonbury 3 Atlantis 2', *I.T.*, No. 104.*

Roberts, Anthony, 'Giants of the Earth', *I.T.*, No. 105, 1971.

Roberts, Anthony, 'The Thing From Fulham — X', *I.T.*, No. 118*.

Roberts, Anthony, 'White Tower and Spiral Castle', *TLH*, No. 25, 1971; reprinted *The Atlantean*, No. 141, 1972.

Roberts, Anthony, 'Historical Perspectives in Ancient America', *TLH*, Nos. 28, 29, 1972.

Roberts, Anthony, 'The Pyramids', *I.T.*, Nos. 125, 126, 1972.

Roberts, Anthony, 'Avalon and Atlantis', *Torc*, No. 5, 1972.

Roberts, Anthony, 'Magic Cambridge', *Arcana*, Feb. 1972.

Roberts, Anthony, 'Shadows of Atlantis', *The Atlantean*, No. 142, 1972.

Roberts, Anthony, 'The Scottish Megaliths', *TLH*, No. 34, 1972.

Roberts, Anthony, 'Shadows Over Glastonbury', *TLH*, No. 38, 1972.

104 Rodger, Ian, 'Megalithic Monuments', *The Listener*, No. 2,122, 1969, page 301.

105 Rodgers, Philip, 'Why Flying Saucers Followed the Leys', *TLH*, No. 8, 1970.

Rudge, E.A. and E.L., 'A Stone Age Trade Route in East Anglia', *Discovery*, July 1952.

* Titles chosen by *I.T.*, not Anthony Roberts, presumably.

106 Russell, Geoffrey, 'The Secret of the Grail', *Glastonbury* (RILKO booklet).

Sale, Jonathan, 'The Spirit World is Now Available Over the Counter', *The Observer Colour Supplement*, 1 Oct. 1972.

Samson, Derek C., 'Excavators and UFOs', *N.I.C.A.P. Journal*, Vol. 1, No. 3, 1970 (earthmoving operations affecting leys?).

Scott, Firth, 'Poles, Priests and Pyramids', *Atlantis*, six parts, 1957/8; part 6 reprinted *TLH*, No. 17, 1971.

Screeton, Paul, 'The Pattern Puzzle', *TLH*, No. 1, 1969 (barrows).

Screeton, Paul, 'Flying Saucer Visionary', *TLH*, No. 1, 1969 (review of John Michell's early work).

Screeton, Paul, 'The View Over Atlantis', *TLH*, No. 3, 1970; reprinted *Time For The Times To Come Together* booklet (review of book 40).

Screeton, Paul, 'Not The Done Thing', *Egg*, No. 3, 1970 (UFOs and S.F.).

Screeton, Paul, 'Bats, Ghosts, Old Mother Midnight and the Wishing Stone', *TLH*, No. 8, 1970 (Hart).

Screeton, Paul, 'Betwixt the Earth and Sky', *Awareness*, No. 9, 1970.

Screeton, Paul, 'Like a Zeppelin', *TLH*, No. 9, 1970 (N.E. England UFOs).

Screeton, Paul, 'Redmire', *TLH*, No. 13, 1970.

Screeton, Paul, 'The (Tentative) Fleet Shot Hill Zodiac', *TLH*, No. 14, 1970.

Screeton, Paul, 'Leys and Orthotenies Symposium', *TLH*, No. 14, 1970.

Screeton, Paul, 'The View Over Ivory Towers', *TLH*, No. 14, 1970 (debate between speculative and orthodox archaeology).

Screeton, Paul, 'Sky Counties/Jesus Christ/UFO', *TLH*, No. 14, 1970.

Screeton, Paul, 'Atlantis Rising?', *TLH*, No. 17, 1971.

Screeton, Paul, 'Visionary Archaeologist', *The Atlantean*, No. 137, 1971 (Alfred Watkins).

Screeton, Paul, 'Searching for the Future in the Past', *TLH*, No. 21, 1971.

Screeton, Paul, 'Nine Weeks and Eighty Two Years', *TLH*, No. 22, 1971 (Hereford picnic).

Screeton, Paul, 'Lines of Inspiration', *Mantra*, No. 1, 1972; reprinted *TLH*, No. 39, 1973.

Screeton, Paul, 'Leys . . . an Introduction', and 'Dee Days', *TLH*, No. 24, 1971.

Screeton, Paul, 'Arthur Lawton and Ley Energy', introduction to Lawton book 27.

Screeton, Paul, 'Great Wryley Revisited', *TLH*, No. 29, 1972 (Wryley Stones).

Screeton, Paul, 'Mystic Northumbria', *Muther Grumble*, No. 6, 1972.

Screeton, Paul, 'For Whom Was The Web Woven?', *Quest*, No. 10, 1972.

Screeton, Paul, 'Terrestrial Zodiacs: A Bibliography', *The Oracle of Albion*, No. 1, 1972.

Screeton, Paul, 'All Along the Leys', *Grope*, No. 2, 1972.

Screeton, Paul, 'The Mysteries of Hart', *Mantra*, No. 3, 1972.

Screeton, Paul, 'Pictures in the Sky/Pictures in the Earth', *Torc*, No. 6, 1972.

Screeton, Paul, '3 Northumbrian Zodiacs', *The Oracle of Albion*, No. 2, 1972.

Screeton, Paul, 'Woodhenge to Woodstock', *TLH*, No. 35, 1972 (tribal gatherings).

Shepherd, C.D.F., 'Why I Love Glastonbury', *Torc*, No. 3, 1972.

Shepherd, C.D.F., 'The Return Road from Avalon', *Torc*, No. 4, 1972.

Shepherd, C.D.F., 'Why is Glastonbury the Cradle of the Future?', *Torc*, No. 5, 1972.

Shepherd, C.D.F., 'Understanding Glastonbury's Temple of the Stars', *Quest*, No. 11, 1972.

Shepherd, C.D.F., 'The Countenance of Michael', *Torc*, No. 6, 1972.

Shepherd, C.D.F., 'Our Atlantean Ancestry', *Torc*, No. 7, 1973 (Glastonbury).

107   Shuttlewood, Arthur, 'Shafts of Suspended Animation', *N.I.C.A.P. Journal*, Summer 1970 (UFOs and magnetism).

Slowgrove, Anne, 'Survival of the British Mysteries', *Quest*, No. 3, 1970.

Smith, Nadine, 'The Ancient Leys of Britain', *Prediction*, Jan. 1972.

Smith, Stephen, 'A Symposium of Leys and Orthotenies', *BUFORA Research Bulletin*, Vol. 3, No. 3, 1970.

108   Smith, Stephen, 'Orthoteny', *TLH*, No. 16, 1970.

Steele, H., 'The Somerset Giants', *Country Life*, 11 Jan. 1948.

Stokes, Derek ('Bram'), 'One Plus One Plus One Equals One',

TLH, No. 16, 1971.

Sykes, Egerton, 'A Bibliography of Megalithic Tracks, Leys and Alignments', pamphlet from Markham House Press, 1948.

109 Sykes, Egerton, 'Gravitic Anomalies', *New World Antiquity*, Vol. 18, No. 7/8, 1971.

Symms, Christine Crosland, 'Who Were the Leymen?', *TLH*, Vol. 1, No. 2, 1965; reprinted *TLH*, No. 24, 197.

Symms, Christine Crosland, 'Atlantis', *TLH*, No. 31, 1972.

110 Tansley, David V., 'The Principle of Perception in Radiesthesia', *Journal of the British Society of Dowsers*, June 1970.

Thom, A., 'The Solar Observatories of Megalithic Man', *Journal of The British Astronomical Association*, No. 397, 1954.

Thom, A., 'A Statistical Examination of the Megalithic Sites in Britain', *Journal of the Royal Statistical Society*, No. 275, 1955.

Thom, A., 'An Empirical Investigation of Atmospheric Refraction', *Empirical Survey Review*, No. 248, 1958.

Thom, A., 'The Geometry of Megalithic Man', *Mathematical Gazette*, Nos. 83-93, 1961-2.

Thom, A., 'The Egg-shaped Standing Stone Rings of Britain', *Archaeologists' International Historical Society*, No. 291, 1962.

Thom, A., 'The Megalithic Unit of Length', *Journal of the Royal Statistical Society*, No. 243, 1962.

Thom, A., 'The Larger Units of Length of Megalithic Man', *Journal of the Royal Statistical Society*, No. 527, 1964.

Thom, A., 'Megalithic Astronomy: indications in standing stones', *Vistas in Astronomy*, Vol. 7, No. 1, 1965.

Thom, A., 'Megaliths and Mathematics', *Antiquity*, No. 121, 1966.

Thom, A., 'Glastonbury as a Possible Megalithic Observatory', *Glastonbury* (RILKO book).

Thom, A., 'The Metrology and Geometry of Cup and Ring Marks', *Systematics*, No. 173, 1968.

Thom, A., 'The Lunar Observatories of Megalithic Man', *Vistas in Astronomy*, Vol. 11, No. 1, 1969.

Thom, A., 'The Geometry of Cup and Ring Marks', *Transactions of Ancient Monuments Society*, No. 77, 1969.

Thom, A., 'Megalithic Geometry in Standing Stones', *New Scientist*; reprinted *Pentagram*, No. 6, 1967.

Thom, A., 'The Megaliths of Carnac', *The Listener*; No. 2179, 1970.

Trench, Brinsley le Poer, 'The International Scene', *Awareness*, March 1970 (possible Anglesey leys).

Trewin, Ion, 'Puzzles in the Grand Design', *The Times*, 23 Nov. 1972 (review of *Mysterious Britain*).

Valiente, Doreen, 'Nine Men's Morris', *TLH*, No. 40, 1973.

Vinci, Enrico, 'Physics – Radiesthesia', *CESPERA Bulletin* 41, 1968, Italy; reprinted *TLH*, No. 23, 1971.

W.A., 'The Track and Stone People', *The Atlantean*, Sept./Oct. 1967.

111 Watkins, Allen, 'My First Ley Hunt', *TLH*, Vol. 1, No. 3, 1965.

Watkins, Allen, 'Beyond Controversy', *TLH*, No. 6, 1970.

Watkins, Allen, 'Belloc's Ley Impulse', *TLH*, No. 12, 1970.

112 Watkins, Allen, 'The Straight Path in Wisdom Teaching', *TLH*, No. 18, 1971.

Watkins, Allen, 'Alfred Watkins, 1855/1935', *TLH*, No. 21, 1971.

Watts, F.R., 'The Prehistoric Trackways of Oxfordshire', *Atlantis*, Vol. 10, No. 2, 1957 (reprinted from *Oxfordshire Times*).

113 Watts, F.R., 'The Ancient Roads Can Still Be Traced', *Witney Gazette*, 16 Dec. 1960.

Watts, F.R., 'Local Antiquities', series of articles in issues of *Charlbury School Magazine*, around 1948/9; several reprinted *TLH*, Nos. 9, 10, 13.

Wedd, Tony, 'A Hunter's Tale', *TLH*, No. 2, 1969; reprinted *Time For The Times To Come Together*, 1970 (Glastonbury zodiac).

114 Wedd, Tony, 'The Way, the Truth and the Light', *TLH*, No. 3, 1970; reprinted *Time For The Times To Come Together* (Stonehenge).

115 Wedd, Tony, 'The Path', *TLH*, No. 5, 1970; reprinted *Time For The Times To Come Together* (orthoteny).

Wedd, Tony, 'Allotechnology', *TLH*, No. 7, 1970.

116 Wedd, Tony, '6° N. of E.', *TLH*, No. 9, 1970.

117 Wheaton, John, 'The Meridians of Man', *TLH*, No. 11, 1970.

Wheaton, John, 'The Control of Energy in Man', *TLH*, No. 27, 1972.

Williams, John G., 'Notes on Prehistoric Monuments', *Journal of the British Society of Dowsers*, May 1969.

Wilson, Colin, 'Worlds of Magic', *Books and Bookmen*, June 1972 (review of *City of Revelation*).

Wintle, Douglas, 'The Old Straight Track Club',pamphlet, Sept. 1948; reprinted *TLH*, No. 28, 1972.

118 Wood, Betty, 'What is Clairvoyance?', *The Atlantean*, No. 130,

1970 (elementals).

Wood, Betty, 'Expect a Miracle', *The Atlantean*, No. 139, 1971 (Findhorn).

Wood, R.G., 'Ley Dowsing', *TLH*, No. 34, 1972.

Woods, K.F., 'Circles – Clocks, Calendars, Computers', Institute of Post Office Electrical Engineers' Association Section *Journal*, Spring, 1970 (astro-archaeology).

Wright, Ian B., 'Straight Lines, Zodiacs and Antiquity', *TLH* No. 22, 1971.

INDEX

Winchester 102, 122, 208
Wing 122
Winstone 49
Wirral 135
Witches 198
Woe Waters 91
Wold Newton 91
Wolfe, Theodore P. 226
Wood, Betty 248, 249
Wood, James 30
Wood, K.F. 120

Woodburn 50
Woodhenge 48, 76, 122, 221
Worcester 99
Wrekin 179

Yarnbury Castle 48
Yeovil 208
Yetminster 208

Zodiacs 134-141, 207, 219, 221